POWERTIMING

POWERTIMING

Using the

ELLIOTT WAVE SYSTEM

to Anticipate and Time

MARKET TURNS

ROBERT C. BECKMAN

PROBUS PUBLISHING COMPANY
Chicago, Illinois
Cambridge, England

This publication is designed to provide accurate and authoritive information in regard to the subject matter covered. It is sold with the understanding that the publisher is not engaged in rendering legal, accounting or other professional service.

ISBN 1-55738-273-5

Printed in the United States of America

BB

1 2 3 4 5 6 7 8 9 0

Contents

Introduction

Power, in its most basic form, is the ability of one or more individuals to exert their influence and designs on a far greater number of other individuals. There are three types of power, each of which varies in quality—power that comes from exerting force, power that can be achieved through the deployment of wealth, and power that comes from knowledge. Knowledge will be the power that dominates the remainder of this century and beyond.

The first eco-cultural changes in the use of power took place in the Fertile Crescent and in the Far East about ten thousand years ago, altering all of the basic concepts of Neanderthal man, Cro-Magnon man, the Ice Age, the Stone Age, and the Bronze Age. The world of power in accordance with territorial imperative became redundant. Out of the Fertile Crescent emerged a world of energy, the deployment of beasts of burden, and the cultivation of fruits and vegetables. Of course, there were many who could not adapt to the changes, never advancing beyond the concept of maintaining the Old World order of territorial imperative. The Agricultural Revolution continued just the same without them.

The Agricultural Revolution changed the way the world thought, worked, and invested. During the 9,750 years that followed the start of the Agricultural Revolution, there was merely an extension of the upward momentum from the launching pad. Nothing really happened to change the way the world worked, thought, or invested until about 250 years ago, when the second mega-eco-cultural quantum leap appeared; as a result, power involved the creation of wealth rather than armies. This major change has now become known as the Industrial Revolution. The Industrial Revolution began in Europe and quickly engulfed huge tracts of the occupied areas of this planet Earth.

The Industrial Revolution provided a system by which growth could be sustained dynamically, changing human nature and personal motivations along with completely altering, once again, the way people lived, thought, behaved, and invested. The Industrial Revolution represented the springboard for industrialized civilization, with machines being used for energy rather than beasts of burden. During the course of the Industrial Revolution machines produced clothing, financial manias, stock market panics, stress, cancer, heart disease, the pacemaker, artificial limbs, and contraceptives.

The Industrial Revolution gave us Fulton, Whitney, Pasteur, Rockefeller, Ford, Einstein, Nils Bohr, John Maynard Keynes, Nicolai Kondratieff, Charles Dow, Graham & Dodd, Warren Buffet, Larry Tisch, asset allocation, and quantitative and qualitative analysis.

The process of wealth creation also involved the transfer of wealth from one party to another, which took the form of buying and selling portions of profitable enterprises. The genesis of dealing in the shares of companies on Wall Street was a buttonwood tree, under which buyers and sellers used to meet. That tree perfectly fulfilled the function of a marketplace. It became a well-known spot where industrial man could go to transact financial business. Soon, as the number of companies grew and business expanded, the dealers in shares moved from under the tree to a nearby coffee-house and began adding the business of prophecy to the business of dealing in stocks. It wasn't long before the prediction business almost swamped and ruined the business of dealing in stocks. Efforts to improve the situation had been made by Graham & Dodd, Paul Cootner, Charles Dow, and others. These efforts have not been overwhelmingly successful.

There are many leaders engaged in a power struggle, harboring the notion of a territorial imperative as their primary conceptual focal point. There are others wedded to the idea that power and wealth remain a matter of cultivating fruits and vegetables and other agrarian resources. There are even a large number of industrialists who are not yet prepared for the major changes that lie ahead, which are now under way and which represent the biggest changes yet. The conceptual approach to investment is even more antiquated and redundant than that which is shared in other areas of enterprise.

The changes in the manner in which power is deployed and the way the world works will have a greater impact in the years ahead than either the Agricultural Revolution or the Industrial Revolution. For want of a better definition, we can call it the "Knowledge Revolution." It will be post-Agricultural. It will be post-Human.

The "Knowledge Revolution" will lead to a transformation of the way you work, the way you live, the way you invest, and the way your children are reared and educated. The nature of this revolution will decide who will be left behind and who will move ahead. Although generally, life on this planet will cease to be a zero-sum game where for every winner there is a loser, investment life will remain a zero-sum game and there will *not* be an equal distribution of benefits. Many of the "winners" of recent years are likely to be left out of the "Knowledge Revolution" along with the territorialists, agriculturalists, industrialists, and those investors who continue to fight the battle for investment survival with the weapons of a previous war. The conceptual foundations of bygone days are no longer capable of supporting and propelling our society any further forward. In the period ahead, the field of investment will not be an equal opportunity employer.

The most successful entrepreneurs, innovators, and investors of our time have been directing their efforts in this new scheme of things without necessarily understanding the new and revised principles. Indeed, without knowing it, our best and brightest investment banks, economists, and investment analysts have not only moved the goal posts, but they've begun playing a new game in a vastly changed stadium. The roots of the "Knowledge Revolution" stretch back to the 1960s, when the transition first started in a very modest way. The period has since seen the decimation of many of the Old Guard strategists while producing T. Boone Pickens, Sam Walton, H. Ross Perot, and a revival of interest in the work of Ralph Nelson Elliott. For investors, the Elliott Wave Principle represents the most dramatic advancement in price forecasting since investors began attempting to anticipate the price movement of tulip bulbs on the Amsterdam Exchange during the seventeenth century.

The Wave Principle, as developed by Ralph Nelson Elliott, is about as advanced as the field of investment analysis will ever be able to achieve. The Wave Principle, originally defined by R.N. Elliott as "The Law Of Nature," can be found operating in the areas of nuclear physics, quantum mathematics, the Theory of Sets, Catastrophe Theory, Fournier Analysis, and Chaos Theory, the latter being among the most far-reaching mathematical concepts of our age. The effect begins with a sub-minuette wave and doesn't end until there is a correction of a grand super cycle. The Wave Principle is the investment tool of the Knowledge Revolution. It is the only tool I know of that is capable of coping with the changes that lie ahead in markets.

No more than a handful of professional investors and investment analysts seem to be remotely aware of the direction the world is taking toward a cultural, economic, financial, and geo-political infrastructure that will leave only the remnants of the system as we have known it. There are certain indications that suggest the nature and shape of the financial system toward which we are heading. But, nobody knows for sure. What is fairly certain is that the next three decades are going to produce changes in the way the world transacts business that will be far more dramatic than was witnessed at the early stages of either the Agricultural Revolution or the Industrial Revolution. The changes will also be far more rapid. The most dramatic changes of the next three decades are likely to take place during the next five years. Not only is the Wave Principle equipped to deal with changes of this type, but a quantum leap in the very near future is the current message of the Wave Principle in an analytical context.

The changes that are approaching will certainly have a major impact on the field of investment analysis. Investment techniques that are vague, involving low levels of persistency and unquantifiable outruns, will be ruinous for those investors who are not able to adapt themselves to the evolving financial environment.

Investors have been taught to believe that the future must in some way repeat the static, traditional, repetitive past. Consistent with this inflexible belief system is the idea that investment parameters and principles that have been established over the years will continue to offer useful guidelines. This is the logic of the static force. There is no place for this irrelevant and useless logic for those who employ the Wave Principle. Those who watch the tenets of the Wave Principle unfold become acutely aware that the world and markets are dynamic affairs, never static, always changing.

It is an unfortunate reality of the field of security analysis, along with many other professions, that the techniques that become the most popular and acquire the widest following are those that appeal to the lowest common denominator of intellectual achievement. Some of the most outstanding, informative, information and investment principles have been relegated to sitting on book shelves, gathering dust or never published, because the average investor has found, or might find, the material difficult to assimilate intellectually.

The populist in the field of investment analysis will habitually try to convince people of what investors want to believe to start with. Most investors want to believe that by reading a book, or attending a course on investment, they can master a do-it-yourself system in a couple of days or a couple of weeks that will put them on the road to easy riches. A great deal of the educational material on the subject of investment is directly responsible for perpetuating this myth. The promise of quick and easy money—without working or thinking—appears to have become the norm. Investors are rapidly receiving the impression that ignorance is a hard-won accomplishment, the absence of which will impede investment performance. While the logic may be comforting, the results are not reassuring.

Overriding the frustrating, costly, misleading trivia and minutiae of the populist investment advisers is the irrefutable rule in the zero-sum game of markets that says successful investment results rely on the assumption that investors will continue to make the same mistakes in the future that they have made in the past. This is a fairly safe assumption. Before the introduction of the Wave Principle, very little progress had been made in developing investment techniques that were likely to produce useful and meaningful results for those who deployed them. The concept of progress itself is only in its infancy. Progress began in earnest as a byproduct of industrial society. The concept of progress is less than three hundred years old, slightly more than the duration of one grand super cycle, according to the Wave Principle.

Today, as we move closer toward tomorrow and post-Industrial society, there is the continued tendency for the investment community to cling to that which is safe and familiar, regardless of the uninspiring results produced by those investment techniques that have not served the investment community particularly well. The future demands a change in perceptual allowance if progress is to be made. The problem remains one of narrow perceptual horizons that has kept the investment world in the Dark Ages for far longer than was ever necessary. The conceptual basis of the Wave Principle offers a strict departure from the perpetual straitjackets of the past, providing a kaleidoscope of opportunity for those who gain a working knowledge of this amazing investment tool.

For many decades, the Wave Principle had been relegated to the annals of obscurity. This is not surprising due to its conceptual complexity and the manner in which the resolution of various configurations lends itself to a variety of interpretations. Most investors seek absolutes. They want to know on what day and at what time a market, a stock, or a commodity is going to move, precisely how far it is going to move, and for how long. The Elliott Wave Principle offers none of this. The Elliott Wave Principle offers what is realistically achievable. No more and no less. This in itself places the Wave Principle light years ahead of other investment techniques. It is necessary for the investor to revise his perceptions and techniques in order to appreciate and make use of precisely what the Wave Principle has to offer.

The Wave Principle has recently acquired a sudden upsurge in interest among those who have been searching for answers to explain market movements that could not be found elsewhere. This may seem like a step forward. Unfortunately, in many cases, the interest recently shown in the Wave Principle represents a step backward. Many have distorted Elliott's tenets beyond recognition in an effort to find an easy, quick method of applying his work to the day-to-day movements of markets.

I first became acquainted with the Wave Principle during the 1950s, through a series of articles written by A. Hamilton Bolton for the *Bank Credit Analyst,* along with a book by the same author entitled *The Elliott Wave Principle—A Critical Appraisal.* What interested me most was the conceptual approach to the anticipation of share price movements inherent in the Wave Principle that I found in no other technical tool. Although I had become fully versed in the methodology of the major academic, fundamental, and technical approaches to investment analysis by that time, there were many aspects of the investment nomenclature that I found intellectually unsatisfactory. The techniques and logic of Ralph Nelson Elliott were like a breath of fresh air.

I quickly discovered the Wave Principle was no mere trend-following technique that would be useful until it became useless. There was no element of repetitive periodicity upon which so many technical methods rely—and fail. The Wave Principle was not a "system" that suggested markets would follow a fixed pattern, which is simply not the way of markets. Within the Wave Principle lies the only element of market behavior that was consistent with the manner in which markets behaved in the real world, that ever-elusive pattern of stochastic activity.

In the Wave Principle I discovered a method that broadened perceptions and made an attempt to qualify and quantify the various possibilities and probabilities that market price behavior was capable of developing over varying time frames, in a way never before attempted by any other stock market methodology since Dow Theory. In my mind, the Wave Principle was the investment equivalent of Einstein's Theory of Relativity. Ralph Nelson Elliott began where Charles Dow ended.

I then began an intensive effort to acquire everything that had ever been written about the Wave Principle by Ralph Nelson Elliott and others. I managed to get hold of the two original works of R. N. Elliott, *The Wave*

Principle and *Nature's Law*. I found there were two versions of *The Wave Principle*, the second version containing certain revisions of Elliott's original concepts that were made before his death.

I also discovered that for a time R.N. Elliott published his own investment service based on the Wave Principle. The manner in which R.N. Elliott distributed his service was as unusual as the Wave Principle itself.

Elliott was indeed a pragmatist. His service was simply called the Wave Principle and involved the distribution of a series of *Interpretive Letters* which would only be issued on the completion of a Wave. The first of these *Interpretive Letters* appeared to have been published on 10 November 1938, the last in November 1941. The *Interpretive Letters* were not written with the benefit of hindsight. The results Elliott had achieved with his investment service acted to vindicate my enthusiasm for the Wave Principle even more. I continued my search for whatever material could be found on the Wave Principle with an even greater fervor while attempting to make applications of the Wave Principle to my forecasting activities and market dealings.

After working with the Wave Principle for nearly twenty years and collecting as much data as I could find on the subject, in 1976 I produced what I believe to be the first definitive work on the Wave Principle since Elliott's original work and that of A. Hamilton Bolton. The book was entitled *The Elliott Wave Principle As Applied to the UK Stock Market,* and pub-lished by Tara Books.

It was certainly not my intention to produce a "Bob Beckman version" of the Elliott Wave Principle or any watered-down substitute that would make the deployment of Elliott's tenets easier to assimilate for the financially unwashed or financially unwashable with limited experience and time constraints. I introduced the Wave Principle to Europe, based on the behavior of European markets, the same way that I felt Elliott, its innovator, would have done had he been alive at the time, while simply adding my own observations and qualifications. I have never attempted to improve on Elliott's methods. The Wave Principle is the only technical tool I had ever found that incorporated a concept that was intellectually sound and left little margin for improvement.

During the three years following the publication of my first book on the Wave Principle, I extended my application of Elliott's work to the US Stock Market. In late 1979, *Supertiming* was published by the Library of Investment Study and contained additional observations that extended the material of my first book on the Wave Principle, utilizing the long-term behavior of the US Stock Market during the period following the death of Elliott and A. Hamilton Bolton as a basic model.

Supertiming was my last contribution to the annals of technical stock market studies. Neither *The Elliott Wave Principle As Applied to the UK Stock Market* nor *Supertiming* was a huge success. Due to the complexity of the subject matter, I never expected them to be. The Wave Principle was relatively unknown at the time my two books were published and was not considered among the more fashionable technical tools.

As previously suggested, the norm among stock market technicians is to advocate the use of whatever technical tool appeals to the greatest majority who might be willing to employ a technician. If the use of moving averages suddenly becomes fashionable and the investment community would like to be convinced that moving averages offer the touchstone to investment success, there are many who will stand ready, willing, and able to support such a thesis without the slightest reservation. This exemplary illustration applies to a wide range of so-called technical tools, from the use of trend lines, to patterns, to fixed-periodicity cycles. Yet, it is a fact that tools of this type have been proven to be absolutely useless through the application of academic serial correlation methods that leave very little room for doubt.

The fact that the Wave Principle, in the form intended by Elliott, has never attracted wide popularity is to its credit. There is a fundamental reason why the most valuable tools applicable to forecasting must remain illusive. If an analytical tool for the stock market developed a great track record, everyone would start using it and begin acting on the various outcomes, thereby invalidating the usefulness of the tool. If there was a surefire method for anticipating the next major move in the stock market that required very little time and effort, the word would spread very quickly. If the tool indicated a rise in the market, everyone using the tool would buy simultaneously, pushing up values much more than fundamental conditions warranted. And, it wouldn't end there. After several rounds of such a sequence, some bright folks would anticipate an excessive appreciation in response to the activities of those who used this forecasting tool, sell the market short after its initial run-up, and then drive the market down to unsustainably low levels. And so it would go, with an increasing number of disruptions to the outcomes predicted by this surefire tool.

Fortunately, the Wave Principle does not lend itself to this weakness and never will. But, this does not hold true for certain variations of the

Wave Principle that have recently received notoriety while bearing only a vague resemblance to what R.N. Elliott had originally intended. As a consequence of what I consider to be an irreverent and misleading treatment of the Wave Principle in recent years, I have decided to once again direct my efforts to a third presentation of the Wave Principle in the manner in which I believe R.N. Elliott had intended his tenets to be employed.

Since my last published work on the Wave Principle in 1979, a great deal of my time has been spent managing the financial assets under my control. These include the Beckman International Capital Accumulator Unit Trust, whose assets are in excess of $80,000,000, which is similar to a US-style mutual fund. The Beckman International Capital Accumulator Unit Trust was launched in 1982. In the March 1991 issue of *Money Management Magazine,* it was stated that the Beckman International Capital Accumulator Unit Trust was " . . . the star performer of its sector, having never been below third place in the league tables at any time during the nine years since it was originally launched."

In addition to managing the assets of the Beckman International Capital Accumulator Unit Trust, I am also responsible for directing the asset allocation of the Beckman Reserve Asset Fund, whose assets are in excess of $12,000,000. In a report from City & Financial Services Ltd. the London-based administrators of the Fund, " . . . the Beckman Reserve Asset Fund proved to be the best performing offshore money fund in Britain, while ranking third place among the 257 onshore and offshore money funds in the whole of Europe, during its first year of operation, 1990–1991."

I am also responsible for the timing and selection of the market derivatives held by the $4,000,000 Beckman Option and Warrant Fund that was launched in April 1991. The Beckman Option and Warrant Fund is a unique vehicle. There is nothing you can compare with it. However, based on the success that has been achieved through the recommendations made in my publication, the *Investors Bulletin Warrant Survey,* the response to the initial offering was overwhelming. The minimum investment for any investor had to subsequently be limited to $50,000.

In addition to the public funds under my direction, I also manage the funds of 144 private clients involving total assets of just over $60,000,000. Several of my private clients have had their funds under my stewardship for up to twenty years. I have had clients who have educated themselves and their children from the proceeds of the funds held with me. My clients range from a former captain of British industry to high-net-worth executives in various corners of the world, including the US.

The reliability of the investment techniques I use and the tools I employ are readily quantifiable by the performance of those funds under my direction, the results of which appear daily in the UK financial press. I cannot afford to blithely pontificate on the future direction of markets, using indecipherable technical jargon based on theoretical, irrelevant assumptions that have never been validated. I am not in the position to simply make hedged predictions, while taking previous predictions out of context in order to give myself the appearance of having supernatural investment powers, this seemingly having become the norm in the prediction business.

I am not in the prediction business. I am in the investment performance business with real money that belongs to thousands of other people. If the funds I look after perform well, then the tools, techniques, and methods I use can be considered to be of value. If the funds do not perform well, then any forecasts I might make, along with the methods I use, must certainly be questionable. This is a premise which is inviolate.

In a large part, I can attribute the success I have achieved, along with the performance record of the funds I manage, to my use of the Wave Principle. I have used the Wave Principle as a means of enhancing investment performance, first and foremost, rather than as a method for making predictions, which may or may not be applicable to a real-world market experience.

Under no circumstances should the Wave Principle be approached as a method which can be used in the stock market as a substitute for knowledge and thought, as has been suggested by certain practitioners. It has been demonstrated quite conclusively that R.N. Elliott did not use his Wave Principle as an isolated tool. Elliott had a very keen understanding of geo-political affairs, an economic background, and also was well-grounded in all of the basic fundamental approaches to investment analysis.

Do not expect *Powertiming* to give you a quick and easy method for making stock market profits. You will not find it here. As long as the investor continues to search for quick and easy methods for stock market profits, he will never achieve the understanding and expertise that is needed to produce the type of investment returns that can be achieved.

In *Powertiming* what investors will find is the only method which I believe is capable of tracking the type of markets we are likely to have in the future. The investor will acquire a power to anticipate trends in a manner far beyond the reach of those who are not fully acquainted with the Wave Principle. I am convinced that the principles set out in my latest study of the Wave Principle, if applied, will act to improve the investment returns of all investors, along with producing an efficient approach to markets that most never believed possible.

R. C. BECKMAN

1
The Genesis of Genius

Like all other arts, the Science of Deduction and Analysis is one which can only be acquired by long and patient study, nor is life long enough to allow any mortal to attain the highest possible perfection in it.

—SHERLOCK HOLMES, A.K.A. SIR ARTHUR CONAN DOYLE
A Study in Scarlet

How the Wave Principle Arose

Success in the stock market, measured in terms of money earned, is firmly grounded in the science of analysis and deduction. Prediction is an art. Doubtless, just as in crime detection, what appears to be a little luck helps. But detecting the trends to come, the time to act, and the action to take requires more than luck. Luck is how the envious describe hard work and the successful use of skilled judgement.

In this book I propose to take you with me in search of stock market luck via the study of the Elliott Wave Principle. It will not be easy; mastery of the technique will take a great deal of time, patience, and judgement.

The antecedents of the Elliott Wave Principle are both peculiar and more than a little obscure. In search of his original thoughts, commentary on his theories, and practical experience of it by others, I have had to do quite some detective work. Also, I have had to work hard and long to be able to effectively use the Elliott Wave Principle myself.

The Principle is intellectually appealing to those who know the stock market offers no absolutes, that it will do what it wants to do, when it wants to do it. That what you need for success is a guide to help define probabilities and the knowledge to weight them, followed by the confidence to act on your own judgement and not be thrown off-balance by the arrival of the improbable.

Some sixty years ago, an ordinary man, not very well, spent his convalescence attempting to discover pattern and also predictability in a very narrow sphere—that of US share prices. Ralph Nelson Elliott established the Wave Principle, a guideline for share-price movement, not easy to understand, not easy to apply, but the only "system" that I, in thirty-five years of successful stock market trading and analysis, have found the most consistently useful—because it is most consistently right.

Elliott published his findings in two articles. The first, outlining his new theory called "The Wave Principle," was published in *The Financial World* in 1939. Seven years later, in *Nature's Law*, he published his deepened and updated thesis. Two years later he was dead.

If in 1948 there were Elliott followers, they kept very quiet; the knowledge was either too good to share—or too hard to learn. Only one Elliott student, Garfield Drew, revealed what he knew and yet he only devoted two of the 365 pages (one for every day of the year?) of his book, *New Methods for Profit in the Stock Market,* to Elliott's ideas. He gave no information about the man.

Even the late A. Hamilton Bolton, once president of Bolton, Tremblay and Company, principal enthusiast and exponent of Elliott's work, was never closely associated with him. Perhaps it is just as well for the objective assessment of Elliott's theory; it has to stand on its own merits, uninfluenced by personal likes, dislikes, or garbled memories. But it means that very little original material on the Wave Principle is currently available— his monographs and his quaintly titled "educational letters" are long out of print.

Hamilton Bolton, from his heights as president of Bolton, Tremblay and Company, not only had the authority to make his views known, but also the medium through which to do it: the company published the respected *Bank Credit Analyst.* Bolton's first venture into print on the subject of Elliott and his theory was in 1953. He published a short pamphlet on his interpretation of what the Elliott Wave Principle was saying about the US stock market at that time, five years after Elliott's death.

Enter Charles Collins

Another thirteen years were to pass before a further notable contribution from a newcomer was made to the literature on Elliott. Bolton had regularly printed assessments of the US stock market according to the Elliott Wave Principle in the annual supplements to the *Bank Credit*

Analyst. Then he discovered that Charles J. Collins, editor of a nationally distributed weekly investment bulletin, had actually known and worked with Elliott. He invited Collins to contribute his knowledge of Elliott to the 1966 annual supplement. And so we discovered how Elliott first brought his theory to the attention of the professional investment world.

Elliott wrote to Collins from his convalescent home in California in the autumn of 1934; he stated that a bull market on Wall Street had begun and was likely to carry the Dow Jones Industrial Average for a considerable distance. He suggested that Collins might like to investigate his, Elliott's, work on cycle theory, the basis for his assertion. Probably dismissively, Collins countered with the usual editor's bored request, that Elliott go on record with his predictions, and equally probably, promptly dismissed it from his mind.

Elliott in Action

Now for some history: in March 1935 the Dow Jones Rail Average collapsed below the 1934 low, while the Dow Jones Industrial Average simultaneously shed eleven percent. Classic Dow Theory would pronounce this a definite "sell" signal. In Collins' mind, briefly, another infallible system bit the dust. US investors, still sensitized by the 1929 debacle, were running scared. But Elliott, unperturbed, cabled Collins on the very day that saw, with hindsight, the Dow Jones Industrial Average (DJIA) touch an important low. Elliott insisted that the break was over and that another leg of the bull market had begun.

As Collins read the cable, the DJIA was racing upward. But, the time stamp on Elliott's cable showed that it had been sent more than two hours before the bottom had been touched and the trend turned. Impressed as much by Elliott's insistence as by his accuracy, Collins invited him to be a house guest at the editor's New England estate.

The two men spent several weeks together, engrossed in the study of Elliott's Wave Principle, and a little of Elliott's personal history emerged. He was an American who had spent most of his working life in Mexico as a wireless operator, until forced by illness to retire back to his native California. Most people when convalescing take up reading or knitting, sometimes religion or gardening. Elliott during three convalescent years on his front porch, for want of any other intellectual stimulus, studied the stock market data of the past eight years. As a complete novice his mind was more completely open.

The results show that Elliott was zealous in his work. Elliott read the classical analysts of his time (Charles Dow, Richard Schabacher et al.), but he discovered a pattern of previous share behavior that outdistanced their accepted methods. Behind the repeated outlines that underpinned most technical methods of that time (remember we are in the mid-thirties), Elliott discovered a form that seemed to account for the many times the known patterns failed. He saw a wave; a wave that rose, fell back, and rose again repeatedly and on many time scales.

The fledgling analyst with his new theory wanted to join Collins' organization, but only to work on his own theory. Collins, wisely, never tied himself exclusively to one single method or approach, but was sufficiently impressed with Elliott's theory to help him aquire some risk capital to manage. And Collins then edited Elliott's first monograph, *The Wave Principle*. This Elliott later amplified as *Nature's Law*, which included more philosophical points and touched on the Fibonacci Summation Series, a set of apparently mystical numbers first published in medieval Italy.

The Elliott theory was that all fluctuations in the stock market are fragments of a great rhythmic system of waves and cycles in ascending and descending order of magnitude. This rhythm, he argued, is repeated in the various forms of nature in the universe. Elliott, although agnostic, had leanings toward mysticism as did his great predecessor, W.D. Gann, author of *Truth of the Stock Tape* (1923).

Gann argued that the stock market continually followed a pattern of perfect mathematical balance and that share-price behavior could be seen as mathematically symmetrical when one finally established the starting points of the various cycles. Elliott concurred and also felt that the Fibonacci Summation Series—more on this later—forms the basis of all points of cyclical departure. Curiously, Joseph Schillinger, in a totally different field, arrived at the same conclusion, published in his 1956 book, *The Mathematical Basis of the Arts*.

As this story continues, readers may be amazed at the way in which the concept of mathematical symmetry weaves in and out of the various aspects of human behavior. However, readers of James Gleick's seminal work *Chaos: the Making of a New Science* (1988) perhaps may be less amazed than others.

Elliott's explanation for the historical movement of share prices was based on the theory of irresistible cyclical forces acting over long periods of time. Early economists had already put forward cyclical theories, but Elliott was the first man to apply them to stock market behavior.

The Economics of the Wave Principle

N.D. Kondratieff gave his name to a fifty-four-year economic cycle, which he proposed in his 1928 essay "Die Langen Wellen der Konjunktur" (The Long Waves of the Trade Cycle). In this he confirmed earlier work by the Dutchman J. Van Gelderen who, around 1920, published *Springvloed; Beschouwing over Industriele Ontwikkleling en Prijsbeweging* (Springtide; Observations on Industrial Development and Price Movement), in which he demonstrated a much longer economic cycle than the previously discovered ten-year cycle of W. Stanley Jevans (1878).

In the mid-1930s Harvard professor Joseph Schumpeter brought together the work of the three main cyclical theorists: Kondratieff with his fifty-four-year cycle; Juglar and his eighteen-year cycle; and Kitchin with his four-year cycle. In his *Theory of Economic Development* (1934) Schumpeter argued that each Kondratieff cycle was composed of three complete Juglar cycles and fourteen Kitchin cycles.

We cannot know whether Elliott was influenced by the work of the great cyclical economists; he seemed intellectually honest, yet made no mention of any of these famous studies in his work. Had Elliott come to his conclusions in isolation? It only makes them all the more interesting.

Elliott began with one major long-term force, which he subdivided into lesser short-term forces. But Elliott's sub-divisions were more detailed than those of Schumpeter and notably free of cyclical constraint. Elliott had to coin his own terminology to classify the wave dimensions.

First came the grand super cycle, then the super cycle, compatible in time with the Kondratieff cycle of fifty-four years. Next in Elliott's scale came the cycle which, at fifteen to twenty years, depending on the first, obviously coincided with Juglar's cycle of economic activity. Elliott's shortest major cycle, empathizing with Kitchin's four-year period, he christened the Primary Wave.

Like a Circle in a Spiral

But from there, Elliott parted company with the classical economists. He continued down the scale with an intermediate, minor, minute, minuette, and finally a sub-minuette cycle. Perhaps only the constraints of recorded time, and man's ability to act within defined time scales, prevented further sub-divisions. In London, the smallest recorded movement of the market is hourly, as measured by the Financial Times Industrial

Ordinary Share Index. Wall Street, of course, is perfection, the Stockmaster giving minute-by-minute price changes in the Dow Jones Industrial Average (DJIA), adjusted immediately for every transaction in the thirty shares that make up the DJIA.

And there was more than just symmetry in descending order of scale: Elliott found that the components of cycles of similar size showed specific behavior patterns. Though there was no fixed periodicity or repetition, there was a distinct relationship to the various movements. Elliott concluded that, regardless of size, a complete stock market cycle comprised eight movements.

Let us take the upward, or bull, cycle first. Elliott found three basic ascending waves, which he called *impulse* waves (they gave the direction), each of which was followed by a downwave, which he called *corrective*. The third and final downwave, following the final impulse wave, corrected the entire upward cycle, with one upward corrective wave intervening.

What has Elliott given us? An upward movement of five waves, three up, two down, the former longer than the latter. After the fifth wave, the momentum is downward in three waves, with two down and the one up between the two, but shorter than its predecessor.

This is the essential Elliott shape, but within this apparently finite shape, the detail accumulates and helps us establish targets, devise an investment strategy, and hold on while all others lose their heads.

The advocates of Elliott's work rank it with that of Charles Dow, the granddaddy of all technical market theory. Some would argue that Elliott continues where Dow left off, Dow being more limited in his classifications, though he, too, had determined the cyclical forces that govern share prices. Dow said that the basic force of the market was the primary bull (upward) trend, which contained intermediate moves called *secondary corrections*. He was not much concerned with the smaller movements. Both men defined three upward thrusts in a bull market, but Elliott went further.

There are those, eminent technical analysts to a man, who believe that the Wave Principle offers the only significant explanation of stock market history; describing the upward sweeps of share prices from 1857 to 1929, the massive corrective wave from 1929 to 1949, followed by the surge from 1949 to 1973, and the fourth-wave plunge from 1973 to 1974 on Wall Street, and what may turn out to be the *terminal juncture* of a grand super cycle that began 250 years ago, as we move into the 1990s.

In formulating his Wave Principle, Elliott opened up not only Dow's trend structure, but a Pandora's box as well. He was willing to recognize four trend-categories smaller than intermediate, and four trend-categories larger than intermediate, nine in all, including the intermediate category itself. And he insisted that no trend-category could have more than three components of the next-lower order running in its dominant direction. The idea must have been to set up a rigid standard of definition. But the fact is that trends develop more than three thrusts.

Elliott got around this problem by permitting third legs to become very complex—that is, more thoroughly articulated than second and first legs. But, whether the rigidity of his theory yields a practical benefit or not is debatable. Attempts to implement Elliott's principle quickly run into mind-wrenching frustrations as multiple alternatives of definition suggest

Figure 1
NEW YORK STOCK EXCHANGE   1857–1929

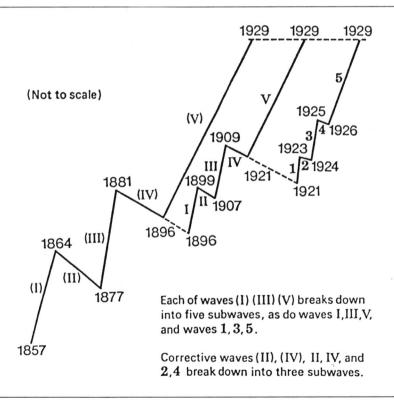

(Not to scale)

Each of waves (I) (III) (V) breaks down into five subwaves, as do waves I,III,V, and waves 1,3,5.

Corrective waves (II), (IV), II, IV, and 2,4 break down into three subwaves.

themselves. One of the most difficult aspects of the Elliott Wave Principle is size classification of the waves and their correct positioning in the cycle.

Let me repeat: the Elliott Wave Principle does not offer absolutes but alternatives; it is a guideline for your judgement, not a substitute. All those who seek absolutes will be disenchanted with all stock market methods. There are no absolutes, and there is no substitute for informed, personal judgement.

This must be accepted by those who wish to successfully use the Elliott Wave Principle; judgement of alternatives, assessed by knowledge of probabilities, will be the basis of their investment strategy. Courage will not be the least of their virtues.

It sounds more difficult than it actually is: imagine, if the *wave count* suggests an upward move is beginning in Wave Three, or possibly Wave Five, then all we need to retain is that the movement is UPWARD, so the downside risks are limited. And so the courageous among us act accordingly. Remember that at a turning point, the precise nature of the Wave is rel-atively unimportant; the fact of change is.

Occasionally, we shall find that several options are offered by the Wave Principle, with risk and reward not clearly defined. Then we stand back and wait for greater definition. Not all price movements can be immediately categorized.

A most rewarding aspect of the Elliott Wave Principle is that when only one option is offered, the probability of success is extraordinarily high. I shall show you. The long-term investor need only deal with the long-term wave developments, whose climaxes are easily recognizable.

There are two points of prime importance when starting to study the Wave Principle. The first and simplest is mastery of its basic tenets; the second and most difficult is how to work with it.

At one of my annual *Investors Bulletin* seminars, James Dines, well-known American investment adviser, goldbug, and newsletter editor, commented: "A genius by the name of Ralph Nelson Elliott developed something called the Wave Principle, but it takes a genius to understand it."

I think I understand it, I think I can help you to understand it. I do not claim to be a genius, but George Louis Buffon said that "Genius is nothing but a great aptitude for patience."

Be patient, bear with me, follow me—and you may become richer.

2
Know Your Stock Market

Between the idea
> And the reality
>> Between the motion
>>> And the act
>>>> Falls the Shadow.

—T. S. ELIOT
Four Quartets

Once, I had a client in New York who turned his life's savings of $2,000 into $1,000,000 through skillful use of the stock market. His system was simple: he went for the substance, not its shadow. Whenever the yield on the Dow Jones Industrial Average (DJIA) rose above six percent, he put all his money in the market; when the yield fell below three percent, he took all his money out and put it in a bank savings account. When the yield was back over six percent, in he went again. And so on.

Of course, he had the magic of compound interest on his side, but the important thing to note is that he had mastered three major principles. He was consistent in his approach; he knew how to be inactive over a long period; and he had a high success ratio as his criterion. But, he was a long-term investor and it did take him thirty years to build his fortune.

As I never get tired of repeating: the secret to stock market success is to find a tool with a high probability of success, to stick with that tool, to be consistent, and to listen to what the market is saying about itself. It is my firm belief that the Elliott Wave Principle is such a tool.

My client was primarily concerned with the long-term, cyclical repetition of the yield factor; he was not particularly bothered by the time scale.

A theory based on cyclical repetition is never very comfortable for those brought up with the traditional outlook on the socio-economic, world-of-finance type of problem. These are those who, when the economy looks gloomy, steer clear of the stock market, and when things look brighter, come back in; and those who buy after a company has announced good results. After all, they argue, the stock market must reflect the economic growth of the nation; the shares of a company that has done well must go up.

All this seems very logical and often, to the small, first-time investor, almost seductive. But the professionals know that share prices often fall after the announcement of good results, that when economies look their most promising, the indigenous stock market is usually on the brink of a disastrous decline.

The stock market deals with the future, it is not a shadow of the past; that is the cardinal rule of stock market behavior and yet one that people find hardest to understand. Information that appears in the daily papers is yesterday's news—the market has already discounted it. There have been academic studies relating stock market behavior to the dissemination of news and these studies have shown that the market is totally efficient. News spreads so fast that there is no advantage whatever in acting on information published for mass consumption.

Stock market profits are made by taking advantage of variations in share prices; business trends or corporate earnings rarely indicate market turning points. Now let us apply a basic Elliott Wave classification and see how it works. Remember the wave shape is of three upward movements with two corrective downward movements in each bull cycle. Let's take a look at the Wave Principle in action.

Amazing Revelations Unfold

For the purpose of illustration, I am using the sequential development of the Financial Times Industrial Ordinary Share Index between the period January 1975 and June 1991. There are very few examples that are available to demonstrate the manner in which the Wave Principle can be utilized along with its revelations with such clarity. The behavior of the Dow Jones Industrial Average during the corresponding period was not as well delineated.

As I mentioned earlier, in order to achieve the best results from the Wave Principle, it is necessary to have a thorough grounding in the various

Figure 2
FT30 1975–1991

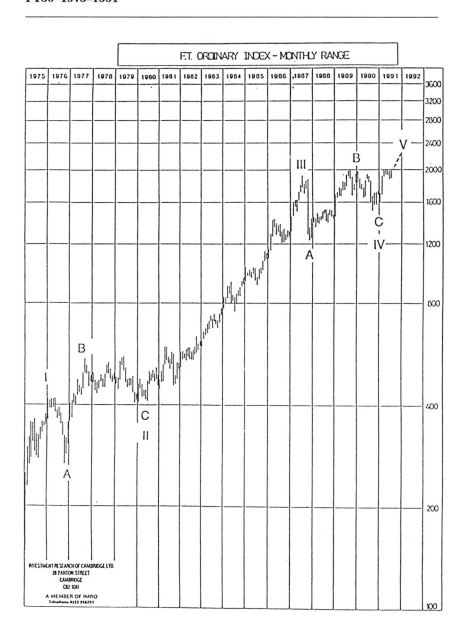

technical studies that have been made over the decades, along with a reasonable knowledge of the fundamental and economic influences on medium- to long-term behavior of markets. In this respect, a study of Dow Theory is no less quintessential to the market operator than a knowledge of scales and chords is to a musician.

Dow Theory tells us that any major movements in the equity market of one major industrialized country is likely to be repeated by those markets of other industrialized countries, with the passage of time. This is Dow's Law of Commonality. This law remains inviolate. We saw that law in operation during the Crash of '87, when not one single market was spared from the ravages initially triggered by Wall Street.

By categorizing the movement of the Financial Times 30 Share Index between the period of January 1975 and June 1991, we see a near completion of the traditional five-wave, bull-market pattern. First we see the completion of the two upward movements and part of a third, signified by (I), (III), and (V). We also see the two downward movements which interrupt the important "impulse" waves, designated by (II) and (IV). Waves (II) and (IV) have the traditional components involving one upward drive (B) and two downward drives (A and C).

In application, there are some startling revelations to be seen from this chart that also offer some amazing possibilities. The price action covers a period of more than fifteen years. This means that when the five-wave pattern is completed, the correction that follows must be greater than any correction that occurred during that fifteen-year period. Strategically, given the amplitude of the correction which is to follow the fifteen-year upward drive, it would have been foolish for any long-term investors to have considered purchasing shares on the London Stock Exchange during the summer of 1991.

Indeed, the Wave Principle was warning that a major bear market of enormous dimensions was approaching quite rapidly during the summer of 1991 and that the cycle factors that acted to propel the British stock market upward for fifteen years had fully spent their force over the period. In addition, according to Dow's Law of Commonality, not only was the UK stock market approaching a major terminal juncture that was likely to produce the type of bear market that was seen in the US during the 1930s, but other markets would follow suit, even though the behavior patterns may not have been as well defined as that of the British stock market at the time.

The application of the Wave Principle to the behavior of the UK equity market, between 1975 and 1991, also provides another interesting revelation. The Crash of '87 is widely considered to have represented some kind of stock market holocaust and has often been compared to the 1929 Crash on Wall Street. Seen in its proper context on a logarithmic scale as the Wave A of Wave IV, that downward drive in 1987 was of normative dimensions, similar in time and amplitude to Wave A of Wave II that took place during 1976.

Many were expecting the Crash of '87 to be the precursor to the type of bear market the US experienced between 1929–1932. The Wave Principle said otherwise. At the time of the Crash of '87, a full five-wave pattern was yet to be completed. There was no element in the structure that called for a 1929–1932-type bear market at that time.

During the summer of 1991, a five-wave structure spanning a fifteen-year period was approaching completion. The Wave Principle tells us that what was widely expected to follow the Crash of '87, by the international investment community during 1988, was promised for a later date. According to the Wave Principle, what remained in store for investors during the summer of 1991 would make the Crash of '87 look like a roaring bull market.

During the summer of 1991, investors in the US and the UK were still waiting for the economic recovery that was promised by politicians to follow the end of the Gulf War. But, patience was beginning to wear thin. There was no genuine conclusive evidence that a recovery was about to take hold in the US, or anywhere else. In the UK, all the signs pointed toward a deepening recession that might lead to a depression. In the US, there were suggestions being made that the spurt in economic activity that followed the Gulf War was an unrepeatable affair and that a "double-dip" recession was in the cards.

In London, the Wave Principle as applied to the British stock market was signalling a decline in share prices of a magnitude that no one believed possible, which would be shared by all other markets, with the attendant economic implications. By the time you read this, you should know whether it was the politicians who were right or the Wave Principle.

News and the Wave Principle

It must be remembered that news items can often cause extremes in the degree of a cycle, can sometimes even affect the time scale, but they never actually alter the cycle itself. If the general mood is pessimistic, a bearish news announcement will reinforce any existing downtrend, but a bullish statement may briefly arrest its downward momentum. On the other hand, if optimism is the mood of the day, a bearish announcement could slow down, but not reverse, an uptrend which, equally, could be given further stimulus by good news. In both cases, it is seen that the overriding major cyclical forces governing the immediate trend of the market dominate the daily fluctuations in prices provoked by news items.

A mid-seventies study, published by Draper Dobie, Toronto, shows that seventy-five percent of the reasons given by investors for their actions relate to foreseeable fundamental events. The rest is attributed to instinctive human response to unforeseeable fundamental events (hurricanes, coups d'etat), which add *specific randomness* to share price movement.

Events, which stimulate the bulk of investor reaction and so have some effect on the overrriding cyclical forces, fall into roughly three categories. They are:

1. Events of an historical nature, which may motivate the buying or selling of shares.

2. Events which can be anticipated, influence the economy as a whole, and have specific effects on industrial groupings.

3. Events which can be anticipated and which affect the performance of a particular company.

Short-term influences which cause *random noise* within the overriding trend, and to which investors attribute about a quarter of their decisions, are those unforeseen events that fall in the following categories:

1. Acts of God, earthquakes, volcanic action, droughts, floods, and other natural phenomena; assassinations, insurrections, and other political action.

2. Conflicting reports which attempt to forecast the unforecastable, such as self-interest reports issued by governments, pressure groups, or members of the securities industry, commenting on or countering longer-term economic forecasts.

3. Reports which are simply ill-conceived. And in this category we have to place most stock market commentary by newspapers and predictions widely disseminated by individuals using a priori judgments that cater to the herd instinct.

These last are frequent and their effect on prices is sudden and pronounced, but ephemeral without much effect on the time scale.

I wish I could hammer it into the head of every investor that major national and international events, which attract mass response, do not, repeat not, dominate stock market activity on anything other than a short-term basis. A study of the cyclical movements in the stock market and the application of the Elliott Wave Principle over long periods should help dispel this false belief. Short of the thought police, it is obviously impossible to determine the real motivations of every investor. But the papers choose the worst option, that of describing today's stock market picture as a reaction to current news or statements by local personalities. I must insist that market action leads the business news events of the day, does not shadow them, and discounts in advance the business cycle.

The impact on market action of any of the above-cited events does not alter the time cycle. Linked markets throughout the world continue to keep time with each other, though temporarily the degree of trend may be distorted. To prove my point even more emphatically, look at Figure 3, which illustrates the Juglar and Kondratieff economic cycles through the period of the US Civil War, and followed by the two world wars. (This is reproduced from the book *Cycles: The Science of Prediction,* by E.R. Dewey and E.F. Dakin.)

From this diagram you can see how the cycles dominate the supply and demand markets (commodities, shares), their origins firmly in the important basic rhythms of the world economy. Charles Dow stated that a bull market that occurs in one major economy will usually have its counterparts in the other major economies of the world.

The cyclicality of price movements, reflected by the DJIA on Wall Street or the FT Industrial Ordinary Share Index in the City of London, is the distillation of all the basic economic rhythms in those countries, as well as the coincidence of the business rhythm of the industries (personified by companies) that go to make up those indices.

This is what produces the dominant trend in the international stock market cycle—general sentiment which then influences all share-price behavior.

Of course, there are deviations from the dominant trend, due to the introduction of random noise created by investors with the jitters caused by reading too many newspaper articles on events of passing importance. As we go through the Elliott Wave Theory you will see how to allow for this random noise.

Figure 3
WAR AND ITS DISLOCATIONS

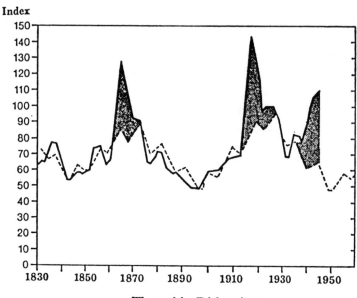

War and its Dislocations.

Fig. 3 shows distortion in the Wholesale Price Index in time of War. The solid line shows the three year moving average of the Index of Wholesale Prices in the U.S., 1830–1945. The broken line shows the synthesis of the regular 9-year and 54-year cycles. The shaded areas show the difference between the Index and the regular pattern for the periods of the Civil War, World War I, and World War II.

The 3-year moving average has been extrapolated to 1945. The shaded areas begin one year prior to the outbreak of wars, since in a 3-year moving average the effect of the first year of war is extended one year backward.

It is interesting to note that in spite of the magnitude of the distortion, the *timing* of the peaks happens to coincide with the normal timing of the 9-year cycle. It is also interesting to note how nearly equal are the distortions.

Elliott and the Academics

The major difference between the work of R.N. Elliott and that of the traditional economists and analysts, who focus on cyclical behavior, was in the area of fixed time frames. Many who have attempted to apply the work of Kondratieff, Juglar, Kitchin, and other cyclical economists have done so by rigidly superimposing fixed periodicities on economic and market behavior. Elliott, in his wisdom, argued that economies and markets could never be subjected to fixed time frames of re-occurrence. Elliott was concerned with cyclical relationships rather than any element of a fixed time frame.

Elliott was convinced that markets did not lend themselves to repetitive sequences within given time frames and that the use of such cyclical tools would do more harm than good. Elliott held the same view of repetitive configurations. He did not believe a "head and shoulders top" meant the market would always go down, nor did he believe that a "rounding saucer bottom" pointed to the end of a bear market or the terminal juncture of a cyclical decline with any useful or meaningful degree of reliability.

R.N. Elliott was primarily concerned with the behavior of the various parts that composed the cycle, since the evidence he collected did not justify the repetition of share price movements over any fixed period, short, intermediate, or long. Nor did his research indicate that the repetition of sequential patterns would give an indication of future prospective price movements.

In order to appreciate the radical implications of Elliott's work, it is necessary to give some consideration to the work of the academics, such as Professor Burton G. Malkiel, Paul Cootner, Eugene Fama, Bachelier, and others. Paul Cootner stood the investment world on its ear with his book, *The Random Character of Stock Price Movements.* Yale University Professor Burton G. Malkiel added to the drama with his lucid and influential *A Random Walk Down Wall Street,* where the "narrow" or "weak" form of the efficient market hypothesis was outlined.

According to the efficient market hypothesis, the history of price movements in the stock market or any other market contains no useful information that will enable an investor to consistently outperform a buy-and-hold strategy incorporating a randomly selected, diversified group of shares.

Essentially, what Burton G. Malkiel said was that you would be far better off building an investment portfolio, based on the results of a tribe of monkeys throwing darts at the financial pages, rather than attempting the timing and selection of your investments with the use of technical analysis.

The work of Cootner and Malkiel is available for all to study. Those investors whose actions are deflected by thought must certainly wonder how the technical analysts and chart players continue to stay in business and maintain their following. There are actually three reasons. First, using charts and technical tools offers the seductive promise of making stock profits by expending relatively little time and energy. Second, the methodology of most technical principles can be assimilated fairly quickly and can be easily understood by the average investor. Last, the technical analysts and chart players have been able to hang on to their credibility simply through revolving cycles of luck! As Malkiel puts it:

"Let's engage in a coin-tossing contest. Those who consistently flip heads will be declared the winners. The contest begins and 1,000 contestants flip coins. Just as would be expected by chance, 500 of them flip heads and those winners are allowed to advance to the second stage of the contest and flip again. As might be expected, 250 flip heads. Operating under the laws of chance, there will be 125 winners in the third round, 63 in the fourth, 31 in the fifth, 16 in the sixth and 8 in the seventh.

By this time, crowds start to gather to watch the surprising ability of these expert coin-tossers. The winners are overwhelmed with adulation. They are celebrated as geniuses in the art of coin-tossing—their biographies are written and people urgently seek their advice. After all, there were 1,000 contestants and only 8 could consistently flip heads. The game continues and there are even those who flip heads nine and ten times in a row. The point of this analogy is not to indicate that investment fund managers can or should make their decisions by flipping coins, but that the laws of chance do operate and they can explain some amazing success stories."

Although I've spent many years attempting to discover the methods used by Elliott to accumulate the overwhelming amount of data that would have been needed for him to develop the Wave Principle, I am yet to determine how Elliott went about collecting and quantifying his data. But, what I do know is that it has taken many years for highly qualified brains with the most up-to-date computer technology to arrive at the same conclusion as Elliott. That is, share prices demonstrate randomness over all of the time periods tested.

The work of R.N. Elliott is certainly not inconsistent with that of Malkiel, Cootner, and the other academics, who provide overwhelming evidence that price randomness is an intrinsic element in market price movements, albeit with a stochastic bias. Many technical analysts and chart players complain that their work has never been sufficiently tested, as if randomness could be eliminated under special circumstances for special analysts. As far as I am aware, only the technical work of Charles Dow and R.N. Elliott has ever been able to stand up to the challenge of the academics.

Where Elliott Rules the Waves

One could argue that the Wave Principle is not truly a cyclical theory, for true cycles are observed repetitions of events at stated intervals. Elliott apparently had no intention of making any further contribution to the many cycles of fixed periodicity, which were being discovered in his day. He flatly refuted the ten-year pattern of Edgar Lawrence Smith unveiled in 1938. Said Elliott: "It will work until it stops working."

As with some of Charles Dow's investigations, any cyclical classification of Elliott's work must allow for psychological derivations. Action and reaction are given more weight than cause and effect by the psychological theorists of market action. Whatever the cause of a change in expectation of share prices, it is the consequence of change—not forgetting the element of uncertainty—that the psychological theorist believes will trigger the next phase of the cycle. Dow and Elliott both recognized that seeking periodic repetition in share price movements, primarily stimulated by emotion, would be irrelevant. Elliott believed that his waves would arise regardless of the time element, with each subsequent wave reflecting investors' response to the extent and duration of its predecessor. This time frame will seem somewhat indefinite to many readers, but it is the most important element of wave classification and offers the most pragmatic approach to cyclicality.

As the Elliott cycle unfolds before us, we find a series of *impulse moves,* which eventually rise excessively, due to speculation. *Corrective moves* then occur, so that the excesses will be eliminated and the cycle continue. The time frame relationship is that a corrective move must be proportionate to that of the impulse move it is countering. So, if the impulse move is two weeks long, the corrective move is likely to be seven or eight days. On a larger scale, such as: an impulse move of two or three years (the suggested time scale of US bull markets), the corrective move would take eighteen months or so.

So we shall see that the time cycle develops according to the periodicity of its components.

Classification of Waves

Probably the best way to gain a perspective of the time frame relationships is the classification of waves that appeared in the April 1974 issue of *Accountancy Magazine,* the Journal of the Institute of Chartered Accountants in England and Wales.

"Elliott's actual classification of the various waves by degree in order of decreasing magnitude—designed to cover everything from the smallest imaginable wave formation involving the hourly moves in the index, to a formation lasting two hundred years or more—were as follows:

"**Grand Super Cycle.** This was designed to cover the longest possible measurable time period. As of our current historical records, we have no concrete evidence of the completion of a grand super cycle, since Elliott's records only go back to the mid-1800s. According to Elliott, Wave I of a grand super cycle began in 1800 and ran to 1850, Wave II from 1850 to 1857, Wave III from 1857 to 1928, Wave IV from 1929 to 1949, and according to the Principle, we remain in Wave V of a grand super cycle, which could stretch for several years more. Obviously, the risks are far greater for investors now than they were when we were at the early stages of the grand super cycle, such as the beginning of Wave III or even the beginning of Wave V.

"**Super Cycle.**   This is the next lower degree. Elliott claims that a super cycle of five waves began in 1857 (Wave III of a grand super cycle), following the depression of the 1850s. The five waves were completed in 1929. There then followed a corrective super cycle, running from 1929 to 1949. In 1949, a new super cycle began. We have completed four waves of the particular super cycle within Wave V of the grand super cycle.

"**Cycle.**   The wave pattern of the next lesser degree to the super cycle is that of the cycle. A breakdown of the 1857–1929 super cycle to cycle dimensions would give us the upmove from 1857 to 1864, the downmove from 1864 to 1877, the upmove from 1877 to 1881, the downmove from 1881 to 1896, and the upmove from 1896 to 1919.

"**Primary.**   The period from 1896 to 1929 represents Cycle Wave V of the super cycle. If we break this cycle wave down to its primary wave components, we find an upthrust from 1896 to 1899, a downthrust from 1899 to 1907, an upthrust from 1907 to 1909, the downthrust from 1909 to 1921, and the big upthrust from 1921 to 1929.

"**Intermediate.**   The intermediate waves of the long and glorious bull market that stretched for eight years from 1921 to 1929 can be subdivided into the upwave from 1921 to 1923, the downwave from 1923 to 1924, the upwave from 1924 to 1925, the downwave from 1925 to 1926, and the massive three-year upthrust that sent share prices soaring until they finally toppled over, from 1926 to 1929.

"**Minor.** By this time, readers may be somewhat suspicious of the historical data used as examples, doubting the application of the Wave Principle to the current environment. If we examine the upwave in the FT30 which began in February 1971 and ended in May 1971, we find the same five-wave pattern in repetition once again. Minor Wave 1 began in February 1971 and was terminated in May 1971. Downwave 2 began in May 1971, ending in mid-June 1971. Minor upwave 3 began in mid-June 1971, ending in September 1971. Minor downwave 4 began in September 1971 and was completed in November 1971. The longest wave, which is practically always Wave 5, began in November 1971 and was completed in May 1972.

"**Minute.** As can be seen, the minor waves will usually encompass the monthly movements of share prices, while the minute waves are likely to relate to the weekly movement in share prices. If we examine Minor Wave 5 of the move from November 1971 through May 1972, we find a Minute Wave I running upwards from mid-November to mid-January for a total of seven weeks. This is followed by a Minute Downwave 2 running down from mid-January to mid-February for four weeks. Minute Wave 3 starts in mid-February and runs until late February for two weeks. Minute Wave 4 runs downward from late February to early March for three weeks. Minute Wave 5 runs upward from early March until mid-May for eight weeks.

"**Minuette.** If we now take the period representing the last eight weeks of the February 1971–May 1972 bull move, this period representing Minute Wave 5 of Minor Wave 5 of Intermediate Wave V, of Primary Wave V of Cycle Wave III, etc., we can break the pattern down into its minuette wave components, which show the daily movements. Minuette Wave 1 began on 10 March at FT30 495.1 and ran for twelve days, reaching FT30 520 on 22 March. Minuette Wave 2 began on 22 March and ran for two days, bringing the FT30 down to 503.1. Wave 3 began on 27 March, running for thirty days, taking the FT30 up to 540.3. Minuette Wave 4 then acted in a corrective fashion for nine days, taking the FT30 back down to 419.6. The final Minuette Wave 5 lasted twelve days until the top at 545.6 was reached on 22 May 1972.

"**Sub-Minuette.** The sub-minuette waves comprising the last twelve trading sessions in the final stages of the bull move of May 1972 reveal a Sub-Minuette Wave I lasting twelve hours, Sub-Minuette Wave II lasting five hours, Sub-Minuette Wave III lasting eight hours, Sub-Minuette Wave IV lasting six hours: the final burst of Sub-Minuette Wave V was nineteen hours long.

"One can readily begin to see how Elliott's method completely supersedes most other forms of pattern categorization of share-price movements and, to say the least, clearly demonstrates the obsolescence of the over-simplified bull-market-bear-market fixation, which tries to establish a constantly recurring periodicity of bull and bear market cycles into two- and three-year repetitions. The randomness of the time relationship in classification amply demonstrates this point. For all practical purposes, we have in the Wave Principle the ultimate in a work-a-day series of stock market sequences."

3
Elliott, the Market, and Its Law

The market has its law. Were there no law, there could be no center about which prices could revolve, and therefore, no market.

—RALPH NELSON ELLIOTT
The Wave Principle (1938)

Although Elliott would seem, from his writings, to have been well read in Dow Theory, and to appreciate both its qualities and its shortcomings, he argued that so much new stock market information had been stored since Charles Dow wrote that new, important deductions could be made from certain behavioral characteristics in price movements.

By the time Elliott had concretized his theory, the theory that Charles Dow elaborated while he was editor of the still-prestigious *Wall Street Journal* was half a century old. Many stock market professionals thought that the Dow Theory had special forecasting significance, but their more modern colleagues recognized its imprecision and laggard nature. For example, following the Dow Theory, a trend is usually well-established before a classic *buy signal* is triggered. Elliott's approach was far more pragmatic.

"Wild, senseless and apparently uncontrollable changes in share prices from year-to-year, month-to-month, day-to-day and even hour-to-hour, linked themselves into a law-abiding, rhythmic pattern of waves." One can detect an almost exultant tone in Elliott's statement, the fruit of many years of statistical compilation of share-price behavior.

The sequence, insisted Elliott, repeated itself continually in sequence, from hour-to-hour movements to massive market movements over decades. So, by establishing the exact position of the current market movements within the major cyclical force, one should be able to determine the degree of maturity of a market drive within any particular trend, and so, with courage, plan one's investments accordingly.

Let us step back a little in time and once again refer to the London Stock Exchange for an example. An Elliott Wave categorization of the January 1975 to March 1976 move would have encouraged investors to remain confident during the subsequent June–August decline of 1975 and the February–March decline of 1976. In Elliott terms only three impulse waves of that particular bull cycle had been completed. The mature stage of that particular movement would not occur until the fifth and final wave was nearing completion. There would have been little need to try to predict when the cyclical drive would end. The Wave Principle indicated the very early stages of a major cyclical drive that could last for years. Strategically, shrewd investors would have confidently purchased during the two downswings cited above, as I had recommended in my publication, *Investors Bulletin,* at the time, while taking the same action for my managed accounts.

There are many compatibilities between Elliott and Dow. Both recognized that long- and short-term swings are part of the same movement. The small swings are part of the swing next up the scale, which itself is part of its greater successor, and so on, up to the grand super cycle. The reverse is also true.

The Tides of Dow and Elliott

The analogy with tides was first chosen by Charles Dow; the waves are subordinate to the tide, the ripples in the water subordinate to the waves, each rising and falling with rhythmic regularity, self-generated and forming cross currents, but the whole governed by seemingly moon-driven tidal forces. This comparison should help one to understand the different trends of share prices, sometimes acting concurrently, sometimes running contradictorily, but always subject to an overriding force.

The flotsam on the stock market ocean is *random noise*—in other words, the shorter-term price movements caused by spontaneous events. This sort of movement, going in two or three directions at once, often opposite to the primary trend, can be difficult to understand. But, bear in mind the basic sub-division of three kinds of cycles, rather simplified as short, medium, and long; then use the long to give perspective to your judgment of the short swings, also vice versa, and you will then soon become more skilled at judg-ing market movement. This phenomenon you must understand before you can understand the basis of the Elliott Wave Principle. To adapt a phrase from James Gleick's book on the new science of chaos, the Wave Principle will give you "periodicity that was disguised in random noise."

There is greater precision in the classification of the various movements in a complete cycle in Elliott's work than in that of Charles Dow. Elliott's separation of larger corrective movements into minor, minute, and sub-minuette categories is one of the most fascinating aspects of the Wave Principle. Elliott's basic pattern repeats itself again and again: beginning with the sub-minuette cycle, upward to the minuette cycle, on up to the minor cycle, still up to the intermediate cycle, a steady continuation up to the grand super cycle of one hundred years and more, spanning major changes in our civilization.

Elliott's Five Important Rules

The basic pattern which is the subject of this cumulative upward progression is quite simple to comprehend. Elliott's work can be summarized in five basic tenets:

1. For every action there is a reaction. Stock market movements in the direction of the main trend are *impulse moves.* Stock market movements counter to the main trend are *corrective moves.* An impulse move is always followed by a corrective move.

2. Generally, all impulse moves have five subordinate waves while all corrective moves have three waves.

3. When the main trend is upward, waves 1, 3, and 5 are impulse moves and waves 2 and 4 are corrective moves. When the main trend is downward, the first and third waves become impulse moves, while the second wave becomes a corrective move.

4. The action of the main trend can be taking place over a time frame of anything from a few hours to many years. When the main trend has completed a series of five waves, it reverses and a *counter move* of three waves is expected.

5. When completed, a move comprising five waves followed by a counter move consisting of three waves is the first cycle movement. This complete cycle movement will represent the first and second waves of a cycle in the time frame of the next higher degree.

That was pure Elliott—now let us try and simplify it further.

Elliott in the Market

Elliott's basic configuration was the five-three pattern; five generally upward waves followed by three making a downward move. For the sake of simplicity, we will assume that the five-wave pattern is only applicable to bull markets, the bear markets having three waves, and act accordingly.

Now, look back to the seventies through your new Elliott Wave spectacles. There were some lucky, or clever, investors who bought into the London market in January 1975, but some got out too early, in June 1975, when Elliott students would have known only one wave of the bull cycle had been completed. Even more got out between February and March of 1976, when only the first and part of a second wave of the bull market were completed. Those confident in their knowledge of Elliott's Wave Principle were still holding on before the Crash of '87, knowing that the fifth wave was yet to be completed.

It was during the summer of 1991 that the completion of the fifth wave began to look imminent.

Figure 4 is a simplified illustration of the five-wave phenomenon. But remember that the stock market is rarely as symmetrical as the diagram; it is an illustration only.

Forecasting with the Wave Principle

I use the Wave Principle as a timing tool for the purpose of enhancing my investment performance, but one can also use the Elliott Wave Principle as a forecasting tool, rather than just as a method for strategic analysis. This is how. Note that the impulse waves in the diagram are parallel to each other, so are the corrective waves. These characteristics will prove very valuable later in the context of *channelling* when applying the Wave Principle (we shall discuss this in a later chapter as we go into more elaborate detail on Elliott Principle-based forecasting).

Figure 4
BASIC FIVE WAVE PATTERN

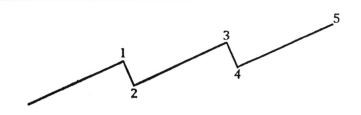

Figure 5
COMPLETE BASIC CYCLE

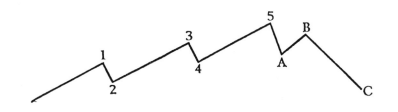

More important at this stage are the bottom levels of Wave 2 and Wave 4: in most stock market cycles Wave 2 will not retrace all the ground gained by Wave 1, but only a proportion of it. (How great a proportion we shall be able to establish, more or less, when dealing with the subject of cycle amplitude.) Nor will Wave 4 retrace all the ground gained by waves 1 and 3; its depth is related to that of Wave 2. As a general rule, during an upward progression, Wave 2 will be shorter than Wave 1 and Wave 4, shorter than Wave 3. Furthermore, Wave 4 will usually turn above the bottom of Wave 2.

Look at it in figures: assume that Wave 1 is, say, 20 points in amplitude; when the downwave comes we can act on the assumption that it will be less than 20 points. Similarly, if Wave 3 is 25 points, we can assume that Wave 4 will be less—in fact, it will relate more to Wave 2 in scale. This gives us both the probable and the maximum extent of the two corrective waves.

The five-wave pattern of Figure 4 illustrates the complete upward phase of a cycle: to round it off, the entire movement, which began with Wave 1, would need to be *corrected*. The next Elliott rule is that once the five waves of the upward phase are completed, the next corrective wave will be larger than the two previous corrective waves. The correction following on Wave 5 acts to correct the previous five waves.

The illustration in Figure 5 is the complete cycle, the three waves of the downtrend (A,B, and C), added to the five previous ones of the uptrend. The first downward thrust of the corrective movement, Wave A, is countered by the rally of Wave B, which is depressed again by Wave C. Thus the cycle is completed. And at the end of Wave C, the cycle begins again at Wave 1.

Applying What Has Been Learned

Now that you have got that under your belts—and confess, it was not that difficult—we shall apply what we have learned.

In Figure 4 we suggested a Wave 1 that could represent a 20-point move in the Dow Jones 30. Following on that, we should assume that the downward Wave 2 would be less than 20 points: that is, had Wave 1 started at DJ 800 to finish at DJ 820, we could *forecast* that the downward move would finish above DJ 800. (The principle that Wave 2 will NOT retrace all the gain of Wave 1, remember?)

To continue the illustration: let Wave 3 be 30 points, let Wave 2 have been 6 points, downwave 4 will definitely be less than 30 points, indeed more likely 8 points.

Now, let us fill in a few more hypothetical numbers and anticipate a crash. On our imaginary DJ30 chart of Figure 4, Wave 1 begins at 800 and turns at 820. Wave 2 takes us down 6 points to 814, but Wave 3 surges up 30 points to 844 before collapsing into Wave 4, down 8 points, leaving us with the terminal point of the wave at DJ 836. But, suppose Wave 5 is on the same scale as Wave 1, lifting the index 20 points to 856. Here comes the crash! Now what, how do we incorporate out Elliott knowledge into our investment strategy?

No Elliott-wise investor would have considered buying on the move up from DJ 836 to 856 because this was the dreaded Wave 5. But he would have been quite happy to buy around 814, his downside risk would not increase beyond 12 points, because Wave 2 does not retrace all of Wave 1. Another comfortable buy-in point would have been at the end of Wave 4, at DJ 836, because his risk was less than 30 points and more likely to be in the 6–8-point range, since Wave 4 would be more like Wave 2, and not likely to devour all the gains of Wave 3. And, remember, the cycle was incomplete, Wave 5 was yet to come. Our Elliott-wise investor would like to dispose of some issues near the top of Wave 5, and would not consider buying in again until the DJ30 had fallen at least 10 points.

The rule we have established is that the correction of Wave 5 corrects not only that wave, but also the entire upward movement! This warns us that the downward wave, after Wave 5, is likely to be larger than either of the previous two corrective waves. On our illustration, the largest corrective wave was Wave 4, dropping 8 points. Therefore, the minimum expectation of correction following on Wave 5 would be more than 8 points. Then we could forecast that the minimum expectation for the next downward move in the DJ30 would be 848 (which being 856 – 8 = 848).

The Futility of Absolutes

By now you will have noticed the absence of absolutism, so beloved of most fanatical chartists in predictions built on the Elliott Wave Principle. Those chartists insist on predicting absolute levels in the DJ30 or FT30.

As we discuss the Elliott Wave Principle, the phrases *maximum probable extent,* or *minimum expectation* and similar, will be applied to market movements. So, when it is said that the minimum expectation of the corrective wave is DJ30 848, this does not mean we expect the market to end up there. It means that the DJ30 may end its correction at that point, but it could conceivably move further.

The strategic aspect of dealing with factors that establish maximum and minimum probabilities is that one never acts counter to the risk factor. In the example above, it would be extremely imprudent to start a buying program (or even think of it) until the market reaches the minimum objective. And it would be equally imprudent to start a selling program until the market was near its maximum objective—in the example, the completion of Wave 5.

If you are wondering why I have chosen to use such small hypothetical movements in the DJ30, which is currently into four figures, the answer is quite simple. The choice of sub-minuette movements was made to present a situation which could be put into immediate practice. It was the smallest feasible amplitude commensurate with hourly developments on the stock market.

In succeeding chapters, I will show how to use these hourly movements as the starting point for wave classification. Why not try a few dry runs with what you have learned of the Elliott Wave Principle to date?

Determine—or try to—the last pivotal point in your favorite stock market index and from there try to build up a wave pattern, starting with the smallest movement. You will need to use an hourly chart of your chosen index.

The smallest moves that one can record are the sub-minuette moves. When you have completed your first sub-minuette cycle (remember the 5–3 configuration), you will find you have also drawn waves 1 and 2 of the minuette cycle, which is the next higher degree. Continue to study the hourly moves in search of a second complete sub-minuette cycle, and that will give you waves 3 and 4 of the minuette cycle, no doubt on a longer time scale. The final move to look for will be a five-wave in the sub-minuette cycle which, when corrected, will produce the first part of the larger wave that will correct the minuette cycle.

The corrective phase of the minuette cycle will be larger than any of the corrective waves in the upward phase (five waves) of your sub-minuette cycle and larger than any of the corrective waves, which complete the three sub-minuette cycles.

And so you will continue to build up with the cycles, higher and higher, defining cyclical forces of greater size each time, and to use the five basic tenets of wave behavior to guide your investment strategy.

You may feel that the tools at your disposal are limited, while the plotting of cycles of ever greater size may seem somewhat confusing. You have got to the difficult point, but, courage: in subsequent chapters, we shall discover the aids that will help you.

4

Nature's Law,
Red in Tooth and Claw

Creative minds through the centuries have done the important work of adapting past gains to an ever-changing present, a work which we must continue.

—THOMAS A. HARRIS

I'm OK, You're OK!

Markets are efficient, but ninety-percent driven by emotion. Every market movement represents the sum total of individual emotional instability—whatever its cause—of the players at that moment in time. Some knowledge of how the mind works certainly helps one understand the rhythm of share-price behavior.

Freudian psychology, like the Dow Theory, has many useful qualities, but also failings. Just as Dr. Eric Berne, by using group free-association for analysis, overcame the major problem of patient-therapist dependence of the Freudian school, so Elliott's method of stock market analysis made it possible to credibly foresee market developments, rather than follow market trends, as Dow Theory or other technical analysis tools do.

The consequences of the in-built, trend-following tendencies of most technical indicators, such as share-pattern analysis, is that the market appears to seem exceptionally strong when, in fact, it is technically at its weakest. A fundamental stock market rule that I would like to inject into the emotional as well as intellectual psyche of all investors is this: markets are technically at their strongest after a sharp decline and technically at their weakest after a sharp advance. I know, I know, I have said this before—bear with me—for it bears repeating, over and over and over again.

Dow Theory departs from trend-following techniques in its approach to the three distinct phases of bull and bear markets, alerting its practitioners to the behavioral extremes that occur at important turning points.

Trend-following techniques lead into a double trap: that of considering further advances likely at the extremes of a bull market, or further declines imminent at the bottom of a bear market. Dow Theory alerts the intelligent investor to the possibility of major and minor turning points.

The major shortcoming of the Dow Theory is the lack of quantitative tools that can be applied in a useful and precise manner between the important terminal points. Elliott gave investors the ability to project movements forward in time, within precise parameters of probability. He examined the technical tools available at the time, thought there must be a better way, and set about the painstaking analysis of thousands upon millions of share-price movements of the previous eighty years, to discover a correlation that had never been discovered before.

The Wave Count

Using hourly plotted movements to form the sub-minuette cycle, you saw how it built up the cycle of the next-highest degree, the minuette cycle; the minuettes constructed the minute cycle, which in turn forms the minor cycle; the building continues upward through the intermediate cycles, primary cycles, and so on, up to the grand super cycle, which can span many decades.

The manner in which the interlinking of these cycles can be used to project future price trends is just one of the many fascinating aspects of the Elliott Wave Principle. It represents the most important development in the field of technical stock market analysis this century.

Now, let us try to see how well you have grasped the basic concept of the Elliott Wave Principle by working it down the Wave classification, within a time frame and using a larger scale.

So, back to Figure 4 of Chapter Three, but now we assume it represents a time scale of many years, a complete primary cycle. (Whatever the time scale, the principles regarding the interaction of impulse waves, corrective waves, and the five-up-three- down sequence, ALWAYS remain the same.)

We start by assuming that impulse Wave 1 represents a move of 600 DJ30 points building up over twenty-four months and impulse Wave 3 is 940 points accumulated over three years. Corrective waves 2 and 4 are 290 points over twelve months and 435 points over nine months. Our final impulse Wave 5 measures 650 points, put on over twenty-five months. This is a picture of a bull market that lasts eight years and ten months, with a total upward move of 1,395 DJ30 points.

If this were happening in real life, conventional market analysts would insist that the first two-year move was a complete bull market and its one-year corrective successor, a complete bear market. And repeat this judgement for waves 3 and 4. According to the Wave Principle, such classifications are unreal, and result in major analytical and strategical errors, which could be costly. Our main interest is in wave relationships and categories. In this respect, the time frame suggests a primary movement, which will be divisible into all the Elliott classifications down to intermediate, minor, minute, minuette, and sub-minuette. It's rather like Mandelbrot's coastline, the infinite within the finite, but, possibly fortunately, we are limited in our sub-divisions by the ability of current technology to register market changes. Wall Street's instantaneous trade recording device, the Stockmaster, is cur-rently the fastest and most detailed.

In Figure 6, we have Primary Wave 1 subdivided into the waves of the next smaller degree, the intermediate cycle. You will see that there are five smaller waves, a to e, whose sum total adds up to the whole of Wave 1 of Figure 4 in Chapter Three. The same will hold true for Wave 3 and Wave 5, each with five smaller waves, a to e, whose parts go to make up its sum.

In the normal Elliott manner, Primary Wave 2 corrects Primary Wave 1, which consists of five waves of the intermediate degree. And so, Primary Wave 4 acts to correct Primary Wave 3, which has five intermediate waves. (The breakdown of primary waves 2 and 4 to the intermediate scale has purposely been omitted here as it requires special treatment. It will be dealt with later.)

Figure 6
PRIMARY WAVE SUBDIVIDED

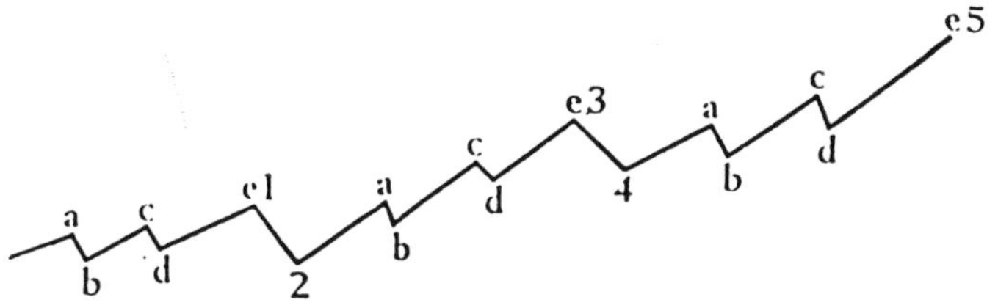

Figure 7
BREAKDOWN OF INTERMEDIATE WAVES

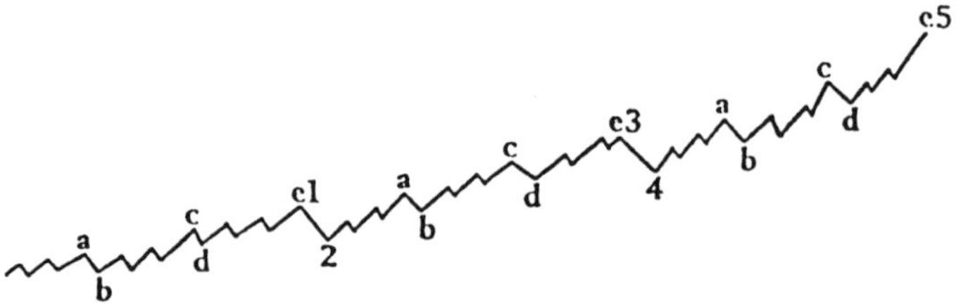

The intermediate waves can be broken down into the five waves of the smaller cycle, the minor wave, as we see in Figure 7. Intermediate waves a, c, and e—which resulted from the breakdown of primary waves 1, 3, and 5, of Figure 4 in Chapter Three—now each have their own five sub-waves. Though limited in number, the Elliott waves are all self-similar.

The primary waves we have just subdivided would be the equivalent to the very long-term bull or bear markets, which span five to ten years. According to currently popular classification, this primary wave would probably cover three bull and two bear markets. The intermediate waves would be the bull and bear markets of two to three years and six to eighteen months, respectively. This makes the minor waves relate to the monthly movements; the minute waves to the weekly fluctuations; the minuette to the daily; and the subminuette to the hourly changes.

The Primary Market Price Cycle

The chart on page 35 shows the breakdown of a primary cycle to the minute waves. The total number of minute waves in the complete primary cycle is 144; the total number of minor waves is 34, the intermediate total is 8. If we wished to break down the primary cycle any further, we would discover that there are 610 minuette waves, and 2,584 sub-minuette waves.

Needless to say, if we started from the grand super cycle down to the sub-minuette, the figures would become astronomical. But for all practical purposes, a three-cycle breakdown is sufficient to count the moves in a cycle and so start to assess probable future developments.

What puts the Wave Principle miles ahead of most other technical, or chartist approaches, is its consistency of form. The shape of the waves and

Figure 8
PRIMARY MARKET CYCLE BREAKDOWN

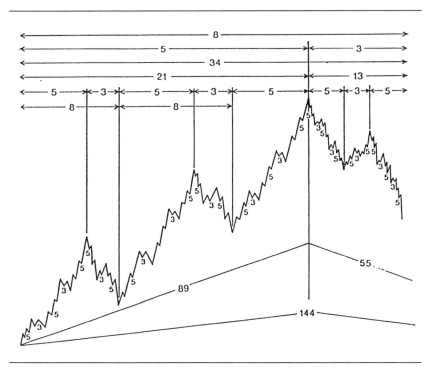

their relationships can be seen as they are plotted out. In theory the shape of the waves can be defined with great precision. Once the degree of a wave—primary, intermediate, sub-minuette, or whatever—has been recognized, the skilled Elliott Wave practitioner can draw the waves of the degrees upward.

He can construct a share-price-behavior model for years into the future. Many have done so and use these models, constantly refined, in their day-to-day trading.

In markets, absolutes do not exist. The only help an investor gets in anticipating future price trends is given by the possibilities and probabilities that are present in all mathematical game theory. The Elliott Wave Principle is not a tool that creates absolute predictions of the future, but with this principle, investors can anticipate a wider variety of price movements and will be able to quantify their possible resolution more accurately.

Terminal Junctures

The Wave Principle shows that there is a continuous repetition of cyclical phenomena within a defined, but flexible framework that allows the knowledgeable user to anticipate the impact of current price behavior by quantifying it on future price behavior. The point of departure is always pivotal—a turning point, such as the start of a new bull market, the beginning of a new bear market, a new intermediate or minor trend. Pivotal points always occur at the end of the classic Elliott five-three sequence; five waves up, three waves down.

Once the Elliott afficionado has successfully identified the pivotal point of a trend, he can project the probable development of the five upward waves of that trend and so the likely dimensions of subsequent corrective waves. Projecting these forward, he can be fairly certain that the next series of impulse and corrective waves will follow a recognizable pattern, riding up into the next-higher degree cycle. Each component wave of the pattern will run in parallel with the first impulse wave, after an important pivotal point on a comparable time scale and of similar size.

On a practical level, the investor should always try to make his purchases as close to the beginning of a primary trend as possible, and, conversely, to sell them as close as possible to its finish. Applying the Elliott Wave Principle can alert the investor to the possibilities for gain or loss at the time he wishes to act. Remember, all primary trends can be subdivided into their intermediate component; so if an investor was to begin his investment program during the first intermediate wave of the first impulse wave of the primary trend, there would be very little danger of any major market reversal in the immediate future—but note the qualification "major."

The ultimate objective of any investor well skilled in the Elliott Wave Principle would be to make his share purchases during the first sub-minuette wave, of the first minuette wave, of the first minute wave, of the first minor wave, of the first intermediate wave of any primary trend.

The reverse being also imperatively true: he would try to liquidate his portfolio when the fifth sub-minuette wave, of the fifth minuette wave, of the fifth minute wave, of the fifth minor wave, of the fifth intermediate wave, of the primary trend, in its fifth wave has spent its force.

Using standard, conventional technical tools, our investor is hardly likely to achieve these aims. With the Elliott Wave Principle, they are within the realm of achievement. But, when all these impulse forces reach their climax and have spent themselves, a formidable top is likely to have been constructed. When a move of such magnitude reaches its terminal stage, the destructive forces become dominant, unleashing a tremendous downward motion, more politely referred to as *corrective* in Elliott terminology.

The Summer of 1987 . . . and Beyond

Now, I am going to use the capabilities of the Elliott Wave Principle to cover a long-term forecast based on developments in the real world. So far, the illustrations have been idealized, presenting a very tidy picture. But when you, the newly Elliott-Wave-armed investor, apply his principles to a real-life stock market, you will be faced with an array of configurations that seem to defy classification in the categories you have learned. Experience over time will teach you that every stock market movement, no matter what, will fall into the Elliott format somewhere.

To digress, but only slightly, my first book on the Elliott Wave Principle was entitled *The Elliott Wave Principle as Applied to the UK Stock Market*. I started that book in 1972, when the UK stock market was experiencing a severe bear market. It began in May 1972 and ended in January 1975, during which time the FT30 Share Index (comparable to the DJIA) lost seventy-three percent of its value.

As I was working on that book, during the last few months of that bear cycle, there was panic in the city of London. Many believed the end of capitalism, as they know it, was in sight. But Ralph Nelson Elliott's Wave Principle gave me a different message.

Obviously, I had been watching the behavior of the FT30 Share Index very closely. I was particularly concerned about the form of the Wave C that the remainder of that bear market might take. Shortly after Wave 2 of Wave C was completed, I published my opinions. According to the Elliott Wave Principle as interpreted by me, the London bear market would take the FT30 down to 146. I based this then-audacious judgement on two elements of the Wave Principle: first, the amplitude of Wave A of that bear market, which began in the summer of 1969. The downward projection of that Wave A also coincided with the first wave of Wave C that began in May 1972.

Of more immediate relevance was that figure for the FT30: 146. Looking back, one saw that the UK stock market began a super cycle in 1932. The bear market born in August 1969 represented, in Elliott terms, the fourth wave of that Super Cycle. The first bull market of the UK super cycle, the first primary wave of that super cycle, ended precisely at 146. According to the ground rules of the Elliott Wave Principle, the maximum probable extent of a fourth wave would be to the peak of the first wave.

On November 17, 1974, I published my findings in *Investors Bulletin*. I had decided, based on the unfolding of the three waves of Wave C, that the bear market would run to its optimal extent while leaving the Elliott Wave Principle inviolate. Though at that time attempting to define an accurate time scale was rather difficult, projecting the bottom of the bear market with the aid of the Elliott Wave Principle was fairly simple, supported by important cross-confirmations.

The bear market that began in 1969—though conventional wisdom of the time had it beginning three years later—would end at FT30 146. This would be the turning point to begin the longest and most glorious bull market in the history of the London Stock Exchange. That was the published opinion of R.C. Beckman, editor-publisher of *Investors Bulletin* and your present guru, in mid-November 1974. Britain's most widely read evening paper, the *London Evening Standard,* promptly took me and my predictions up and published them. This forecast remains a matter of record, a forecast that was made not with the benefit of hindsight, but Wave Principle foresight.

The Financial Times Stock Exchange Index plunged: on January 6, 1975, it closed the day with a sharp loss at 146.5, the lowest level of the day. The day after there was a rally at the open, but share prices ended below their best for the day. But the rally gathered strength in the weeks that followed: in June of that year the FT30 was at 420.

And what was the consensus of popular opinion in the city of London after that tremendous upward drive? That the stock market had just about completed its bear market rally! Dare I tell my Elliott-wise readers that some investors actually sold short, insisting that there was a bear market all the way up from 146.5 to 420? And that many fund managers, now in other employment, used this sharp upward move to liquidate their portfolios? No, you all say, that would be about the most foolish step possible.

Elliott Wave afficionados knew by foresight what others only learned by hindsight: that in the early months of 1975, the UK equity market was starting minor wave 1 of intermediate wave 1, of primary wave 1, of the longest and strongest UK bull market to date.

"Share prices are going to move higher, faster, and for much longer than anybody believes possible," I told the listeners to my daily report, put out by the London Broadcasting Corporation. They certainly did. During the fifteen years that followed my forecast, the FT30 Index moved from 146.5 to 2024, multiplying investors' funds nearly fourteen times. Just as the Elliott Wave Principle had projected in the early months of 1975.

My second book on the Elliott Wave Principle was written in the latter half of 1979, four years after the first. This second book, *Supertiming,* was destined for practitioners in the US stock market. In that book I observed that a new super cycle had also begun in the US, about the same time it began in the UK. In 1979 I concluded that, sometime during the 1980s, the US stock market would witness the final completion of the

fifth sub-minuette wave,
of the fifth minuette wave,
of the fifth minute wave,
of the fifth minor wave,
of the fifth intermediate wave,
of the fifth primary wave,
of the fifth cycle wave,
of the fifth super cycle wave.

Since the 1973–1974 bear market in the US was only a primary-wave correction, the implications of the super cycle wave correction that was to come were fairly obvious—to those who knew their Elliott.

On August 23, 1987—which just happened to be my birthday, it's the same every year—the DJIA touched 2746.65 and then turned down. According to my interpretations of the Elliott Wave Principle on that day, the fifth sub-minuette wave of the cycle Wave III was completed. What followed was a steady technical deterioration of the US equity market and other global equity markets, culminating in the October 1987 meltdown, which has since become known as the Crash of '87.

As the various waves unfolded during the late summer of 1987, into the early autumn, it became obvious that a correction of cyclical magnitude was developing on the Elliott scale, which also offered the possibility of taking on super-cycle and even grand-super-cycle dimensions. Precise categorization of the wave count was difficult during the summer of 1987, since it had been nearly thirteen years since the cyclical terminal juncture of December 1974, when the Dow Jones Industrial Average hit bottom at 569.70.

Figure 9
DOW JONES INDUSTRIAL AVERAGE   1974–1991

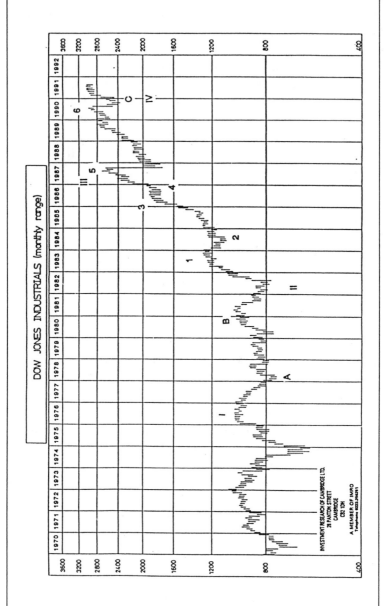

DOW JONES INDUSTRIALS (monthly range)

INVESTMENT RESEARCH OF CAMBRIDGE LTD.
28 PANTON STREET
CAMBRIDGE
CB2 1DH

A MEMBER OF IMRO
Telephone 0223-356251

If the decline that was unfolding were to take on super-cycle dimensions, it would be acting to correct the whole of the fifty-five-year drive that began in the US during 1932, similar in timing and parameters with that of the previous super-cycle corrective wave: that of September 3, 1929, to June 30, 1932. It was during that period that the Dow Jones Industrial Average fell from 381.2 to 40.6, losing nearly ninety percent of its value, while the values of many individual stocks lost more than ninety percent and some evaporated into extinction.

In view of the very long time frame between the pivotal action of December 1974 and that of the summer of 1987, the wave count lent itself to several alternatives. One alternative suggested that the orthodox top of the bull market that began in December 1974 occurred during 1986, placing the drive during 1987 in the category of a fifth-wave extension. While this interpretation offered a low probability, it was not unlike Elliott's interpretation of the 1929–1932 US stock market catastrophe.

Contrary to popular opinion, the peak of the bull market that began from the depths of the 1920–1922 recession did not occur in 1929, but in 1928. Elliott's own interpretation of that era shows that the downward drive from the 1928 peak in the Dow Jones Industrial Average represented Wave A of a super-cycle correction in the savage bear market to follow. The upward drive during 1929 to the peak of 381.2 in the DJIA that was achieved in September 1929 was seen by Elliott to be Wave B of an irregular correction that took the Averages to a new all-time high, consistent with that type of correction. The downward drive from the September 1929 peak of 381.2 in the DJIA to the June 1932 low of 40.6 was considered by Elliott to be Wave C of the super-cycle correction that began a year earlier.

You should now begin to gain a better understanding of the manner in which the Wave Principle adopts itself to real-life situations, unlike the many technical tools that are interpreted on the basis of the erroneous assumption that price relationships are constant, rather than ever-changing.

During the summer of 1987, there were two distinct possibilities. One possibility indicated that a five-wave bull market had been completed, which also coincided with the completion of a super cycle that began in 1932. According to that interpretation, the decline that began in the summer of 1987 would be far greater than any bear market that had been witnessed since 1932, similar in time and amplitude to the 1929–1932 bear market in the US.

The second possibility, which offered the highest probability, was that the peak in the Dow Jones Industrial Average during the summer of 1987 represented the terminal juncture of Cycle Wave III of Super Cycle V and that a stock market decline of cycle dimensions rather than super-cycle dimension was in store. This meant that the subsequent decline would be greater than anything witnessed since 1974, but to a lesser degree in time and amplitude than the 1929–1932 Crash on Wall Street.

Since the October 1987 massacre, there have been so many analysts who claim to have predicted the Crash of '87 that one must certainly wonder how such a crash ever occurred, given the huge number of investors who claim they were prepared for it. I have been given credit for predicting the Crash of '87. To set the record straight, I did not predict a plunge in share prices that would take the Dow Jones Industrial Average from 2746.65 to 1616.21 in a matter of weeks. I am not capable of making predictions of this nature, nor have I ever tried to.

With aid of the Wave Principle, ten days before the one-day massacre in October, I told listeners to my broadcasts on the London Broadcasting Corporation network to expect ". . . a decline in share prices of greater magnitude than anything seen since 1973, which could take on the dimensions of a 1929-type crash." This forecast was also repeated a few days after, in my publication *Investors Bulletin,* for subscribers.

In the final analysis, it's how you make use of the Wave Principle in a strategic, money-making context that really counts. I had no equity holdings of any kind in either of the portfolios that I manage or the Unit Trust whose investment policy I determine. It is a matter of record that the price of the units in the Beckman International Capital Accumulator Unit Trust rose steadily during October 1987 as stock markets all over the world crashed.

As the drama unfolded, the Crash of '87 is yet to take on the dimensions of a full-scale, super-cycle correction similar to that of 1929–1932. But, the verdict is still out. It has now been seventeen years since the last major terminal juncture in the Dow Jones Industrial Average. As the wave count clearly shows, we are confronted with a higher irregular configuration that lends itself to a variety of interpretations.

It may be that the orthodox top of the 1974 bull run was in August 1987, and, not unlike the 1929 crash, the October 1987 crash was Wave A of a 1929–1932-type bear market, in which case the upward drive from the November 1987 low of 1616.21 to the 3057.47 peak reached on June 3, 1991, would represent Wave B.

An alternative count would place the August 1987 peak in the category of the terminal juncture of a Cycle Wave III. Cycle Wave IV could be considered to have spanned the period from the October crash to the 1990 low, leaving the Dow Jones Industrial Average approaching the terminal juncture of Cycle Wave V during the summer of 1991. Should this interpretation be the correct one, the Dow Jones Industrial Average would have a capability of moving to the area of 3,250, but not much beyond that level. There is also the risk of a failure, resulting in a terminal juncture before the level is reached. When Cycle Wave V is completed, a 1929–1932-type bear market can then be expected, involving a super-cycle correction.

There is another possibility that should also be considered. As I am compiling this test, seventeen years have passed since the last terminal juncture of a cycle; sixty-three years have passed since the last terminal juncture of a super cycle; and two hundred fifty years have passed since the terminal juncture of a grand super cycle, which would have been prior to the Industrial Revolution. Many investors have accepted the idea that a super- cycle correction similar to the 1929–1932 bear market is a distinct possibility. Some believe a super-cycle correction is a probability rather than a possibility. Yet, there are few that I know of that have given any thought to the possibility that the market may be approaching a grand super-cycle correction.

A grand super-cycle correction would involve a bear market of far greater severity and dislocation than the 1929–1932 affair. It would be the worst bear market in stock market history, far exceeding the 1929–1932 bear market in time and amplitude. Since the grand super cycle is two hundred fifty years old, it is difficult to determine where the pivotal actions during the early stages of the cycle actually were. There is simply not sufficient data available. Yet, there is evidence to suggest that the world's equity markets are not only in the course of completing—or having completed—Super Cycle Wave V, but also Grand Super Cycle Wave V.

This may sound daunting, but never forget that variant on Murphy's Law that states: no matter how bad things are now, they're likely to get worse. Economically, it would seem that we are rapidly approaching the birth of a new grand super cycle, which will coincide with the death of the old. As the grand-super-cycle correction unfolds, it will involve the self-elimination of all the excesses that have been built into the system since the beginning of the Industrial Revolution—such is the function of the natural economic forces that rule our environment and have done so since the beginning of time. Spend a few moments thinking about the implications. This is a realistic possibility.

There is an entirely new system of wealth creation that is currently under way, unlike anything anyone on this planet has ever witnessed. The new system of wealth creation explains the tremendous upheavals now spreading across the planet—premonitory shudders that herald a collision of wealth creation systems on a scale never before seen.

A grand-super-cycle correction followed by the birth of a new grand super cycle would certainly be consistent with the profound technological and geopolitical developments that are taking place.

5
Beware the
Stamping Butterfly

Then the Butterfly stamped. The Djinns jerked the Palace and the gardens a thousand miles into the air: there was a most awful thunderclap, and everything grew inky black.

—RUDYARD KIPLING
Just So Stories

The Elliott Wave Principle differs from other cyclical theories, particularly economic ones, in that it does not insist on a fixed time scale for the cycles. But it does insist on accurate wave classification. Within its framework waves may contract or expand in time over very considerable periods. The patterns which we have referred to as cyclical phenomena are therefore far more flexible than those associated with more widely known cyclical theories with fixed time scales.

An encouraging factor, even if to be seen over the long term, is that the Elliott Wave Principle is based on continued world growth, even over a grand-super-cycle period. The main direction of the grand super cycle can be considered as always upwards; the inner downward moves always being corrections to some degree.

Elliott's basic concept, that the stock market expands and contracts according to a set pattern in shape and size, but not necessarily in time, is simple enough. One can see some analogies with shock theory: that the degree of reaction is directly related to the scale and frequency of the initial impulse. (Briefly, force produces strong reaction first time applied, second time of application produces a muted response, third time produces a negative response.) The set pattern is of five waves forward, three upward interspersed with two downward corrective waves. And these are followed by an overall corrective pattern of three waves, two downward and one upward between them. This continues up the time scale, constituting normal market action.

Normative Behavior

There is no such thing as normal behavior, not for people, animals, or markets: normal is a convenient fictional yardstick for doctors, teachers, psychiatrists, and scientists, also policemen.

The normal Elliott Wave pattern that we have discussed so far is the foundation for infinite variations on its theme. It is not a true-to-life working model of the stock market, yet in some way or other, all market movements are related in some degree to this five-directionally-up-three-directionally-down pattern, first discerned by Ralph Nelson Elliott. The degree of relationship, or deviations from the norm, in themselves have predictive value for those who fully understand the mechanism of the Elliott Wave Principle.

The diagrams we have discussed so far are strictly for illustration only. They do not refer to any real stock market movements; they are just idealized formations. If, by now, you have begun plotting stock market movements on your wall or chart paper and attempted to apply Elliott Wave classifications to your shapes, you may have occasionally found that it fits neatly into the Wave Principle as so far expounded. In which case, if your predictions followed the Elliott principles, their chances of coming true would have an exceptionally high probability ratio.

More likely, you will have found many price patterns where the Elliott Wave Principle does not appear to fit at all. Trying to analyze the market according to the chart you have plotted, you will find that, in reality, actual price behavior and price relationships leave open many avenues of interpretation, never mind several different predictive possibilities. There will be extra waves that do not conform to the five-three pattern; configurations that do not wish to be categorized on Wave Principle terms.

In Search of Absolutes

At this point those without stamina will conclude that the Wave Principle does not work at all, and they look for something else. If you are remotely tempted to do this, refer to my warning, and remember that consistency is a virtue. Seeking absolutes will be dangerous to your wealth.

It is a necessary trial of faith during which you will discover the sheer magnificence and the pragmatism of the Elliott Wave Principle. You will soon see why all other technical tools are but flint fragments from prehistory in comparison.

When the student of market behavior moves beyond theory into practical application, significant deviations from the model will always be found in reality. The gap between the theoretical and reality must be appreciated. The Elliott Wave Principle allows for deviations, which is what sets it apart from other absolutist tools.

Reading Elliott's original thesis, it can be seen that he had given a lot of thought to the various ramifications of stock-price movements as well as the extent and manner to which real-time behavior was likely to deviate from his framework. Elliott, who was pre-Computer Age, did not classify his information on a yes/no binary basis and would not make it fit the perfect pigeonhole—so beloved of bureaucrats worldwide—if it did not do so naturally.

As we continue to examine the different facets of the Elliott Wave Principle, I will show how Elliott made allowances for all those deviations from his basic theme; how he quantified and categorized them all, in an attempt to provide the analyst, professional or amateur, with a tool that would provide useful probabilities and possibilities in the actual stock market world. We shall consider the many variants, their categorization and quantification, as we go along—a sort of intellectual, specialized form of programmed learning.

Elliott's waves can be broken down into ever-smaller parts until one reaches the sub-minuette cycle. But whatever their size, they all follow the five-three pattern—with exceptions. Impulse waves have five components. Corrective waves have only three components. Both can go either upward or downward, their major difference being the number of components and their inter-relationship.

In an ongoing bull market, impulse waves will be upward, three up and two interspersed; corrective ones downward. These three upward waves will be made of five waves of the next-lower degree. The corrective waves that interrupt the upward impulse waves will also have three components of the next-lower degree. They are all self-similar.

The corrective waves are subject to numerous variations, not least that there are sometimes more than three part which in themselves have aberrations. And the fifth wave of an impulse wave can sometimes harbor nasty surprises.

During a very fast-moving, strong bull market, the fifth wave of any upward impulse wave can extend itself and then become subject to what Elliott called a *double retracement*. Panic! You have sold short on the fifth minor wave,

> of the fifth intermediate wave,
> of the fifth primary wave,
> of the fifth cycle wave.

You think you could not have been more right, short of being a prophet. And then another upwave appears,

> and another,
> and another,
> you feel like a child abandoned in a storm.

Do you cover your shorts? Do you increase your shorts? Do you jump out of the second floor window? Damn Elliott and go back to your yes/no computer system? Or will you take a deep breath and continue your Elliott Wave studies to the end of the book?

Practicing the Elliott Wave Theory is not like learning to drive a car: here you must get to know how the engine works, after you have admired the bodywork and before setting off at top speed down the motorways. There are no shortcuts, and there are many refinements yet to be appreciated.

Random Noise

Wave classification poses a major problem to those only newly initiated, or partly educated, in the mysteries of Elliott. The precise order of wave formation can often seem obscure, riddled with random noise, leaving you totally confused as to the position of the market within the framework of the overriding Elliott trends.

Imagine that you are trading at a time when there appears a corrective wave in a bull market. It is going to be vitally important for your future strategy (possibly your job) to identify whether that corrective wave is a "2" or a "4" wave of a primary uptrend. If it is a "2," you will want to pick up some of the favorite shares at its end. But, if it's a "4," you will want to look at the second rank of favorites at that point and perhaps increase you leverage to increase your performance. Courage, it is not quite as difficult as it seems, though vital, given the necessity for correct categorization to avoid multiplying the error up the scale.

Meteorologist Edward Lorenz, working in the early sixties on models for weather forecasting, with the aid of very primitive computers, discovered the horrors of compounding minute errors. (And so, unintentionally, launched the new science of Chaos, just defined in the eighties.) At that time, most professional meteorologists regarded forecasting as something less than a science, more seat-of-the-pants witchcraft by technicians, much as contemporary stockbrokers regard their backroom analysts. But both very much want reliable forecasts.

Elliott always insisted that his wave theory was a precise one with neatly dotted i's and crossed t's, and now I have introduced a margin for error, unreliable variants, and other nasties. And yet, for fear of compounding even the minutest of butterfly errors, we must be very precise in our classification of the waves.

In the thirty-five years that I have been using the Elliott Wave Principle as a guide to my investment policy, I have been able to forecast the precise size of major and minor movements in various stock markets to within one tenth of a point, weeks or months before the objectives were achieved. Other skilled Elliott users have also emulated my feats.

And in those thirty-five years I have also failed to forecast correctly, because I did not define the wave correctly which, with hindsight, I subsequently could. The forecasting error was not due to Elliott's Wave Principle but to my misuse of it, judging facts on insufficient data.

The further we get away from important market turning points, the more forecasting errors (due to incorrect classification) are compounded. For the further away we are from the unmistakable turn, the greater the number of possible variations, interpretations, and possibilities offered for classifying the wave under study and the cycle of which it is part. However, with the Crash of '87 just under our belts, easily recognizable to all, this problem will not be as acute, but there still remains considerable margin for error.

We are involved here in an art, not a science; markets represent dynamic forces with continuing variables, to which constants, or absolutes, can never, ever be applied. You do not need a Ph.D. in the mathematics of the unreal to understand the Elliott Wave Principle. But you do need to be pragmatic—that is a nice way of saying a hands-on, sleeves-rolled-up, mucky kind of everyday investor. While you may not have to be a genius to understand the Elliott Wave Principle, and to be able to use it well, you will have to study hard. As a reward I promise you that there is some beauty in the reality of market-price movements—and your new, improved bank accounts.

Are there times when I have seemed to you to be a stopped clock, or a faulty compact disc? Sorry, but I will continually repeat the basic Elliott precepts, over and over, approaching them each time from a different hideout. This is intentional; I feel that no opportunity should be lost to help you understand this extremely valuable and potentially highly profitable investment tool.

I want you to think, live, and breathe Elliott and his Wave Principle for as long as it takes you to bring your yacht alongside mine in Monte Carlo (incidentally, once the home of the world's top gamblers). How nasty of me to appeal to your greed and avarice; gentlemen (and ladies) of course study such matters as the Elliott Wave Principle for its academic interest—if they already have money. I sincerely want you to be rich.

Winning Isn't Everything . . . Losing Isn't Anything

But, you have to work for it, and now I shall dampen your spirits again. At no time would I like to suggest that the Elliott Wave Principle is an easy way to move from rags to riches. I have called up from the vast deep all the problems associated with the incorrect use of the Elliott Wave Principle, but hopefully lit the lantern at the end of the tunnel for you all.

Pronouncement: markets and the Elliott Wave Principle are like the Delphic Oracle; neither are ever right or wrong, they just are.

It is important now to make a sacrifice of one's ego: if your analysis of historical price movements does not fit in with the Elliott Wave pattern, then *you* are wrong—not history, not Elliott. This humbling of the self may be painful—but it may make you richer.

You must have faith in the tools you are using. How would you drive your car to the station were you to worry every inch of the way about its brakes, combustion ratio, fuel consumption, exhaust pipe, or lighting system? Badly, is the answer. You need cool money to make money in markets, but you must maintain your perspective. Winning may not be everything, but losing isn't anything! Who wants to be like the guy in the traffic accident, right but dead right? Be realistic—that is the best way to achieve optimum results from the Wave Principle.

When in Doubt . . . Stay Out

However, life, despite Delphic Oracles, is not all gloom. I do most strongly feel that even the slight acquaintance with the Elliott Wave Principle that you have thus far will reinforce your performance as an investor. Before you would have been petrified by falling markets; now you can place them in context—a mere corrective wave, possibly time to buy in with both hands. Before, you might have been tempted to become wildly enthusiastic about bull markets, getting yourself (or worse, your clients) right in at the top of the market every time. Now, if you see that the prices are rising in the fifth wave, of a minor wave, which is the fifth wave of an intermediate wave, which is the fifth wave of a primary wave—you are not going to be a willing buyer at all. You will be jumping out rather than climbing in.

If, with your present skills at plotting stock market movements, you sometimes find yourself lost in a surge of waves, sub-waves, and wavelets, it would be as well to suspend judgement for a while, at least until a cycle of the next-highest degree completes itself. This may take some time, but when the full five-wave pattern does show itself, the picture could be much clearer. You may have to wait for a minuette cycle, which is in tune with daily movements, whose pattern may be clearer than one based on hourly movements. It may be possible that even the minuette cycle does not present a distinguishable formation. You will then have to wait for the less-sensitive minute or minor cycles, until you are confident in what you see.

If you are a longer-term investor, you are likely to be less interested in the sub-minuette and minuette cycles anyway. But, I suggest you keep a record of them also, as these smaller—butterfly?—cycles can greatly help interpret and clarify the picture of the longer-term cycle.

As your confidence in your ability to use the Wave Principle grows, it would be as well, at this stage, to keep a wary eye for the possible terminal stages of the completion of five-wave patterns, especially the minute, minor, and intermediate time frames. Meanwhile, maintain a policy of *masterly inactivity* as you await the completion of these five-wave movements.

When there are strong indications that a five-wave pattern has been completed, you will be in an excellent position to consider your selling objectives. The time frame of the cycle that is closing will prove a valuable reference point when it comes to disposal; it can be related to the percentage of your holdings that you may want to sell.

Obviously, it matters what kind of trader or investor you are: are you nearer those who trade the very short term, thinking in terms of hours and minutes—or to the truly long-term investor, who holds on to his shares for years, if not decades. Only the very short-term traders, for example, would be interested to sell, because the fifth wave of a subminuette cycle had completed its move, which, in time, might have covered four, five, or six trading days. For the ordinary short-term trader, seeing the completion of a minuette cycle, over perhaps eight to ten trading days, liquidation at this point would be good timing. And, unless he knowingly chose to play the downside of the following correction phase, he would not start buying in again until the completion of a full three-wave-minuette correction. Trading on this basis places the odds more in favor of the trader. And, in line with keeping those odds in his favor moreover, unless purchases had been made at the beginning stage of a minuette cycle, or during the third wave in the corrective move of a minuette cycle, our short-term trader would not make an otherwise attractive trade.

Intermediate traders would probably ignore both the two smallest cycles, merely watching their movements in order to establish a point of reference for other cycles. He would wish to sell only upon completion of the minor and intermediate cycles, spanning months or years.

The amount of cash to be raised would be governed by the size of the cycle that was being corrected. A correction of a three- to four-month cycle would suggest that prudent traders would liquidate about a fifth of their holdings. If we are talking correction of an intermediate cycle that spans a year or more, the prudent would raise their liquidity levels to fifty percent.

But, in the event of corrective action developing in a cycle whose five waves are each a year or longer—with the whole cycle spanning some seven or eight years—then it is time to take your money out and find a low-risk, capital-protected investment for it until the storm is over.

6
Fibonacci and
the Nomad Scholars

The rare scholars who are nomads by choice are essential to the intellectual welfare of the settled disciplines.

—BENOIT MANDELBROT
(as quoted by James Gleick in *Chaos*)

Let us cease the mind-wrenching exercises revealed by the Wave Principle, with thanks in passing to John Schulz for the pithy description. Let us soothe our minds.

Consider the beauties of nature, the mystery of the universe, the vastness of the galaxy. Admire the achievements of man in all fields of scientific endeavor: nuclear theory; miniaturization, enabling you to have a computer in your pocket; penicillin keeping you alive; the electronic transmission of data; rocket engineering; the invisible bugs that give you allergies; the visible beauty of flowers and butterflies.

All these, and those I have not named, have one thing in common: the *Fibonacci Summation Series,* which is also the mathematical grounding of the Elliott Wave Principle.

The series first surfaced in the twelfth century A.D., published by an Italian mathematician, Leonardo Bigollo Fibonacci of Pisa. Fibonacci took a sabbatical holiday in the Middle East, surprising to us now, but logical then, for we owe the origins of our numbers and mathematics to the early Arab scholars. The series of numbers, later to be named after him, Fibonacci discovered in Egypt. Since his time it has never attracted much more than passing curiosity from scholars, something for the mind to fiddle with while their real work was on the mental back burners. But recent theoretical developments in the field of nonlinear mathematics—the mathematics of the improbable—place the series in a different light.

The Series

The Summation Series itself is relatively simple, as is the entire Wave Principle concept. Starting with the number 1, the series develops as follows: 1, 2, 3, 5, 8, 13, 21, 34, 55, 89, 144, 233, 377, 610, 987, 1597, etc., stretching to infinity.

SEVERAL EXTREMELY UNUSUAL PROPERTIES AND
RELATIONSHIPS SOON EMERGE.

1. The sum of any two numbers in sequence forms the next number in the sequence, viz. 1 + 2 = 3; 2 + 3 = 5; 3 + 5 = 8; 5 + 8 = 13; 8 + 13 = 21; 13 + 21 = 34; 21 + 34 = 55; 34 + 55 = 89; 55 + 89 = 144; 89 + 144 = 233; 144 + 233 = 377; 233 + 377 = 610; 377 + 610 = 987; 610 + 987 = 1,597.

2. If we divide any number into the second number above it in sequence, we will find the quotient of 2, with the number that is left over equal to the exact number resting immediately before the original divisor. For example, if we divide 21 by 8, the quotient is 2 with 5 left over; 5 is the number immediately before the divisor, 8. If we divide 55 by 21, we get 2 with 13 left over; 13 is the number immediately before the divisor, 21. If we divide 5 by 2, we get 2 with 1 left over; 1 is the number immediately before the divisor, 2.

3. The ratio of any number to its next-highest number works out at 1 to 1.618. If we divide 987 by 610, the answer is 1.6180327. If we divide 144 by 89, the answer is 1.6179775.

4. The ratio of any number to the number below it works out at 0.618 to 1. If we divide 34 by 55, the answer is 0.6181818. If we divide 21 by 34, the answer is 0.6176470.

5. The ratio of each number to the second number below it is 2.618. If we divide 144 by 55, we get 2.6181818. If we square 1.618, we come up with 2.618 (2.617924). The reciprocal (1 divided by 1.618) equals 0.6180469.

6. We can classify the series as each number being related to the number before it by the formula: $1/2 \, (\sqrt{5} + 1) = 1,618$.

7. The formula relating each number to the number above it would be: $1/2 \, (\sqrt{5} - 1) = 0.618$.

W.D. Gann's Numerical Approach

The 1920s stock market theorist W.D. Gann attempted to apply mathematical balance to the stock market. In Gann's work we find time and size of share-price movements related to simple numerical subdivisions. For example, one of Gann's principles deals with the high probability of a rally effort taking place when a share has fallen from its high to a point midway between its extreme high and extreme low over a protracted period.

When dealing with time studies, Gann attempted to anticipate changes in trend by linking the duration of a share-price movement to the duration of the trend that immediately preceded it. He also used the subdivision of ascending and descending angles, subdividing them in terms of their probable importance, to represent a possible pivotal point for a change in trend.

These were the first attempts at applying a system of mathematical balance to share-price behavior, and, looking at W.D. Gann's record of achievement with his method, the results were far superior to most other stock-market-trading formuls. But, his work has always been difficult to quantify, and the simplistic mathematical principles used leave many questions unanswered.

Gann formulated his principles in the 1920s and 1930s; the Elliott Wave Principle was not published until the late 1930s, so it is likely Elliott was aware of Gann's work, though he only ever cited that of Charles Dow. However, it seems there is a much stronger reason for using the Fibonacci Series as a common denominator of universal balance than the simple subdivision of numbers employed by Gann.

Is this simple numerical series actually the mathematical nucleus of universal motion as Elliott suggested? Some will find this idea intellectually unacceptable. It is certainly beyond the scope of this book to prove or disprove. The proofs that are offered seem to go beyond mere coincidence, so they should not be totally rejected.

The advantage of the Fibonacci Summation Series, for those wishing to apply it to share-price behavior, is that it deals in finite whole numbers. It is a method of analysis which takes into account the characteristics of the available data.

The Fibonacci Series in Art and Nature

In *Nature's Law* Elliott refers to the Great Pyramid of Gizeh. Many people interested in the occult insist that the pyramid holds a divine message of revelation still to be disclosed!

The pyramid's properties do have some astonishing relationships to the Fibonacci Series. The height of the pyramid is exactly 5,813 inches, our numbers in the Fibonacci Series (5, 8 and 13). The ratio of the base of the pyramid to its elevation is exactly 61.8 to 100.

Peter Tomkins, in his splendid book, *Secrets of the Great Pyramid,* examines the Fibonacci relationships visible in the structure of the pyramid even further. The mathematics of the pyramid's structural relationships seemingly have resulted in the impossible function of squaring the circle. As students we were taught that the squaring of a circle offers an insoluble problem, when we use the irrational value of π. However, the problem can be resolved if we use the Golden Ratio as a function. In the Great Pyramid of Gizeh one finds the function of the Golden Ratio in the relationships found in the triangle formed by the height, the half-base, and the apthem. Fibonacci himself seems to have only used the series principally to explain a progression of numbers, such as the multiplication of rabbits from a single pair. Elliott notes many repetitions in nature. In Jay Hambidge's work *Practical Application of Dynamic Symmetry* to which Elliott refers, it is noted that the pattern made by the seeds at the center of a sunflower has eighty-nine curves. There are fifty-five winding in one direction of a logarithmic spiral and thirty-four in an opposing direction.

Other observers have noted the manner in which the series carries over into a myriad of man-made objects, living plants, and animals. In a pine cone, the "grid" of opposing swirls that can be observed is composed of five lines in one direction and eight in another. In a pineapple husk, one can find the ratio of opposing spirals to be thirteen to eight. Examine a daisy head, and you will no doubt discover the ratio of the swirling spirals of petals to be twenty-one to thirty-four. There are similar relationships in the logarithmic or equiangular spirals in sea shells, the rings marking tree growth, elephant tusks, and the horns of the American Rocky Mountain goat.

The Fibonacci Series and its relationships can be found in architecture through the "Golden Rectangle," in the shape of the Parthenon in Athens. As Joseph Schillinger observed, in his work *The Mathematical Basis of Arts,* the Summation Series appears in the paintings of Leonardo da Vinci, the music of Bach, and the pulse of Keats' poetry.

The most fascinating aspect of all is the manner in which the series can be used in the studies of "shock and instability," a concept instrumental to Niels Bohr's discovery of the process of cognition, which guided him in developing atomic theory. Before becoming a scientist, Bohr was a student of the philosopher Kierkegaard. Kierkegaard taught that "in life, only sudden decisions, leaps, or jerks can lead to progress. Something decisive occurs always only by a jerk, by a sudden turn which neither can be predicted from its antecedents nor is determined by them." Bohr must have been influenced a great deal by this philosophy.

Examples from *Nature's Law*

The areas in which one can find examples of the Fibonacci Summation Series and the 1.618 (Golden Ratio) relationships stagger the imagination. In *Nature's Law*, Elliott's magnum opus, which he sub-titled *The Secrets of the Universe*, he cites further examples:

1. Our personal anatomy follows the Summation Series, in accordance with the five-plus-three pattern which characterizes a complete stock market cycle. From the torso there are five extremities: the head, two arms, and two legs. Each extremity can be broken down to the "cycle of the next- smaller degree," of three sections. The legs and arms can be broken down into the next-smaller degree also, the arms terminating in five fingers and the legs in five toes. These fingers can be further extrapolated into three sub-sections, the 5-3 pattern remaining through-out. (One may find an anomaly with regard to the big toe. However, in the case of monkeys, apes, and other similar forms, the fingers and toes are the same in anatomical structure. The big toe of a monkey breaks down into three sub-sections, as do the other minor extremities.)

2. In music we have the octave of eight diatonic notes. We have the chromatic scale with thirteen notes, while the staff has five lines. There are three basic elements in music: melody, harmony, and rhythm. Natural harmonies follow the Golden Ratio.

3. There are three primary colors. The blending of these three primaries produces all other colors.

4. The Washington Monument in Washington, D.C., has a capstone with a base measuring thirty-four feet square with a height of fifty-five feet. The ratio is 0.618. The base of the shaft of the monument measures

fifty-five feet square, while the rim of the shaft measures thirty-four feet. The foundation has eight steps. There are eight windows. The monument has three basic components: the base, the shaft, and the capstone, the latter being in the shape of a pyramid.

In *The Mathematical Basis of the Arts,* Schillinger contends that what we refer to as talent is probably an innate sense of mathematical proportion peculiar to individual artists. This *mathematical proportion* can be seen in all great works of art, music, literature, etc. It is Elliott's claim that such proportion has its roots in the Fibonacci Summation Series, the mathematical basis by which all activity is related.

Fibonacci and Cyclical Behavior

Of greater interest to the student of share-price movements—who should fully realize that such movements are the result of emotional rather than rational responses to day-to-day news events—is the manner in which the Fibonacci Summation Series can be found in the emotional cyclical behavior patterns we experience.

For decades, theorists have been attempting to relate sunspot cycles and astronomical forces to share-price movements. It has only recently been discovered, through the work of Dr. R. Burr in his treatise "Blueprint for Survival," that sunspot activity has a direct effect on geo-physical, magnetic earth cycles. These in turn affect the behavior of various forms of life on this planet. The predictive value of this information is uncertain; however, it should be noted that sunspot cycles do conform to the Fibonacci Summation Series, as do movements of planets and planetary relationships in our solar system. Furthermore, shifts in the earth's magnetic field alter the amino-acid balance in the bloodstream, which can be related to shifts in temperament, which are likely to have an influence on mass behavior patterns.

Brilliant or Ludicrous?

Obviously, the sceptics, particularly the academics who refute the idea of anything other than randomness in share prices, can find many objections at this point. Reference to the Golden Ratio, the Great Pyramids, etc., hints at numerology and mysticism, both anathemas to the pseudo-sophisticates of share-price movements. We are certainly on the brink of pseudo-science. Naturally, if one makes a point of searching for examples of the Fibonacci Summation Series, they can be found in innumerable areas.

In all probability there is a far greater number of phenomena in which the Fibonacci Summation Series will not appear. Many will question the logic of comparing stock market trends with the proportions of animal life and the structure of flowers, buildings, music, and art. An appraisal will invite screams of "Where is the connection?" Such comparisons are likely to be deemed speculative and mystical.

However, a prejudiced intellectual suffers an extremely serious blind spot. The farmer in the fable of the boy who cried wolf did not suffer from such a prejudice. He felt, in view of the boy's repeated false promise of the presence of a wolf, that empirically, it was highly improbable. At the same time, he was not so self-opinionated as to deny the proposition further consideration.

The correct attitude to the Fibonacci Summation Series and the work of Elliott as a whole is best summed up by William O'Connor in his brilliant work, *Stock, Wheat, and Pharaohs:*

> He apparently embodied ingenuity and brilliance, as well as the ridiculous and the erroneous all at the same time. Should readers ever come upon any new revival and up-to-date revisions of Elliott's original works, it will be very advantageous to remember that this man eludes a unified classification as regard credibility. What he has given us is capable of revival and revision into foolishness, capable of revival and revision into brilliance, again both at the same time.

> It is customary to unify our attitude concerning the intellectual credibility of men. If a man doesn't know where Broadway is, there is a tendency to take that into account when he directs us to which way is Uptown or Downtown or the East Side. But applying such an attitude to Elliott's Wave Principle may cause us to discount the most brilliant aspect of him. His work will not stand classification either wise or unwise, for it was both. But, on balance, the wisdom far outweighs its pardonable impurities.

Open Mind—Successful Investment

Probably the most important intellectual quality for successful investment is the ability to keep an open mind, to recognize the finite nature of man's knowledge generally, and one's own in particular. The biggest mistakes are made by those who "do not know what they do not know." Students of modern capital market theory preach of the efficiency of stock market behavior and the randomness of share-price movements, assuming their computers are now capable of producing the final answer, not unlike the medical practitioners of years past, who believed a headache could be cured by drilling a hole in the sufferer's head. The problem in both cases is the attempt to carry the technique of the period beyond its capabilities.

To accept the Fibonacci Summation Series as the final answer to share-price relationships over time and amplitude would require faith as well as judgement based on empirical proof. However, when one considers the empirical evidence produced to support various other aspects of stock-market theory, one must come to the conclusion that we remain in a very grey area, which remains to a great extent unquantifiable. So the only proofs that are of value are those related to achievement.

The achievements of the Elliott Wave Principle as shown by its various practitioners go far beyond those which have ever been produced by any other method.

7
Using the
Summation Series

The more extensive a man's knowledge of what has been done, the
greater will be his power of knowing what to do.

—Benjamin Disraeli

There were these two market analysts who meet in a lunatic asylum.
One says to the other, "I'm better than mortal men! I can see the future!"

Says the other analyst, "Where did you get this great gift?" First man
says, "The Lord gave it to me!" Second analyst says, "Like hell I did!"

That story has been kicking around financial circles for quite some
time, along with a number of others that are not quite so friendly in their
nature. It has become the norm for investment advisers to claim or insinu-
ate they are the possessors of some special prophetic gift, a claim that has
always amused the more hard-headed denizens of the investment community. What amuses Wall Street even more is that many investment advisers
often fall victim to actually believing their own advertising.

It should be obvious to any investor who thinks about it for a little while,
that speculative markets, like almost everything involving human emotions, are basically unpredictable. We may be able to anticipate with vague
accuracy in a way that will help improve investment performance. We
cannot predict. He who predicts is lost!

Speculative markets are like huge, wild hurricanes of random events
that are themselves unpredictable. Some are public events: wars, strikes,
government actions. Some are private events: a man may be forced to sell
his shares because he is hit with an unexpectedly large tax bill. Another

man may sell his shares because he is afraid of losing his job. If the economy appears to be turning sour, a number of people may be frightened into selling their shares for fear of losing their jobs, withdrawing to the safety of savings accounts like frightened mice scrambling into a hole.

Even if the events I've just outlined could be predicted, the investor could never really be certain about the manner in which they would be reflected in the behavior of speculative markets. How many times have markets risen on bad news and plunged on good news? It was generally expected that a war in the Persian Gulf would decimate the stock market. Instead, shortly after the war broke out, the stock market staged one of its strongest rallies ever.

It is a fact that most of the investment advice that is produced is not based on any real knowledge of any kind. It is based on sheer guesswork. That guesswork is often the product of wishful thinking, and, on far too many occasions, the invention of vested interest.

The problem that faces the majority of investors involves an unwillingness to abandon fantasies and a refusal to be educated. The average investor believes what he wants to believe, rather than what the markets or history is telling him. As an industry, the securities industry is fully aware that it is a simple task to convince people of what they want to start with. It then becomes a simple matter of peddling the advice that people want to be told.

Investors want to believe that someone, somewhere is able to predict the behavior of share prices with absolute accuracy. Many investors are almost fanatical in their belief, spending the whole of their investment careers—or until their money runs out—searching for that someone, somewhere. Nothing the market ever does to these worshipful dunderheads will make them lose faith.

Chart Techniques

Without a doubt, the most fanatic of all the faithful are those who call themselves technical analysts or chartists. These are the fellows who, surrounded by sheer, thundering chaos, wander about muttering to themselves, "I know there's a head-and-shoulders pattern in here somewhere!" They will insist the market only appears to be chaotic, but it really isn't. They cling to the belief that the only reason the "pattern" has been conspicuous by its absence is that nobody has been smart enough to find it . . . yet!

The technical analysts and chartists are the victims of their convictions. Like a drowning man clinging to a life preserver, with desperation, they clutch to the belief that this howling wilderness, these speculative markets, are orderly enough, so that their movements can be charted on graph paper in such a way as to predict future price movements, and so that the line that has already been drawn will follow the path of the line undrawn.

The chartists believe that patterns repeat themselves. They think that if the market, a commodity, or individual stock begins to repeat the beginning of a pattern they saw a few years ago, or that appears in the textbook of chart patterns, the market, commodity, or individual stock will go on to repeat the pattern in its entirety. Since the chartist is convinced that he knows what the pattern is going to be, he is equally convinced that he knows something about the future price of the speculative item he is dealing with.

When things don't work out the way he predicted—which in general they don't—the fanatical chartist will humbly blame himself. He will kick himself in the backside and invite you to stick pins in his eyeballs, admitting his temporary lack of acumen. He knows that his charts are capable of predicting the future . . . if only he can figure out how to plot them correctly at this stage of the market cycle. The difficulty, he will argue, is that the market, though orderly, is so stunningly complex that its internal pattern hasn't yet been elucidated with sufficient clarity.

What the chartist will never admit is that the problem might lie within speculative markets themselves. The chartist and majority of technical analysts will blind themselves from the simplest of all truths, in the same way that Dracula cringes at the sign of the cross. The stock market has no repetitive patterns that occur with unfailing frequency. It almost never repeats itself and never does so in reliably predictable ways. There is near-total price randomness, nearly perfect chaos. There are relationships within the chaotic framework which can be useful to the astute investor. These relationships do not fall into the category of repetitive patterns.

Why Markets Go Up and Down

What causes speculative markets to go up and down? A basic recognition of the appropriate elements is vital if the investor is to acquire a conceptual approach to markets, which is consistent with a winning strategy. It is equally important to be aware of the factors which are not a particularly meaningful influence over an extended period, such as the day-to-day news events which I define as *random noise*.

There are essentially two groups of forces that investors must come to terms with. First, there are fluctuations of supply, along with public and institutional demand for commodities, stocks, and bonds. These are influenced in turn by a myriad of other forces. wars and threats of wars, peace and promises of peace, economic recessions and depressions, economic recoveries and promises of economic recoveries, pronouncements by industry, pronouncements by union leaders, pronouncements by government officials, economic statistics, business surveys, inflation, inflation prospects, interest rates, interest rate prospects, rates of joblessness, consumer confidence, etc., etc., ad infinitum, ad nauseam. The list of transient and semi-transient market influences could fill this book and a few more volumes to follow. The list could stretch from here to eternity.

Cycles of Optimism and Pessimism

It is possible to make reasonably accurate forecasts on a number of transient influences that will have an unquantifiable effect on markets. The result of such forecasts usually constitutes the basic, fundamental nomenclature that is fed to investors by the investment industry. This diet of irrelevant minutiae and trivia often does more harm than good, serving to distract the investor's attention away from what markets are really made of. Markets are not made of pure, cold numbers. Markets are also made of emotion. They are influenced by the irrational behavior of lunatics. Markets reflect all kinds of thinking, from the very smart to the ineluctably dense. Corporate profit projections and economic forecasts, inter alia, get lost in markets like a paper airplane in a cyclone.

We look through a glass darkly when we attempt to peer into the future of markets. By attempting to brighten the glass with the wrong illuminators, we often become so mesmerized by the cracks, flaws, and colors of the glass that we actually lose complete sight of the glass itself.

According to the work carried out by L. Peter Cogan, economist and scientist, in his study *The Rhythmic Cycles of Optimism and Pessimism,* there is a relatively high correlation between the timing, sequence, and amplitude of share prices, leading business indicators, private borrowings, and major business contractions, with idealized patterns of rhythmic repetition that seem to confirm the existence of cyclical rhythms related to peaks in optimism and pessimism, which govern mass behavior patterns. In other words, the overriding force for all markets, at all times, is a psychological force.

R.N. Elliott was firm in his conviction that his *Nature's Law* represented the distillation of human activity. The mathematical basis for Elliott's work was represented by the unstable numerical sequence of the Fibonacci Summation Series, which he claims has always functioned in every human activity, reflected in the evolution of rhythmic waves of varying degrees. When suitable data is compared with the cyclical pattern discovered by Elliott, the waves then become visible to the experienced eye.

"All human activities have three distinctive features," said R.N. Elliott, "pattern, time, and ratio, all of which observe the Fibonacci series."

Cogan's research produced the conclusion that monetary and fiscal policies did not appear to be the primary cause of the business cycle, but merely acted to modify the amplitude of the cycle, and to some extent the timing and frequency. The work of Cogan adds further credence and fortification to the long-term economic cycle theories of Schumpeter and Kondratieff. In his two-volume, monumental effort, *Business Cycles,* Schumpeter stated that within the context of the long-wave cycle—that could stretch from forty-five to sixty-five years—shorter-term cycles would vary in amplitude and duration depending on the general level of confidence and liquidity in the system and on the timing, strength, and ingenuity of political leaders, while the infrastructure that would determine the terminal juncture and shape of the longer-term economic cycle would remain virtually intact.

Apparently, the period 1929–1932 would have represented a major turning point in history, regardless of who was president of the United States at the time, or the methods deployed to pull the economy out of recession. Is it not ironic that 1920 and 1974 represented periods of peak commodity price inflation, in spite of the lessons that were supposedly learned during the intervening years? As we move along into the 1990s, many of the world's economies are in deep depression while others are experiencing severe recession. The international banking system is in chaos. Residential and commercial property prices are plummeting. We seem to be approaching an action replay of what took place sixty years ago. During those sixty years, the global authorities are yet to devise a method of eliminating these dislocations.

Despite the accepted importance of military and political decisions on the US economy, along with the myriad of changes that have taken place during the last sixty years, with the US economy becoming subjected to increasing government intervention, the longwave economic cycle—noted by Schumpeter to have applied to wheat prices ever since the fourteenth century—still persists.

This long-wave economic cycle has an average time frame of fifty-five years, an integer of the Fibonacci Summation Series—more than just coincidence? If we were to assume the beginning of the Industrial Revolution occurred in the year 1760, the Fibonacci Summation Series would suggest an end to the Industrial Revolution in the year 1993, accompanied by a grand-super-cycle correction. The Industrial Revolution would have changed the face of society over 233 years, another Fibonacci integer, which may also turn out to be more than mere coincidence.

Elliott's Choice of Data

You can construct a chart of the results of a long sequence of coin-flipping. On that chart, you will find patterns and rhythmic sequences. If you stick a label that says, "Dow Jones Industrial Averages" on the chart and hand it to a chartist, he will try and figure out what numbers are coming out next by studying the sequences. The chartist will invariably give you some answers.

The Wave Principle cannot be applied to coin-flipping patterns, along with other data where application would not be practical or possible. Elliott was quite specific on the type of data to which the Wave Principle could be applied.

Examples of data which would be suitable for the deployment of the Wave Principle would fall into the following broad classifications:

1. Extensive commercial activity represented by corporations whose ownership is widely distributed.

2. A general marketplace where buyers and sellers may affect rapid transactions through representatives.

3. Any auction market that is the subject of mass participation on a national or global basis, involving the immediate execution of transactions.

Accordingly, economic activity does not lend itself to Wave Principle application or the quantitative use of the Fibonacci Summation Series.

Commercial real estate activity would also not be applicable to forecasting techniques involving the Wave Principle, nor would individual share-price behavior, especially those with a narrow market. Elliott did believe that the behavior of share prices on the Stock Exchange provided an ideal vehicle for the application of the Wave Principle. But, this would only seem to apply to the stock market indices, which reflected and induced mass response. In this connection, the Dow Jones Industrial Averages would be a far better index for the application of the Wave Principle than the Standard & Poors Index. Although the Standard & Poors Index is more broadly based, the DJIA is a much more emotive indicator, with a far wider following worldwide.

In *Nature's Law*, Elliott states, "In order to best illustrate and expound this phenomenon it is necessary to take in the field of man's activities, some example of which furnishes an abundance of reliable data, and for such purposes there is nothing better than the Stock Exchange."

The choice is obvious, since in no other area has there been so much time and effort expended on predicting the future with such poor results. Elliott focuses on the examples of 1929. Despite the many forecasting methods then available, the bear market of 1929–1932 still managed to wreck the investment community. Logically, forty additional years of research should have done something to blunt the effect of the bear markets experienced worldwide during the early 1970s. However, just as in 1929, hordes of investors were wiped out by the bottom of the decline and many investment companies, trusts, banks, etc., were annihilated. Forty years of stock market research produced very little reward indeed. Nearly sixty years' work and study showed no better results . . . witness October 1987. The second reason given by Elliott for choosing the stock market as an area to illustrate the wave impulse common to socio-economic activity is, of course, the great reward attendant on successful stock market forecasting.

"Even accidental success in some single forecast has yielded riches little short of the fabulous," says Elliott. "From July 1932 to March 1937, for illustration, an average of thirty leading and representative shares advanced by 373 percent. During the course of this five-year movement, however, there were individual shares whose percent advance was much larger. Lastly, the broad advance cited above was not in a straight upward line, but rather by a series of upward and downward steps, or zigzag movements of a number of months' duration. These lesser swings afforded even greater opportunity for profit."

The Rhythms of the Mind

Elliott's recognition of the true forces behind share-price behavior gives additional credibility to his Wave Principle. The fact that most individuals do not succeed in their speculation, and the generally poor performance of the forecasters in the securities industry, is primarily because most attempt to relate stock market behavior to current events, whereas those events have little to do with future stock market performance. Today's news has nothing whatever to do with today's share prices, even though journalists continually feature various news items in an attempt to make them conform to stock market action (see Chapter 4).

Elliott felt this aspect made his Wave Principle that much more important. He said:

> Despite the attention given the stock market, success, both in the accuracy of prediction and the bounties attendant thereto, has necessarily been haphazard because those who have attempted to deal with the market's movements have failed to recognize the extent to which the market is a psychological phenomenon. They have not grasped the fact that there is regularity underlying fluctuations of the market, or stated otherwise, that price movements in shares are subject to rhythms, or an ordered sequence. Thus, market predictions, as those who have had any experience in the subject well know, have lacked certainty or value of any but an accidental kind.

> But the market has its law, just as is true of other things throughout the universe. Were there no law, there could be no center about which prices could revolve and therefore, no market. Instead, there would be a daily series of disorganized, confused price fluctuations without reason or order anywhere apparent. A close study of the market, however, as will be subsequently disclosed, proves that this is not the case. Rhythm, or regular, measured, and harmonious movement, is to be discerned. This law behind the market can be discovered only when the market is viewed in its proper light, and then is analyzed from this approach. Simply put, the stock market is a creation of man and therefore reflects human idiosyncrasy.

The Wave Principle and its companion, the Fibonacci Summation Series, represent this rhythm of man's response to external stimuli, which shows itself in price fluctuations in the stock market and other markets, where mass-behavior patterns react to the forces of supply and demand. Once the waves have been interpreted, the knowledge can be applied to any movement, as the same principle affects the price of shares, government securities, grains, metals, cotton, coffee, and other mass markets.

When the movements of these markets are studied with the intention of applying the Wave Principle, three distinct features must be noted. Every series of actions and reactions will comprise pattern, time, and ratio, all of which will be found to follow the Fibonacci Series.

"Patterns," Not Patterns

Dealing with the subject of pattern, the Fibonacci Summation Series will be applied to the actual "wave count." For example, normal behavior of a complete stock market cycle, consisting of a bull move and a bear move should involve the completion of eight waves. The bull cycle consists of five waves, of which three are impulse waves and two are corrective waves, while the bear cycle will consist of two downward impulse waves and one corrective wave, all of which conform to the Summation Series. When we go down in the cycle, the cycle of the next-lower degree should also have a breakdown of waves conforming to the Summation Series. In other words, the first impulse wave of the bull movement should have five inner waves, whereas the second wave, which is a corrective wave, should have three waves, just like the longer-term cycle.

Should the impulse-wave continue beyond the count of five, normal behavior has gone by the board, and we are on the alert that a further series of Elliott tools should be employed. These are to be met in subsequent chapters.

Basically, any impulse move should end with a wave count equal to one of the numbers in the Summation Series. An upward move that develops beyond five waves is likely to continue for three additional waves. A downward move which exceeds three waves is likely to develop two more waves; if these two waves are exceeded, a further three waves can be expected. If a count goes beyond thirteen waves, counting both up waves and down waves of similar dimensions, we can expect the move to continue in the direction of the main trend, until twenty-one waves have been completed.

To forecast, we can thus use a study of the wave pattern in order to tell us how much further a move is likely to develop, before a counter-trend gets under way. Generally, any move in a particular direction will continue until such time as a number in the Fibonacci Summation Series is complete. A major uptrend comprising four intermediate waves, two up and two down, which in turn comprises sixteen minor waves, would be an incomplete move, and the major uptrend would have to develop at least five more waves before the uptrend was complete and the next number in the Fibonacci Series reached.

A major bear market consisting of one intermediate down wave, comprising five minor waves; one intermediate up wave, comprising three minor waves; and part of an intermediate down wave, comprising two minor waves would also be incomplete. Three additional minor waves will be necessary, bringing us to the number thirteen in the Summation Series, in order to complete the move.

To verify the wave count, one can begin with the waves of the highest degree observable, then descend downward to the intermediate, minor, sub-minor, and even lower categories. Until the last wave in the lowest category reaches a number in the Fibonacci Series, it is unlikely that the direction of the move in the wave category, which formed the starting point, will reach its endpoint.

Ellliot states in *Nature's Law*, "From experience, I have learned that 144 is the highest number of practical value. In a complete cycle of the stock market, the number of minor waves is 144, as shown in the following table:

Number of:	Bull Market	Bear Market	Total	
Major Waves	5	3	8	Complete Cycles
Intermediate Waves	21	13	34	" "
Minor Waves	89	55	144	" "

All are Fibonacci numbers and the entire series is employed. The length of waves may vary, but not the number."

The phenomenon and breakdown is best illustrated by the diagram in Chapter Four, Figure 8, page 35. It must be remembered that this chart is a model, and one must never expect the stock market to behave in such a precise manner.

Time

The Fibonacci Summation Series is designed to place further emphasis on the timing aspect of stock market behavior. In Chapter Three, I briefly touched on the time span relationship and the way it was used to place the market in the wave cycle. It would be unreasonable to classify a two- or three-week movement in the stock market as part of the cycle, which spans several months, even though the amplitude of such a short-term move may appear compatible with a cycle wave of a higher degree. The *time* relationship would be the deciding factor in this case.

Using the Fibonacci Summation Series, superimposed on the time cycle, we can gain not only a clearer perspective with regard to cycle degree classification, but can also use the series to project turning points and the degree of action likely to follow.

Investment Educators of Chicago, Illinois, was one of the few firms to develop the Elliott Wave Principle and present it in a form that could be taught to students. It referred to Elliott's time concept as representative of *isochronic time,* or, according to Chamber's Dictionary, "a line on a chart joining points associated with a constant time difference." While we do not have a *constant time difference* in the case of Elliott's work, we do have a constant time relationship in the form of the Summation Series.

When dealing with the time factor, we must only make consistent comparisons. If we wish to project the important turning point of an intermediate move on the time scale, we must use the terminal juncture of the preceding intermediate-term move to make our projections. Similarly, a minor-trend change can be projected in time when one uses the previous minor-trend change as a date for measurement. This is true for all scales.

When dealing with time, price levels or the size of waves is totally ignored. Time is measured on a horizontal basis. There are only three important time periods to consider: the durations of the major trend, the intermediate trend, and the minor trend. As you gain experience in looking at the various chart formations and dissecting the wave relationships, you will be able to recognize the different terminal junctures in their various degrees. By bringing the Summation Series into your analysis, you will be able to perceive those points of measurement, enabling you to anticipate approximately when the various degrees of movement should end.

When attempting to determine approximately when a particular move will stop, we expect the time sequence, whether it be hours, days, weeks, or months, to follow the Summation Series. There is the possibility of very short-term inter-day rallies or declines ending within three hours, if such moves are counter to the overriding cycle. Any sub-minor move that runs beyond three hours will then offer a strong possibility of extending to five trading hours, the number five being the next number in the Summation Series. Should the particular move extend beyond five hours, a reversal is unlikely until the move draws close to its eighth hour. Obviously, an eleven-hour move would be incomplete, as eleven is not in the series. Using this phenomenon in your short-term strategy, you should immediately notice superior results, as you will avoid action during those hourly movements which lie within the longer time intervals of the sequence.

The same holds true for daily movements. No firm conclusion can be drawn during the first three days of a movement, in the context of a trend that is likely to be sustainable. The series suggests a sub-minor trend is established, nothing more. A completed sub-minor movement can take place on any one of the first three days, the sequence of 1, 2, and 3 all being part of the Summation Series. However, when the movement goes beyond a third day, there is a high probability that such a movement will enter its fifth day before completion. Carrying beyond the fifth day presents a further probability that such a move will extend for another three days. Therefore, one should not consider action until the eighth day of the move occurs. By now, one can see how a move picks up additional staying power as it develops, until the force is finally spent.

When dealing with longer time spans, the same method of approach should be adopted. A minor trend, which develops into the fourth week of its movement, will usually have at least one more week to go before reaching a terminal phase. Similarly, an intermediate-term move of ten months is likely to continue in the same direction for a further three months. A major bull cycle of more than two years should continue for a further year. If such a bull cycle exceeds the three-year time span, another two years of the bull move are likely.

The manner in which the Summation Series can be seen to have been applied to previous market cycles is a matter of history. The following explanation will give you just a brief synopsis of the manner in which the Summation Series would have served the investor in the past.

The period from 1929 to 1942 (thirteen years) produced a bear market spanning three years (1929–1932), a major bull market spanning five years (1932–37), followed by an extended bear market spanning a further five years (1937–42). Elliott places special emphasis on this period from 1929–1942. The entire pattern of development over that period comprises one massive *triangle*. Each wave of the triangle is perfectly proportionate to its predecessor, in accordance with the Golden Ratio of 61.8 percent. All three factors—pattern, time, and ratio—are perfectly in accordance with the Fibonacci Summation Series.

In view of the dogmatic insistence on prediction in favor of probability and anticipation by many who use chart patterns to predict price moves, when using Elliott's time concept with the Fibonacci Summation Series and the Elliott Wave Principle as a whole, *anticipate* is the operative word. When a particular move stretches beyond the time sequence or wave sequence compatible with the Fibonacci Series, one does not predict the move will stop at the next-higher integer in the sequence, for, quite simply, in accordance with the tenets of Elliott, it may not. One anticipates a terminal juncture at or near a sequence number and seeks evidence for support when it appears to be taking place. It must be recognized that, should such a turning point not happen, the move could stretch to the next-higher integer in the series. The longer the move and the more advanced the wave count, or the time count, the greater will be the probability of a turning point. Fixed judgement and absolute predictions have no place in the Elliott Wave Principle approach to stock market behavior.

I shall repeat the warnings I gave you in Chapter 4. And remember, the longer the projection in time span, the greater the chance of errors and multiple errors. It will prove far more satisfactory to make the projections as time moves along.

The Golden Ratio

We now come to the final aspect of the stock market behavior to which the Fibonacci Summation Series is applied: the *ratio*, or the proportionate relationship of one wave to another, both in time and in amplitude. Here we are only concerned with two mathematical factors, 1.618 and 61.8. This mathematical relationship is implicit in the wave count itself. As we know, a five-wave movement is followed by a three-wave movement running counter to it, three approximating to 61.8 percent of five. An upward impulse wave of 144 minor waves will be followed by a counterwave of eighty-nine minor components, 89 being 61.8 percent of 144 in accordance with the series relationship.

When dealing with the size of relationships, rather than wave count relationships, Elliott cites several examples. For instance, the number of points registered by the Dow Jones Industrial Averages between 1921 and 1926 (i.e., the first three waves of the bull move) was precisely 61.8 percent of the number of points during the last wave of the move between 1926–28. (It should be noted that according to the Elliott Wave count the orthodox top of the bull move began in 1928.) This relationship was repeated in the five waves up from 1932–37. The wave from the market top in 1930 (297 in the DJIA), to the market bottom in 1932 was 1.618 times the move from 40 to 195, which took place during 1932–37. The bear market decline that took place from 1937–8 was 61.8 percent of the 1932–37 advance.

In 1960, when A. Hamilton Bolton published the first definitive work on the Elliott Wave Principle, entitled, *The Elliott Wave Principle—A Critical Appraisal,* he stated: "Should the 1949 market to date adhere to this formula, then the advance from 1949 to 1956 (361 points in the DJIA) should be complete when 583 points (1.618 percent of the 361 points) have been added to the 1957 low of 416, or a total of 999 DJIA."

In 1966 the DJIA advanced to marginally above the level of 999, but closed at 998.5, thus completing the long-wave 1949–66 cycle, and, unable to achieve this level again until many years later. Obviously, those who were anticipating a trend change in accordance with the principle of this proportionate projection would have profited handsomely.

Fibonacci Applied

When applying the Golden Ratio to stock market behavior, one assumes that since a bull market has five waves and a bear market three waves, the three-wave corrective move would be equivalent to approximately 61.8 percent of the preceding bull wave in time and/or size. A bull market producing an index move of, say, 100 points over a time frame of, say, two years, would thus be followed by a bear market involving a down move of approximately 62 points, stretching over a period of about fifteen months.

The simple formulas for calculating the ratio of time and size relative to the various waves are as follows:

$$\frac{\text{Number of points in corrective phase}}{\text{Number of points in impulse phase}} = \text{Size Ratio}$$

Periodicity of corrective phase
(hours, days, weeks, months, or years)
$$\frac{\text{Periodicity of corrective phase (hours, days, weeks, months, or years)}}{\text{Periodicity of impulse phase (hours, days, weeks, months, or years)}} = \text{Time Span Ratio}$$
Periodicity of impulse phase
(hours, days, weeks, months, or years)

It is vitally important to recognize the particular cycle time frame when attempting to forecast the end of that particular cycle. Time span projections for a minor cycle will only apply to minor-cycle time frames; the same holds true for intermediate and longer-term cycles.

When using the formula, be sure to account for trends of similar dimen-sions. To measure the termination of a current upswing, one uses the time frame of the last down wave in the cycle of the same scale. Conversely, to anticipate a likely ending for a downswing in both time and amplitude, we use those previous upswings as a guide.

When dealing with the Wave Principle, one seeks to establish future normal-behavior patterns from which to draw broad guidelines. On many occasions these patterns of normal behavior will be translated into precise market action. However, more often than not, these behavior patterns will either be exceeded or fail to materialize, due to a change in the character of the nature of price action. This in itself should provide further guidelines for students of the Wave Principle. The subject of failures (be warned . . . this is not what it sounds like) will clarify this point.

A corrective wave of sub-normal amplitude will generally indicate exceptional strength during the next impulse wave. An abnormal correction in amplitude will indicate the contrary. A sub-normal correction on the time span will act to sap strength from the succeeding impulse wave, making it shorter than usual. An abnormal correction on the time span will produce an extended period of consolidation, providing a springboard for the succeeding impulse wave.

When there is a divergence between the size ratio and the time-frame ratio of a corrective phase, the extent of the price swing should dominate for the purpose of future projections. In essence, the shape of the pattern and the wave count should always be given the greater weight when attempting to establish future projections based on this particular aspect of the Wave Principle.

Note that the use of both the Fibonacci Summation Series and the ratios which are implicit in the series are intended as a cross-check against projections based on aspects of Elliott's theory. The mathematical basis for the Wave Theory should not in itself be used to make absolute projections, but rather to establish frames of reference, which act as parameters for establishing subsequent behavior.

Historical Examples of the Summation Series

Stock market history comprises endless repetitions of the series. The 1921 bottom in UK share prices was twenty-one years from the 1942 bottom. Similarly, the 1928 "orthodox top" was twenty-one years away from the 1949 bottom. The bull market from 1932 to 1937 lasted five years. The bear market from 1937 to 1942 also lasted five years. The 1921–29 bull market lasted eight years. The first wave of the 1937–42 bear market lasted thirteen months. The bear market from 1929–32 lasted three years. It was precisely eighty-nine months from the bear market bottom of 1921 to the "orthodox top" in 1928. (More recent examples are the thirteen-month move from the bear market low of 6 January 1975, to the peak of the third wave in February 1976. As mentioned previously, the first wave of that particular bull market was five months in duration, the combination of the succeeding two waves being eight months in duration.)

When dealing with the ratio, Elliott pointed out that the number of points gained during the first three upwaves, between 1921–26 of the 1921–29 bull market were 61.8 percent of the last wave 1926–28 preceding the "orthodox top." In the five waves up from 1932–37 a similar pattern can be noted. The wave from the 1930 peak of 297 in the Dow Jones Industrial Averages to the bottom of 40 in 1932 is 1.658 times the 1932–37 advance, which took the DJIA from 40 to 195. Not only was the first wave of the 1937 bear market thirteen months long, but it spanned 61.8 percent of the 1932–1937 advance in DJIA points. (In London we found the first three waves of the bull move from January 1975 to represent 68 percent of the decline, which took the FT30 down from 545 in May 1972 to 145.5, while the corrective phase was nearing 61.8 of the time span noted for the August 1975–February 1976 rise.)

The series obviously occurs with astonishing frequency. However, it can be seen in the examples quoted that at times an important market bottom is found by measuring the time span between the two preceding tops, and at other times a top can be found by measuring the time span of the bottoms. On other occasions the time span of a down wave is found by measuring that of the previous up wave, while the periodicity of an up wave is found by measuring the time span of the preceding down wave.

The student of the Wave Principle should carry out all of these measurements in order to determine the various possibilities that can exist. The important factor to remember is that corrective waves should be approximately 61.8 percent of the preceding impulse wave, both in time and amplitude, while the succeeding impulse wave should be approximately 1.618 times the preceding corrective wave, in both time and amplitude. When using the Summation Series itself, corrective waves should be related to the preceding number in the Summation Series in time and size. For example, if an impulse wave comprises thirteen minor waves, the corrective wave to follow should have eight minor waves. Should a corrective wave last five months, the succeeding impulse wave should span eight months.

8
Fine-tuning the Wave Principle

The grand thing about the human mind is that it can turn its own tables and see meaningless as ultimate meaning.

—JOHN CAGE

The Wave Principle, as conceived by Ralph Nelson Elliott, is undoubtedly the most unusual analytical tool ever devised for anticipating the future behavior of price action in markets. Following two decades of painstaking research, Elliott had perfected his theory by 1938. It was Elliott's view that the Wave Principle, like no other, adequately reflected the behavior pattern inherent in human nature.

It was Elliott's contention that price trends take place in basic, *five-wave rhythms*, with three separate waves in the direction of the primary trend and two corrective waves against the primary trend. This five-wave rule applies to both bull markets and bear markets.

In commenting on the observed fact that a completed movement—up or down—consists of five waves, Elliott wrote in 1938:

> Why this should be five rather than some other number is one of the secrets of the universe. No attempt will be made to explain it, although, in passing, it might be observed that the figure five is prominent in other basic patterns of nature. Taking the human body, for example, there are five extensions from the torso—head, two legs, two arms; five extensions from the head—two ears, two eyes, and the nose; five extensions in the form of fingers from each arm, and in the form of toes from each leg; five physical senses—taste, smell, sight, touch, and hearing; and so the story might be repeated elsewhere.

Essentially, the Wave Principle is a cyclical theory. Yet, it is unlike any other cyclical theory ever employed. Most cyclical theories involve fixed-cycle periodicity in an inflexible manner. Generally, cyclical theory involves the apparent tendency of such phenomena as price movements, weather habits, sun spots, cattle production, etc., to continue in one trend for a fixed number of weeks, months, or years, before reversing to the opposite direction. There is certainly a great deal of value in some of the fixed-cycle periodicity work of many reputable public and private agencies. But, there are many drawbacks in attempting to incorporate fixed-cycle periodicities with investment analysis. To begin with, fixed-cycle periodicity research is not the type of work that can be carried out with ease by the average investor. Complicated records and extremely specialized skills are necessary in order to obtain any kind of accuracy. The biggest drawback of all is that modern computer technology and the use of serial correlation has produced overwhelming evidence to demonstrate that the behavior of prices in markets do not lend themselves to any form of fixed-cycle periodicity analysis.

The Wave Principle, on the other hand, can be applied to all types of long-range or short-range price charts, as long as the subject involves mass behavior. Although there can be extreme difficulties in interpretation during certain periods, when the waves can be clearly defined, the rules are simple and the projections work. The Wave Principle is a far better tool for indicating or *positioning* and defining to what state a trend has developed than anything else available. Those who have studied and used the Wave Principle over the years insist, among other things, that the Wave Principle is alone among cyclical attempts to project what has actually happened since World War II in the stock averages.

Ralph Nelson Elliott died in 1947. It was during the mid-1930s, as a result of some of Elliott's own amazing forecasts, along with the uniqueness of the Wave Principle, that Elliott first became known to analyst Charles Collins and then to an ever-wider audience.

If Elliott's forecasts were spectacular, so were the basic tenets underlying his theory. One of the many fascinating aspects of the Wave Principle is that each wave can be broken up into sub-waves of its own (either three or five waves) and that these waves, in turn, break down into smaller sub-waves, and so on, like the wheels within wheels, circles within spirals, and ripples in the tide of the ocean. In principle, the waves can thus be carried down to the level of the split-second timing for an individual trade.

The Wave Principle can also be extended to a far larger scale of immense dimensions, where each wave is a sub-wave of a larger wave and that wave the sub-wave of a still-larger wave. These larger waves can span years, decades, and generations. Elliott actually believed that some waves in prices were centuries long, during what he defined as the Grand Super Cycle.

In theory, a grand super cycle began at the time of the Industrial Revolution and was reaching its final stages during the summer of 1991. Those who subscribe to this theory may visualize a sequence of five waves, which carried prices up to their peak on the New York Stock Exchange during the summer of 1991. The investor who would be desirous of pinpointing the final peak of the market would have begun counting the waves in detail at the end of the fourth wave, expecting the fifth and final wave to break down into five sub-waves. Once the fifth wave of the fifth wave of the fifth wave became apparent, possibly on a weekly chart and then a daily chart, or an every-price-move chart, it is possible to pinpoint the final peak of the fifth wave of the fifth wave of the fifth wave of that final fifth wave in preparation for a retracing of all the gains made since the first-wave peak of the Industrial Revolution . . . theoretically of course! The Wave Principle approach, which has become increasingly popular in recent years, certainly is most unusual and can result in some bizarre considerations.

During the time that Elliott was using his method, he compiled a spectacular record of forecasting short-, medium-, and long-term price action for the US stock market. During 1934, Elliott went on record to say that a bull market had begun in the US stock market that would carry for quite some time and some distance. In March 1935, the Dow Jones Rail Average crashed below its 1934 low. At the same time, the Dow Jones Industrial Averages plunged by eleven percent. Wall Street was bearish to the man, having the 1929–1932 catastrophe still fresh in mind—along with the depleted bank accounts of most investors. Yet, Elliott was dogmatic in his insistence that the bull market was far from over and that another big leg up in the bull market would soon be on the way. At the very bottom of the eleven-percent decline in Wall Street during 1935, after the Dow Jones Rail Average had levelled off for four days, Elliott affirmed in a telegram to one of his associates that the break was over and that the major upswing that he had anticipated was just getting under way. Looking back at Elliott's interpretation, the eleven-percent break in the DJIA was merely

Primary Wave 2 in a bull market that had two more major impulse waves to go.

Charles Collins, A. Hamilton Bolton, and William O'Connor followed in the footsteps of R.N. Elliott as the leading practitioners of the Wave Principle following Elliott's death. Some of the forecasts made by these three individuals were no less astonishing than those of Elliott while he was alive. Using a "side-effect" of Elliott's concepts, Bolton was able to forecast the level of a key stock market top with an accuracy of 99.6 percent. In his book *The Elliott Wave Principle—A Critical Appraisal*, Bolton predicted in 1960 that the super-cycle high for the Dow Jones Industrial Averages would be at 999. The actual level of Elliott's super-cycle peak was 995; that was reached in January 1966.

In the annual supplements to the *Bank Credit Analyst*, which featured Bolton's work with the Wave Principle, there were many explicit forecasts of general stock market behavior that turned out to be fantastically accurate and which were written without the benefit of hindsight, as is the case with so many seemingly accurate forecasts. "Market Ebb Tide," which was published in *Barron's* during March 1970, contains some of the very accurate predictions of Charles Collins, who correctly forecast several important major bull and bear markets when using the Wave Principle.

William O'Connor, author of *Stocks, Wheat and Pharoahs*, was one of the first traders to successfully utilize the Wave Principle in commodity trading. O'Connor, whose remarkable track record is outlined in his book, placed great stress on the use of daily charts for identifying Elliott waves over the short run.

In recent years, Bob Prechter, a Yale graduate with a bachelor's degree in psychology who had spent some years playing guitar on the road with a rock band, was catapulted to fame as a result of his exploitation of the Wave Principle. Prechter drew increasing attention with a remarkable run of successful market calls in 1983–1984. He also entered and won the United States Trading Championship competition organized by Norman Zadeh, running his real-money option account up from $5,396 to $29,269 in the four months ending May 1984, during which time he traded some 1,400 options and paid $35,000 in commissions.

The achievements of those who have used the Wave Principle certainly make impressive reading, while arguing strongly for the viability of Elliott's theories. It must also be recognized that the investment community's recent fascination with the Wave Principle readily lends itself to an example of the Hidden In Man syndrome in action: the compulsion investors have to believe that somewhere, sometime, some esoteric genius understood what's been going on.

Interpretative Problems Galore

I would be the very last to deny that working with the Wave Principle is not without problems. Some of those problems can be monumental.

The five-waves-up-interrupted-by-two-waves-down concept is simple enough to grasp. Great! Reachey peachey! MacVowtie! O'Rooney! All you have to do, when the market begins a new move after an important downtrend is complete, is to start counting the waves. Until you have two up waves interrupted by two down waves, you do nothing but hold your positions. As soon as the third up wave ends, you sell everything and go short. If only . . . the sad truth, however, lies in the complications. It is often difficult to determine when a new move is actually getting under way. On many occasions it will also be difficult to decipher whether three identifiable upwaves complete the total move or are only components of the first of three larger waves. If the latter turns out to be the case, sales in anticipation of a cyclical downtrend would have been premature and short sales positively disastrous.

That's where your problems may begin. They certainly won't end there. Elliott was able to observe that in many instances, following the third up wave and preceding a decline, the market frequently took off on a wild spree, involving a fourth up wave, which is reached at a higher level than the third up wave, which was supposed to represent the ending of an important move. Undaunted, Elliott referred to this action as an "irregular top," with the new high ground that is entered actually representing a portion of the corrective movements. The categorization of Elliott is certainly useful, but of little consolation if you happen to have sold your stocks and started selling short at the end of the third wave.

Jesse Livermore, considered to be the greatest short-term market operator of all time, did just that. In 1928, Livermore felt the bull market in the United States had come to an end and started selling short. By the time the market rallied to another all-time high in the summer of 1929, Jesse had been decimated. According to Elliott's interpretation of the 1928–1932 affair, the "orthodox top" of the bull market was during 1928, as Jesse had thought. The drive to the 1929 high was the Wave B of an irregular correction. The total collapse in the US stock market from 1929–1932 was the Wave C.

Elliott does note that following irregular tops, Wave C is quite extensive and devastating. Jesse's short positions would have worked out magnificently in the end. It's a pity the Wave Principle had not yet been devised at the time.

Elliott insisted that every stock market movement of every type could be categorized within the tenets of the Wave Principle. Given this all-inclusive system of categorization, it is therefore theoretically possible for the investor to know where prices stand at all times. Elliott believed in *counting* and *labelling* the waves of advances and declines in price movements. These waves, he felt, fell into finite, repetitive sequences so complete and so comprehensive that the investor could accurately be aware of where prices stood in their development during any period and how much potential they had on the up side or down side, roughly how much longer an existing trend was likely to persist, and how much further it would go.

But, what is true in theory does not always work out in practice. Elliott's system of labelling the waves can involve extravagant complexity and often does. The entire concept of Elliott's Wave Principle rests on counting waves. What is a wave? Elliott himself, with all of the extensive work he produced on the subject, gave no answer to this question. This means that the investor is often forced to exert a highly subjective judgement to label a wave on his chart and an equally subjective judgement to identify the time scale in which the wave might fit.

If you conduct a study of a wide range of price charts, you will often find that the final wave of a major bull run will often break up into many more than five sub-waves. It has been suggested that either the theory is wrong or some of the sub-waves should not be counted for some unknown reason. This problem frequently occurs in Elliott's own personal analysis.

Probably the most frightening aspect of the Wave Principle to the average investor always seeking absolutes is its flexibility. It is possible and probable to obtain several radically different wave counts from the same exact price data. The leading practitioners of the Wave Principle are in almost constant disagreement as to the precise wave count at most times. A particularly disturbing corollary to all of this is that the more back data the investor using the Wave Principle has accumulated, the greater the number of possible alternative counts in the price sequence. In most endeavors, additional information can just as easily add to the confusion. We know that a little knowledge is a dangerous thing. With Elliott, a lot of knowledge can be even more dangerous.

I previously touched on the manner in which the final wave of a major bull move seems, more often than not, to break up into many sub-waves which defy categorization. A further flexible aspect of Elliott's theory is the fluid concept of *extensions*; for example, a five-wave move can, under Elliott's tenets, extend itself without warning into nine waves. These and other features of the Wave Principle make it difficult to come to any decisions at any given moment. While it may often be easy to see the correct count—along with the right decisions that should have been made—quite frequently, this expertise appears after the fact.

Elliott, without question, intended that his Wave Principle would mold current price action into a comprehensive structure that would provide guidance at all times. Yet, any cursory perusal of a comprehensive range of price charts will reveal long, blank spots, in which it is impossible to get any sort of wave count. Since one of the fundamental tenets of Elliott's Wave Principle is that all waves be counted, labelled, and categorized, the existence of these "blank" spots means either that the fundamental premise is flawed or invalid, or that the count at these times is subtle enough to escape most or all, observers.

James Dines, one of the most talented investment advisers ever to appear on the US investment scene, speaking at one of my seminars said, in reference to the Elliott Wave Principle, "Unless it can be computerized, I doubt its value." Since then, several attempts have been made to computerise the Wave Principle, the latest being a software package called The Wave Timer. I have monitored the results of these computerized efforts, including the latest software package. I have yet to see any conclusive evidence to indicate that the results achieved through computerization are as consistently accurate and meaningful as those demonstrated by Elliott himself, A. Hamilton Bolton, Charles Collins, William O'Connor, and others who I know have amassed considerable wealth using the original non-computerized tenets of the Wave Principle. Until such time as artificial intelligence advances to the state where a computer is capable of dealing with unstable numbers and where infinity remains an innumerate integer for programming purposes, I am of the opinion that the Wave Principle in its intended form defies computerization.

Finally, dealing with the difficulties that many will encounter when attempting to deploy the Wave Principle in their investment activities, there may also be a severe philosophical problem that invites scepticism. It is not generally realized that Elliott was a mystic—like Aldous Huxley in his later years—who also believed in numerology. In his monograph, *Nature's Law*, Elliott discussed how mathematical relationships in the Great Pyramid of Gizeh not only predicted future world events, but tied in with his own wave theory as well! Although investors should always keep an open mind on most things, many are unable to master this accomplishment. Those who are traditionally minded may find it difficult to accept a method of analysis that is in agreement with pyramid numerology.

Isolating, quantifying, and successfully dealing with non-random elements in markets requires unusual determination and discipline. The efficient market is a worthy adversary, and, in attempting to forecast price movements, the investor must always beware of trying to get more out of an experience than is in it to begin with. There seems to be an overwhelming urge among investors for stock market forecasting to develop a simple, mechanical system that works with near-perfect accuracy. I can now state in no uncertain terms that the Wave Principle will leave that search unfulfilled. The search is a futile one.

Having acknowledged the difficulties in dealing with the Wave Principle, it should be clear that the Wave Principle is a far cry from providing an investment tool that will guarantee outstanding performance. Yet, it is my assertion that the Wave Principle is simply the very best tool you could possibly use. Considering all of the anomalies, dichotomies, and philosophical difficulties, comparing the Wave Principle with other stock market tools is like comparing an Exocet missile with a bow and arrow for optimal effect.

Useful Hints for Wave Counting

Ralph Nelson Elliott was a genius. Of this there should be little doubt. The imagination that has gone into his most intricate system certainly reaches beyond the psychic confines of most people. Genius manifests itself in different ways with different individuals. While Elliott may have had a capacity for genius in his chosen area of endeavor, this did not include the field of literary acumen. When reading through Elliott's original material, over and over, at times I felt as if I were reading the Bible, attempting to decipher its hidden meaning, which was not apparent on the surface.

In addition to dissecting all of Elliott's original work, including the stock market advisory notes he had written while he was publishing his stock market service entitled *The Wave Principle,* I also covered a great deal of the material that was written by those who attempted their own interpretation of Elliott's Wave Principle. With the exception of the annual supplements to the *Bank Credit Analyst* and William O'Connor's magnificent work, *Stocks, Wheat, and Pharoahs,* most of which I found was of little use, often adding to initial confusion.

"No two movements are exactly alike, nevertheless, the phenomenon of the Wave Principle invariably applies as described in the Treatise. Likewise, the same analysis applies to cycles of whatever size," said R.N. Elliott in *Interpretative Letter No. 1 of The Wave Principle.* "The phenomenon and its practical application becomes increasingly interesting because the market continually unfolds new examples to which may be applied unchanging rules." It was obvious that during his development of the Wave Principle, Elliott had encountered the same problems that anyone who would subsequently use his method was likely to come across. Elliott had found solutions to these problems and was able to categorize each and every price movement to his satisfaction. Due to his limited literary abilities, he was unable to adequately explain his method in its entirety. A. Hamilton Bolton contributed a great deal to taking Elliott's theory into the realm of lucid comprehension. Yet, even with A. Hamilton Bolton's work and the work of those who contributed to the annual supplements of the *Bank Credit Analyst,* there remained many questions unanswered. I intended to take matters a bit further. As I re-read Elliott's material, over and over again, I began to pick up clues in comments that he had made out of context, which helped clarify a number of obscurities while facilitating the counting of the waves.

Elliott never fully experienced the degree of emphasis that was to be placed on the Fibonacci Summation Series or whether it was to be used in a confirmatory capacity or a predictive capacity. Several of Elliott's practitioners seem to place more emphasis on the series than on the wave count itself.

Indeed, the series has some very interesting properties. The 1968 *Elliott Supplement of the Bank Credit Analyst* includes a mathematical analysis of the Fibonacci Series by W.E. White. A brief article on the series designed for the layman entitled "The Fibonacci Numbers" appeared in the April 1969 issue of *Time* magazine, containing further references. It has been affirmed that both living and inanimate objects obey a number of laws that revolve around the mathematical properties of this series. Using the 1-2-3-5-8-13-21-34-55-89-144-233-377-etc. sequence, which is Fibonacci summation, it is possible for scientists to predict how populations of animals will multiply, how plants will grow, how crystalline structures will form naturally, and a great many other things. This series also yields the Golden Ratio that is used in architecture. It is evident that a study of this series discloses mathematical relationships that hold in real-life situations. It has been hyphothesized that these relationships are so all-inclusive that they extend into the psychological arena as well, with price fluctuations in markets reflecting their subtle but all-pervasive influence.

Although Elliott wrote extensively about the Fibonacci Summation Series in *Nature's Law*, there is very little reference to the series in either his other work, *The Wave Principle,* or in his interpretative letters. I continue to find Elliott's interpretative letters the most useful of Elliott's writing when attempting to use the Wave Principle in the same manner as its innovator intended. It has become clear to me that the Fibonacci Summation Series, while establishing the mathematical foundation for Elliott's work, was used by him as nothing more than a cross-reference in his categorization of the waves.

"When in doubt, stay out!" should be indelibly inscribed in your psyche when using the Wave Principle and when dealing in markets generally. Another useful adage is that of the K.I.S.S. principle: keep it simple, stupid! Many Elliott Wave theorists involve themselves in mind-wrenching intellectual labors in an effort to define every single movement, allowing low- probability wave counts of waves where there is very little delineation or symmetry. This practice is unnecessary. My rule has always been, never strain for a count. When dealing in markets, the most beneficial results from our wave analysis will occur when the waves are obvious to quick inspection, and especially when their development seems symmetrical to the eye. There is a law in physics stating the angle of incidence is usually equal to the angle of reflection. This law applies to the Wave Principle as well.

Using the Wave Principle should not be treated as an intellectual adventure in prediction. I assume you are going to be dealing with real money. You will be staking your real money on the Wave Principle, and you're going to want to win. Winning isn't everything, but losing isn't anything. If the wave count is not clear, avoid taking action. You will only want to take action when the probabilities are in your favor. If the wave count is not clear, the probabilities will not be in your favor. During such times, you may wish to consult alternative principles of investment. Elliott certainly did. Elliott did not use his Wave Principle to the exclusion of all other investment considerations. This is obvious in his interpretative letters. It is also obvious in the work of A. Hamilton Bolton. The Wave Principle is not intended to encourage you to take action undeflected by thought, nor to act as a substitute for knowledge.

> Production recently completed five major waves upward. Industrial stock prices are lowest since March 1938. Utility averages at record low; production of electricity at highest level. New corporate financing near zero. Federal debt highest ever and going much higher. We are participants in the world's most serious conflict. Inflation is feared by many. A reliable hedge is unknown—certainly 'cash' would be the least desirable refuge.

That was Elliott's personal message to his followers in *Interpretative Letter No. 20 of The Wave Principle* covering the period November 1940 through December 10, 1941. It was obvious that Elliott was acutely aware of the fundamental influences governing markets and that he incorporated these fundamental factors as cross-references for his analysis. Elliott was certainly not a "pure chartist," who locked himself in a room without windows, avoiding communication with the outside world, as some technical analysts advocate.

In the same interpretative letter, Elliott wrote,

> Graph (3) demonstrates the divergence of the Dow Jones Industrial Averages and the Federal Reserve Production Index. Investors who are unfamiliar with triangles and were guided by the Production Index suffered severe losses which they found expedient to register tax-selling losses recently on account of high taxes, both present and prospective. This selling created additional downward pressure with the result that, on a comparative yield basis, stocks are cheaper today than they were in July 1932, as is graphically demonstrated in Interpretative Letter No. 19.

Elliott was also concerned with traditional stock market values, as can readily be seen in his writing. It should now become patently clear that a mechanical approach to the Wave Principle will not yield satisfactory results. It should also become abundantly self-evident that no-think computerized approaches to the Wave Principle involving expensive software packages that inject inflexibility when the maximum flexibility is required are utterly useless.

It is at the terminal juncture of an old trend, which coincides with the emergence of a new trend, that users of the Wave Principle are presented with some of their greatest difficulties. Identification of the first wave of a new trend is the most difficult problem. There are several hints in Elliott's writings which suggest this difficulty can be mitigated. The suggestions are as follows:

1. Identify the reflex point which occurs after a well-delineated, five-wave major trend is apparently completed. The reflex point is the peak or trough of the last ostentatiously obvious rise or fall before the trend changed.

2. When the price movements from the last peak or trough exceeds the reflex point, count the price movement.

3. If a minor count can be made: 1-2-3-4-5, you have probably seen the start of a new, major five-wave trend, opposite to the prior trend. What had previously been three-wave corrective moves in the opposite direction of the main trend will have become five-wave impulse moves in the same direction as the new trend.

4. If the count (after the reflex point is exceeded) is only 1-2-3 and both waves 1 and 3 are of equal dimension in space and time, the implication is strong that no new and opposite trend is developing, but rather that the old trend is merely in a resting stage, or that not enough work has been done to constitute a reversal for the time being.

There are no measuring devices implicit in the Wave Principle, as those who use the Wave Principle for predictive purposes may infer. However, the calculation of price objectives—which should not be treated as predictions—can assist in confirming the count. For example, one of Elliott's basic tenets is that Wave III (the second major move, up or down, in the direction of the trend) is never smaller (shorter) than both Wave I and Wave V. If there is a count where Wave III appears shorter than Wave I or Wave V, that short Wave III must fall into the category of a corrective wave. This rule will help prevent miscounting when applied.

Another rule of Elliott's is that the extremity of Wave IV should never overlap the extremity of Wave I. If, in a falling market, what you believe to be the Wave IV of a bull market dips below the peak of Wave I, start recounting. It's unlikely that you have Wave IV. It is more likely that the bull market you think you're in has ended. For some strange reason, Bolton, Collins, and O'Connor seem to be the only practitioners of Elliott's theories who adhere to this vital rule laid down by Elliott: that Wave IV must not, under any circumstances, overlap Wave I. Every other Elliott theorist that I am aware of seems to have ignored this rule, with no word of explanation. This implies that a considerable number of distortions may have crept into Elliott's basic tenets over the years by those with only a second-hand knowledge.

It is vital to examine the price history of a market over the intermediate and long term before attempting to establish a short-term count. Keep in mind that the wave count is taken after a change in trend from either the base point or the top breakout peak. Elliott was very flexible in his own counting when it came to exact terminal junctures of a trend. It would therefore be useful to exclude the basing or topping activity from the wave count.

In a strong market, each up wave will probably increase in scope over the previous one. In a weakening market, the waves will become progressively truncated. Conversely, a progressive truncation of down waves in a falling market indicates an imminent end to the decline, whatever our count may be.

Point and figure charts can also be very useful for determining longer and intermediate wave counts, since a considerable amount of random noise is eliminated from the price structure of a point and figure chart. The point and figure chart has an automatic built-in filter system. However, point and figure charts should only be used in a confirmatory manner, as a cross-reference, never to establish a final count.

Returning once again to the element of price objectives to help you validate your wave count, the length of Wave V may be roughly projected by averaging the lengths of Wave I and Wave III. This method frequently provides a close estimate of the actual resulting move. If the existing structure, according to your count, is at variance with this measurement, it would be wise to reconsider your count.

Another quasi-price-objective corollary of the Wave Principle that may help you to verify your wave count has to do with contrasts between waves. It is common that the three major impulse waves in the direction of the primary trend will have a contrasting appearance. The first of the three major waves may be composed of five sub-waves that are perfectly delineated. The second major up move (Wave III) may be much smoother, with only one or two visible jiggles on a daily range chart. The third major wave up (Wave V) may appear as a straight line where the sub-waves may only be apparent on an hourly chart or an every-price-move chart.

This principle of contrast which Elliott described as *alternation* also appears in the reactions or corrective waves against the major uptrend (or downtrend) in Waves II and IV. Corrective waves fall into four basic categories of which the *flat* and the *zig-zag* are the most common. The zig-zag is steep and sharp. The flat is a sideways movement that can be many months in duration. If Wave II is a zig-zag, it becomes highly likely that

Wave IV will be a flat, and vice versa. As it happens, the zig-zag is most common to Wave II and the flat to Wave IV.

Obviously, by remembering the contrast corollary—Elliott's theory of alternation—wave identification and correct counting can be simplified and made with greater assurance.

Another very useful tendency, which should help you with your wave count and also assist in anticipating the probable extent of a subsequent price movement, is based on one of the most inviolate of Elliott's observations.

As mentioned previously, a corrective Wave IV in a bull market will reach a terminal juncture at or above the peak of Wave I of the cycle of the same degree. Elliott also observed that the correction that follows the completion of a five-wave upward movement comes to an end above the trough of Wave IV of the next-higher degree with similar persistence. It was this rule of Elliott's that helped me several months in advance to anticipate the precise point at which the 1972–1975 bear market in Britain would end.

The bear market began in May 1972, when the Financial Times 30 Share Index reached the level of 545. The Financial Times 30 Share Index travelled downward throughout 1972 and 1973 after having completed a five-wave count at the peak in May 1972. By the autumn of 1974, the Financial Times 30 Share Index had broken below the trough of Wave IV of the cycle, the peak of Wave I, and the trough of Wave II. This was truly a bear market of cyclical dimensions, acting to retrace the bulk of the entire thirty-four-year cycle. The only place to look for the possible end of that bear market was at the level of the trough of Wave IV of the cycle of the next-higher degree. That trough was at the level of 145 of the Financial Times 30 Share Index.

On 6 January 1975, the Financial Times 30 Share Index plunged on heavy volume, amidst an atmosphere of gloom that was so thick you needed a mega-power laser to cut it. Suddenly, at mid-session, on 6 January 1975, downside volume contracted, the market turned; upside volume began to swell dramatically. The Financial Times 30 Share Index ended the session at 146.5, merely .5 below the trough of Wave III of the cycle of the next- higher degree that had occurred several decades before.

The manner in which the tendency for a correction that follows the completion of five waves will hold at a level above Wave IV of the next-higher degree can be seen by the action of the Axe-Houghton-Burgess Index during the long super cycle spanning 1857 to 1932. The decline that

Figure 10
THE AXE-HOUGHTON-BURGESS INDEX 1896–1932

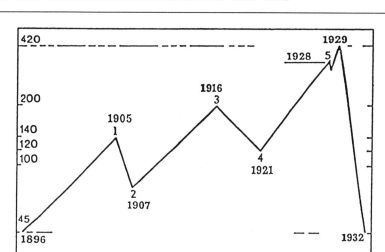

marked the end of that cycle—the crash of 1929–1932—was acting to correct not only the excesses of the primary bull market of 1921–1929, but also the excesses of the 1896–1929 cycle, along with with the excesses of the super cycle that began in 1857.

The Axe-Houghton-Burgess Index was the predecessor of the Dow Jones Industrial Averages in the United States. I have chosen this index since it represents the largest cycle degree for which records are available.

In *Nature's Law*, Elliott produced a breakdown of the 1896–1928 movement, which is divided into the normal five-wave pattern. As seen on the chart spanning the period, a further breakdown of the 1921–1928 fifth wave of the movement, which is not shown, also reveals a perfect five-wave count. In analyzing the 1921–1928 bull market, Elliott also makes cross-reference to the Fibonacci Series. Wave I and Wave III of the 1921–1928 bull market combine to total just under sixty-two percent of Wave V in amplitude, the Golden Ratio of 61.8 percent in action.

On this chart we can also see the phenomenon of Elliott's *irregular correction* that exceeds the upper limits of the trend channel. The orthodox top of the 1921–1928 bull market was achieved in 1928 and was confined to the upper limits of the trend channel. The Wave A of the ensuing bear market took place during 1928–1929 in normal fashion.

Figure 11

THE AXE-HOUGHTON-BURGESS INDEX 1857–1932

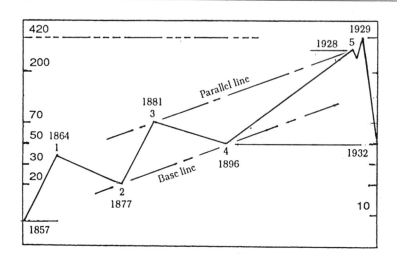

The rally during 1929 was a Wave B of the 1929–1932 bear market, which acted to correct the excesses of the entire 1857–1932 super cycle.

When an irregular correction occurs in the same cycle following the completion of five upward waves, the bear market that follows, according to the tenets of Elliott, is likely to be exceptionally severe. The bear market that included the irregular correction following the completion of the five-wave bull market of 1921–1928 certainly lived up to form, retracing the whole of the gains that had been made during the previous thirty-four years of stock market history.

The 1921–1928 bull market represents Primary Wave V of the cycle that began in 1896. The movement from 1896–1932 represents cycle Wave V of the super cycle that began in 1857.

The charts that have been presented have been drawn on the log scale, since inflation was present during most of the period. As you will soon discover, inflation was a major concern of Elliott's and played an important part in his thinking.

The chart of the Axe-Houghton-Burgess Index spanning the seventy-five years from 1857 to 1932 provides an ideal example of the manner in which the Wave Principle transcends long periods of time. The chart also demonstrates another area of Elliott's arsenal of confirmatory tools—that of the trend channel, an important element of the Wave Principle. The entire movement contains five waves, with Wave 2 and Wave 4 resting on the lower limits of the trend channel and Wave 5 reaching the upper limits of the trend channel. When Wave 5 reachs the upper limits of the trend channel, an orthodox top begins to develop.

In this long-term chart, we also see the Fibonacci Series acting as a confirmatory tool once again. During the period from 1857 to 1928, a more detailed breakdown will show seven primary bull markets (there were two bull markets during the 1921–1928 drive) and six primary bear markets. The number 13 is one of the Fibonacci Series which serves to confirm the accuracy of the seventy-one-year count.

A number of important observations can be made by studying the long-term behavior of the US stock market in these charts. But, for the purpose of illustrating the rule that says a correction following the completion of five waves will hold above the trough of Wave IV in the cycle of the next-higher degree, note the manner in which the bear market from 1928–1932 was halted at the precise trough of Wave 4 of the super cycle that began in 1857. The behavior of this long-wave movement certainly lends further credibility to the Wave Principle and the amazing results this tool is capable of producing when properly applied.

A Four-Part Program

Mastery of the Wave Principle is a full-time endeavor. The first part involves a knowledge of the basic rules and tenets of Elliott, incorporating the basic five-waves-up-three-waves-down structure along with the way these waves relate to each other, e.g., Wave 3 is always longer than waves 1 and 5; the bottom of Wave IV will never overlap Wave I; corrective waves will alternate so that if Wave 2 is a zig-zag, Wave 4 will be a flat, and vice versa; five-wave movements are always in the direction of the main trend, while three-wave movements are counter to the main trend; and, most important of all, is the manner in which the waves sub-divide while retaining their basic relationships.

Essential to the mastery of the Wave Principle is the ability to obtain an accurate wave count. This is the second most important part of the four-part program. To assist in this connection, Elliott devised a system utilizing confirmatory devices, such as the Fibonacci Summation Series, channelling techniques, the treatment of triangles, extensions, double retracements, etc. Elliott was perfectly aware that markets would rarely, if ever, demonstrate the visual perfection of his basic pattern. Elliott's confirmatory devices are intended to render the more obscure price movements—that seem to defy categorization—less obscure, falling within defined parameters of categorization. Determining the wave count, knowing when Wave 5 becomes the first wave of a cyclical bear market, or a serious decline; or when Wave C becomes the first wave of a major bull market on an important advance—is the quintessential element of the second part of this four part program.

The more inflexible an analytical method, the less likely its suitability for application to speculative markets. Speculative markets are subject to very few constraints. Speculative markets can do anything they like, any time they like . . . almost! Elliott was aware of this. Elliott concentrated his efforts isolating the non-randomness of the "almost." There are deviations from the basic rules that will defy categorization even when using the confirmatory devices. Five-wave counts may stretch to seven, nine, and thirteen. Three-wave counts will become double and triple three-wave counts, seemingly in devilish contradiction to all of the basic tenets of the Wave Principle. Yet, here, too, you will find order in chaos, stochastic sequence in another time dimension, in what may appear randomness. There are no exceptions to Elliott's rules, only deviations. These deviations are incorporated in other tenets of Elliott which comprise the whole of the Wave Principle, whose integration is the third part of the four-part program designed to assist you in mastering the Wave Principle. Elliott was adamant when affirming that no market-price movement could occur outside the relationship to the broader structure, whether it be a movement that lasts an hour, a day, a week, a month, a year, or a century.

Finally, the last and most important element of the four-part program is the application of the Wave Principle in your investment dealings. Even if you only master the basic tenets of Elliott, without dealing with the confirmatory devices and refinements, there should be an immediate improvement in your investment returns. By now, you realize that when you see a five-wave upward drive you should respect it and at least stop chasing the trend. You should also be aware that it is not the time to start selling into a rally, when there's been a three-wave downward drive and the market turns up.

I will be offering further suggestions on applying the Wave Principle to the real world of investment. Those of you with an innovative bent may even find applications that I never thought of. With the Wave Principle, the horizons are exceptionally wide.

9
Elliott's World
of Reality

He who does not know the mechanical side of a craft cannot judge it.

—GOETHE

Another device Elliott used in order to assist him in his classification of the waves was the *trend channel*, a tool of conventional technical analysts. As would be expected, Elliott's utilization of the trend channel had a slightly different twist.

In *The Wave Principle*, the first of Elliott's works that was published in 1938, Elliott states: "To properly observe a market's movements, and hence to segregate the individual waves of such a movement, it is necessary that the movement, as it progresses, be channelled between parallel lines."

The operative phrase in that quotation is *and hence to segregate the individual waves of such a movement.* Unlike traditional channelling methods (wherein the chartist draws a trend line and assumes the primary trend is intact as long as the trend line is intact, and then assumes the primary trend is over when the trend line is penetrated), in Elliott's treatment of trend channels, the object is to segregate the wave components, to add confirmation to the all-important wave count.

Clearly, there is always scope for considerable variation in interpretation, when merely a wave count is employed. The incorporation of these trend channels goes a long way in helping to clarify the position, while limiting the variation of interpretations.

Before dealing with the subject of trend channels in detail, it is vital that we consider the real world in which we live and the manner in which events in the real world affect markets. Elliott was the ultimate pragmatist in his market analysis. There was no place in the Wave Principle nomenclature for esoteric tenets that could not be rationalized by Elliott in the real world of real market activity. I cannot overstress that Elliott had an excellent grounding in the field of economics, statistics, mathematics, and the fundamental determinants of investment values. All of these played an important role in his development of the Wave Principle.

Elliott's concept of dealing with trend channels was originally introduced in *The Wave Principle* previously referred to. In *The Wave Principle*, Elliott was quite insistent that all data be maintained on graph paper with an arithmetic grid. Yet, it would appear that by 1939 his insistence had waned somewhat. By the time his magnum opus, *Nature's Law,* was completed, his view had been completely revised. Elliott probably found that the upper limits of his trend channels were being habitually violated. This was evident when in *Nature's Law*, Elliott stated: "When semi-log scale becomes necessary, inflation is present. If semi-log scale is used and inflation is not present, Wave 5 will not reach the parallel line by a good margin."

In *Nature's Law*, Elliott is as equally emphatic about the use of both arithmetic and logarithmic scales when applied to the channelling technique as he was about using arithmetic scales in *The Wave Principle*. The reasons are obvious. When compiling *The Wave Principle*, Elliott was working in a deflationary global economic environment. By the time he finished *Nature's Law*, inflationary elements were creeping into the global economic environment once again.

In our era, "permanent inflation" has been accepted as the norm. This is primarily due to the fact that inflationary trends represent the longest cyclical force in the economic time series, registering approximately fifty to sixty years from peak to peak. Anyone who was born during the post-1930 era will have experienced nothing but inflation, which grew slowly during the first twenty years of the cycle, the major acceleration taking place during the decade of the 1970s, particularly in commodity prices.

Those individuals who are still around and are able to recall conditions during the early 1900s will have experienced inflationary trends similar to what developed during the second half of this century. There was moderate inflation during the early 1900s developing into accelerating inflation, similar to that of the 1970s, during the decade of 1920–1930. Inflation peaked during 1920, as it appears to have done in the late 1970s. Between the 1920s and 1930s, there was a period of continuing deflation, which those who were around at the time thought would be a new "permanent" way of life. There is a message there for the 1990s and for the manner in which the Wave Principle may be adjusted for the future.

Elliott has stated that the presence of inflation during the 1920s was indicated by sub-normal bear markets and extended bull markets during the period. Elliott breaks down the 1921–1928 bull market as comprising three major impulse waves in an upward direction and two corrective waves in a downward direction. Reflecting the inflationary trends at the time, Elliott focuses on the sub-normal size of the corrective waves. According to Elliott, inflationary trends can be forecast by stock-market behavior and the behavior of commodity markets, when the following sequence appears:

1. Wave 1 of normal amplitude and duration.

2. Wave 2 of sub-normal amplitude.

3. Wave 3 of normal amplitude but extended duration.

4. Wave 4 of sub-normal amplitude and duration.

5. Wave 5 supra-normal duration, involving a penetration of a trend channel on the arithmetic scale, along with an extended number of waves.

When the financial and economic environment begins to turn deflationary, a reverse phenomenon develops. If this occurs at the final stages of a bull market, the fifth wave will become truncated, while subsequent downward impulse waves will become protracted, with the rallying action that intersperses the downward wave being of sub-normal amplitude and duration.

Nature's Law is Elliott's final word on the subject of the Wave Principle. Rather than a revision of his previous work, *Nature's Law* would seem to be an expansion of the tenets. "To employ one without the other, as a general practice, is erroneous and deprives the student of their value and utility," says Elliott. "The arithmetic scale should always be employed until log scale is demanded."

While Elliott still maintained that arithmetic scales must be used for short-term movements, in the case of long-term movements, inflation was cited as a cause for violations of the upper parameters of trend channels and fifth-wave extensions. According to Elliott, when the upper parameter of a trend channel was violated by the fifth wave of a long-term movement, circumstances demanded re-plotting on a logarithmic scale.

"If Wave 5 exceeds the parallel line considerably, and the composition of Wave 5 indicates that it has not completed its pattern, then the entire movement, from the beginning of Wave 1 should be re-graphed on semi-log° scale. The end of Wave 5 may reach, but not exceed, the parallel line." (R.N. Elliott, *Nature's Law*, 1946).

Logarithmic Comparisons

For the larger formations, involving extended time periods, Elliott used almost exclusively logarithmic charts in order to make his calculations. For periods involving moves of twelve months or less, Elliott used arithmetic scales. Initially, Elliott called for arithmetic scales as the standard, until he discovered that as the long-term cycle unfolded, the channelling technique began to lose its usefulness with the upper limits of the trend channel being broken.

As a general rule, when starting with a study of short-term movements, one should plot the price action on arithmetic scales. As the price history moves along in time, extending beyond twelve months, it would then be wise to re-plot the price action on a logarithmic scale. If, during the early stages of a move one finds difficulty in establishing the upper limits of a trend channel due to a market that may be highly volatile, showing a great deal of two-way price action, it would be well worth the time spent to use two graphs: one with an arithmetic scale and one with a logarithmic scale.

Figures 12, 13, 14, and 15 reveal the totally conflicting results that can occur if the same data is plotted on arithmetic scales and logarithmic scales.

If one were to plot a short-term move involving the price action as depicted in Figure 12 on a logarithmic scale, as in Figure 13, it would appear as if the trend channel was broken, whereas in reality, it would not have been. The case for the long-term price action would be similar if one were to use arithmetic scales rather than logarithmic scales, as can be seen in figures 14 and 15.

°Elliott uses the terms *log* and *semi-log* inter-changeably.

Figures 12, 13, 14, 15
ARITHMETIC SCALES AND LOGARITHMIC SCALES

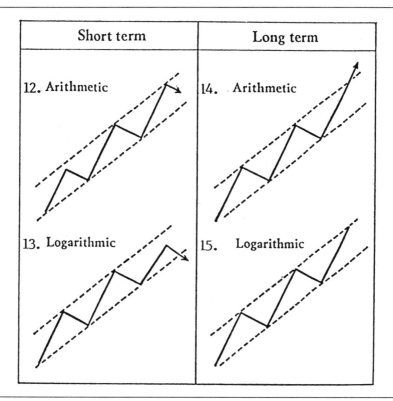

Short term	Long term
12. Arithmetic	14. Arithmetic
13. Logarithmic	15. Logarithmic

Using Trend Channels

In the article written for *The Financial World* on channelling (see Appendix), Elliott concentrates on the forecasting value of establishing a trend channel.

When starting a trend channel, one must first establish a suitable turning point, either by the completion of a previous three-wave corrective phase or five-wave impulse phase. This should be checked and re-checked, in accordance with the rule for establishing time span, the wave count, the previous wave amplitude, etc., generally using all the tools introduced thus far and yet to be introduced.

Once the terminal point of the preceding move has been established, wait for the development of two complete waves of similar degree in the current cycle. These two waves will provide three tangent points from which to form the trend channel.

The tangent points will represent the end of the previous wave, the end of the first wave of the new formation, and the termination of the second wave of the new formation. Naturally, every available cross-check must be used in order to verify that actual terminal points in the cycle are being dealt with.

In Figure 16, we find two completed waves, leaving three exposed contact points, which are readily identifiable. The first exposed contact point would represent the end of the preceding wave and the start of the first wave of the new cycle; the second exposed contact point is formed by the end of the first wave in the new cycle, which also acts as the pivotal point for the beginning of the second wave. The third contact point is the end of the second wave, which presumably will be the starting point of the third wave.

Figure 16
CONTACT POINTS - 2 COMPLETE WAVES

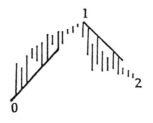

Figure 17
UPPER AND LOWER TREND-CHANNEL LINES

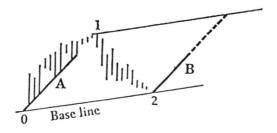

For the purpose of illustration, these contact points have been labelled *0*, *1*, and *2*.

Always wait for the completion of these two waves before drawing your trend channel. A trend channel cannot be formed until the first two waves of a cycle are complete.

When preparing the channel, a tangent, which will be referred to as a *base line*, should be drawn using the contact points of *0* and *2*.

Once this base line has been drawn, a line parallel to it should be drawn, using *1* as the contact point, and extended some distance to the right, as in Figure 17. This line will establish the upper limits of the trend channel.

It will also be found useful to draw a trend line tangential with the bottoms of the entire first-wave movement, subsequently using contact *2* as a point from which to draw a further line parallel to the trend line, between contacts *0* and *1*, as seen in Figure 17. The upper trend-channel line will help establish probable targets relative to the size of the succeeding waves; the channels within the channel will help establish time-frame references. These channels have been labelled *A* and *B*.

When you have finished drawing the necessary lines, the completed trend channel should appear as in Figure 18.

A further line has been drawn between contact points *1* and *2*. This line has been established by using the peaks of the downtrend between *1* and *2*, whereas the trend line between contact points *0* and *1* has been formed by drawing a line tangential to the bottoms of the uptrend. Generally, when drawing trend lines we use the troughs as tangent points in an uptrend, and the peaks as tangent points in a downtrend.

Figure 18
COMPLETED TREND CHANNEL

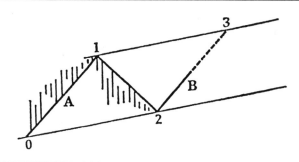

Figure 19
POSSIBLE TERMINATIONS

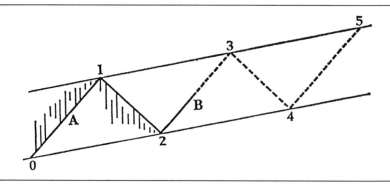

We can now establish a probable target for the end of the third wave in price and time, based on normal, market-behavior patterns.

It is assumed the student is plotting line charts in the normal manner, with price on the vertical scale and time on the horizontal scale; logarithmic paper in the case of long-term price movements and arithmetic paper in the case of short-term price movements. (The use of point and figure charts is not suitable for this type of analysis.) The likely end of the third wave can thus be found by extending line *B* to the top of the trend channel, and parallel with line *A*. The vertical scale will give the price level at which the third wave will end, and the horizontal scale will give the approximate date of termination, i.e., at contact point *3* in Figure 18 and Figure 19.

Assuming that normal, market behavior continues and the third wave terminates at the top of the trend channel, at the price and time coordinate established, one can then use the channel for plotting the possible terminations in price and time for the fourth and fifth waves. Using the end of the third wave as contact point *3*, one draws a line parallel to that drawn between contact points *1* and *2*. The point at which this line contacts the bottom of the trend channel will establish a probable price target and date of termination for the fourth wave, as shown in Figure 19.

In the same manner, once the fourth wave has been completed, and a contact point formed, a line is drawn parallel to the first and third waves. The point at which this line touches the top of the trend channel will provide the target for the fifth wave in both price and time, also shown in Figure 19.

Probabilities Rather Than Predictions

The entire process of channelling appears quite neat and tidy. Given the first two waves of any movement, the average chartist will now assume that the rest of the entire movement can be predicted. Much to his disappointment, he will soon discover such is not the case. While the process of channelling is indeed useful, it is certainly not intended that one should use it for making predictions and acting upon them. Initially, the channel is constructed in order to establish targets in price and time, not unlike the way in which economic forecasting bodies will establish targets for a particular phase of a growth cycle. A frame of reference is established.

As the action of the market unfolds, we adjust our targets in order to compensate for deviations in the trend action. In essence, we establish a model which represents normal, market behavior, and then make adjustments to the model in order to comply with the action of the real world.

Most technical analysis insists that markets form a repetitive pattern, and, by awaiting repetitions of this pattern, one can predict the future. This is not the approach of the Wave Principle. Elliott recognized that share-price behavior can take on grotesque formations, without any historic precedent . . . at any point in time, the market can do anything it likes. Regardless of the behavior of the share-price movements, Elliott's theory states that a basic form remains throughout, whether short-term, medium-term, long-term, or very long-term. Recognizing the basic form is the first step toward successful forecasting. Categorizing and measuring the deviations from the basic form as the action unfolds is the second step.

Temporary Divergences

(Elliott continually used as in Part III of the Appendix, figures 8, 9, and 10). In employing the channelling technique, normal behavior indicates that Wave 3 of a movement should terminate in the vicinity of the upper trend-channel line that was drawn upon completion of the first two waves of the movement. Should Wave 3 end above the upper limits of the trend channel, the movement has taken on temporary strength, and therefore modifications to the trend-channel structure should be made. In the event Wave 3 terminates below the upper limits of the trend channel, a *failure* occurs, and once again adjustments must be made. (The subject of failures will be discussed at greater length in a subsequent chapter.)

In the event of a significant deviation taking place in the price movement, with the end of Wave 3 at a level which is two percent or more above or below the trend-channel line, the old channel is abandoned in favor of a new one.

The new channel is formed by connecting the peaks of Wave 1 and Wave 3. A new base line is formed by using the bottom of Wave 2 as a contact point, then extending this line parallel to the newly formed upper trend-channel line. In Part III of "The Wave Principle," which appears in the Appendix, Figure 8 shows both the old trend channel, shown dotted, and the newly formed trend channel. The original target for the bottom of Wave 4 is thus discarded, and a new target at a higher level supersedes the original target. Naturally, the converse would be true should Wave 3 have terminated two percent or more below the top of the trend channel. The adjusted trend channel would show less momentum and the target for Wave 4 would be lower down. Obviously, if Wave 3 terminates within a two-percent margin of the original trend channel, we will not discard the channel, and the initial target for the bottom of Wave 4 would remain.

The object of every investor is to buy as early as possible at the beginning of every new, major five-wave up move and to sell upon the completion of such a five-wave movement; results in the stock market are achieved this way. Establishing a target for Wave 5 is the most important aspect of Elliott's Wave Principle. The original targets that were formed following completion of waves 1 and 2 gave us frames of reference from which to operate. The completion of Wave 3 may require re-adjustment of these original terms of reference; the subsequent targets established by re-drawing the channel are likely to reveal a greater probability of achievement than those anticipated during the earlier phase of the movement, when the data was less complete.

When we have reached the endpoint of Wave 4, which could be either at the adjusted base line, above, or below it, the final adjustment in the trend channel is made, helping us to pinpoint the all-important peak of Wave 5.

The final and most important channel is thus drawn by using the bottoms of Waves 2 and 4 as contact points, adjusting and extending the base line forward. The peak of Wave 3 is used as the contact point for the start of the new upper limits of the trend channel. The line drawn from the peak of Wave 3, parallel to the base line drawn by connecting the bottoms of Waves 2 and 4, will thus provide the new upper limits of the trend channel and the target in price and time for Wave 5.

An important factor neglected by Elliott, not only in the articles written for *The Financial World* but also in the 1938 version of *The Wave Principle* and *Nature's Law*, is the special treatment required for pinpointing the peak of Wave 5, the time being the most important factor. The illustrations in Part III of the Appendix show parallel behavior of all three impulse waves. This is very seldom the case and must not be treated as normal behavior. Usual behavior within a trend channel will show Wave 3 as being longer in both price and time than Wave 1. In this respect, it is most unlikely that Wave 3 will run parallel to Wave 1, although both upper and lower trend-channel limits may remain perfectly in parallel.

The Almighty Wave V

The question then arises: When drawing a hypothetical Wave V, what references are used? We can either:

(a) Wait until the behavior of the market shows an advance to the top of the channel, assuming further upward price action will continue, until such time as we reach the upper limits of the trend channel. In that case we would not be anticipating either at what level or at what period Wave V would end. In fact, we would not be drawing a hypothetical Wave V at all.

(b) We can draw a hypothetical Wave V by drawing a line parallel with Wave III, using the bottom of Wave IV as a contact point. Where the hypothetical Wave V touches the upper limits of the trend channel, we would check the price co-ordinate to determine approximately where the move will end, checking the time co-ordinate to determine approximately when the move will end. Or,

(c) Instead of using the angle of incidence of Wave III, for establishing a parallel reference for hypothetical Wave V, we can use Wave I. If we use Wave III for our parallel, we would anticipate a rather long, drawn-out ending to the bull move. However, if we use Wave I as the suggested angle of incidence from which to draw hypothetical Wave V, a very fast-moving market would be anticipated with behavioral characteristics similar to Wave I.

The answer can be found in the normal characteristics of wave relationships. According to Elliott, the dimensions of Wave V should resemble those of Wave I in both price and time.

Figure 20
INCORRECT CO-ORDINATES

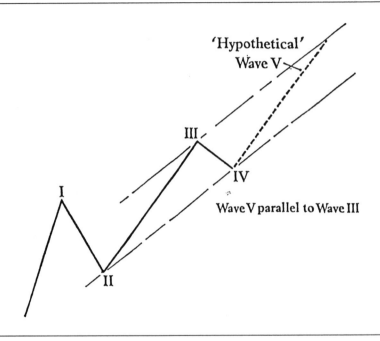

'Hypothetical'
Wave V

III

IV

I

Wave V parallel to Wave III

II

Therefore, in constructing our hypothetical Wave V, we connect the top and bottom of the trend channel by drawing a line parallel to Wave I, which gives us the minimum probable extent of Wave V, both on the price co-ordinate and the time co-ordinate. Figures 20 and 21 illustrate the point.

To most students of technical analysis, Elliott's treatment of channelling will open up entirely new horizons. Much of the value of Elliott's work lies in his close attention to detail and his examination of aspects of market behavior which had previously gone unnoticed. One may be rather surprised at the way in which a simple concept, such as channelling, can be teased into extravagant complexity, and to most, the discussion of channelling up to this point may suffice. Yet, Elliott observed further characteristics of market behavior which extend the concept even further. These characteristics were noted with particular regard to the most important movement of the bull market, the final *fifth wave*. Normally, the fifth wave will terminate at the top of the trend channel; therefore, establishing

Figure 21
CORRECT CO-ORDINATES

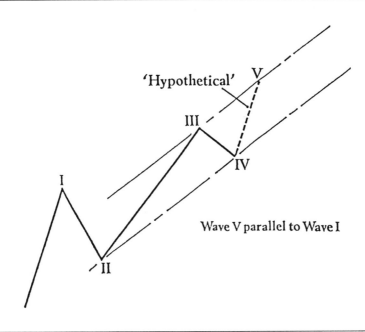

'Hypothetical'

Wave V parallel to Wave I

targets at that level will, on most occasions, prove helpful. However, on several occasions the fifth wave will produce a *throwover* above the top of the trend channel, referred to by Elliott as an *extension*; such extension being subject to Elliott's theory of *double retracement*.

10
The Fifth Wave
of the Fifth Wave

Even divergence deserves to be cherished, simply because it widens
the bounds of life.

—KABEL CAPER

Professor F.J. Hayek says, "The secret of life is life." Charlie Brown
says, "Happiness is a soft, warm puppy." Practitioners of the Wave Principle would generally agree that both the secret of life and happiness rests
with identifying the end of the fifth wave of the fifth wave. It is the most
rewarding pursuit you could ever possibly engage in. It's the genii in the
bottle, Aladdin's lamp, Ali Baba's cave, the pot of gold at the end of the
rainbow, and a turkey wishbone, all rolled into one. Not surprisingly, the
pursuit of this objective in dealing with the Wave Principle is as elusive as it
is rewarding. Make no mistake. Indeed, special emphasis should be placed
on identifying that fifth wave of the fifth wave.

If I accomplish anything in this, my third important attempt at rendering the Wave Principle a tool that can be employed in a manner as equally
rewarding as my precedessors, I hope it is to bring into focus the Wave
Principle as it was originally conceived by its author. I am saddened by the
manner in which the Wave Principle has been diluted and prostituted in
the interest of mass appeal. As I have been wading through some of the
contemporary material produced by those interested in marketing paper
piffle rather than useful investment literature, I see omissions of valuable
tenets and distortions of others, completely devoid of any meaningful
application to the real world of investment, or what Elliott had ever
intended for his theories.

Among those who must share the majority of guilt for taking the Wave Principle into the realms of yet another useless stock-market system are the computer buffs. The efforts of those who have been attempting to produce a no-think trading system, based on the Wave Principle, are as persuasive as they are prodigious. The fact of the matter is that it is totally impossible to computerize the Wave Principle without desecrating some of the basic elements while obliterating the conceptual foundation. There are simply too many variables—the variables are components of the world in which we live. Some of the variables are peculiar to the user of the Wave Principle, while being an intrinsic expression of the principle itself.

It would be a simple matter to predict the nature of the economy five or ten years in advance, with absolute accuracy, if you could predict the behavior pattern of every human being on this planet for the next five to ten years. If that were a possibility, you would simply stuff all the data into your PC, convinced you had the market beat. But, guess what? Even if you were capable of performing that miraculous feat, you might still have a considerable number of problems with your investments. The correlation between stock-market behavior and economic behavior has nothing like the synchronous commonality that investors think it has.

Computer technology has indeed come a long way. There is now a software program that crunches ideas instead of numbers and words. It has been described as the world's first associative lexicon, a new development in thinking. The program promises to turn your PC into a brainstorming tool. Its 665,000 entries combine a database of words and concepts linked by association. Yet, in spite of the tremendous advances in computer technology, the computer remains nothing more than the equivalent of a moron with total selective recall. The four-step program outlined in the previous chapter requires considerable thought, flexibility of mental attitude, practice, and fortitude. The computer cannot provide you with any of that. The computer will not be able to find the fifth wave of the fifth wave with any useful or meaningful degree of accuracy.

Using our maximum efforts to establish an accurate wave count will take you a long way toward defining that all-elusive fifth wave of the fifth wave. But, even when you find it, you might still have problems. I am amazed at the lack of attention given by contemporary practitioners of the Wave Principle to the special characteristics of impulse waves, especially fifth waves of a count. This could be due to the tendency for Elliott buffs to become so mesmerized with the basic principle, the wave count and the

Fibonacci confirmations, that they neglect the refinements of the Wave Principle that are as much a part of Elliott's theories as the five-up-three-down structure itself. Elliott was quite clear on this point.

> While the Wave Principle is very simple and exceedingly useful in forecasting nomenclatives, there are refinements within the principle that may baffle the student, especially when wave movements are in the process of formation. In my forecasting service, I have frequently warned subscribers that in the current position of the Grand Super Cycle, movements may be sensitive to current news and therefore erratic in many ways, such as, for example, the failure described. One of the many advantages of the Wave Principle is, that it discloses irregularities. Without the Wave Principle, there are just two movements, "up" and "down." The Wave Principle is not a "method," nor a "theory," but simply the behavior of a phenomenon. (R.N. Elliott, *Interpretative Letter No. 4*, January 13, 1939)

Elliott's refinements deal with the various cross-references that can be made to verify and validate the wave count through the use of the Fibonacci Series and other nomenclatures. "Every Cycle has twenty-one waves of the next lower degree" (R.N. Elliott, *Interpretative Letter No. 1*, November 30, 1938).

A wave count can be verified and validated by consulting the cycle of the next-lower degree, which should have twenty-one waves, or at least a Fibonacci integer. When confirming a longer term count, a study of the wave of the next-higher degree can be helpful, based on the same Fibonacci Summation Series premise.

Trend channelling is also an aid in segregating important trend reversals from random noise in wave counts of lesser degrees. Amongst this random noise are *incomplete waves* and *failures,* which Elliott is also cognizant of and which calls for special treatment under his category of *refinements.* "Incomplete waves are neither common nor rare—unusual is perhaps the proper term" (R.N. Elliott, *Interpretative Letter No. 2*, November 25, 1938).

Elliott makes a special distinction between waves that are considered to be incomplete and waves that fail to conform to normal relationships, such as a fifth wave that fails to reach the top of a trend channel, or fails to reach the proximity of what would be expected of an impulse wave in time and amplitude. "Failures are exceedingly rare" (R.N. Elliott, *Interpretative Letter No. 7*, April 11th, 1939).

Elliott was unflagging in his determination to categorize all price movements within a composite structure. To Elliott, when it came to the categorization of incomplete waves and waves that failed to meet normal dimensions, both had predictive value within the context of the Wave Principle, this concept being amongst Elliott's many refinements. "I expected that Wave C would be composed of five smaller waves, the same as Wave A. Instead, however, an abbreviated D Wave appeared. I do not recall a similar incompletion. Experience vindicates that incomplete corrections are bullish" (R.N. Elliott, *Interpretative Letter No. 4,* January 12, 1939).

Tactically, the objective is to remain with the trend throughout the duration of a primary movement, while maintaining a constant awareness that the overriding objective is to accurately pinpoint the fifth wave of the fifth wave of a primary uptrend, or the fifth wave of the C Wave in a primary downtrend. If not, all or most of what had been accumulated during your excursion with the primary trend could be forfeited . . . which, of course, is the experience of the majority of investors and fund managers alike.

Extended Wave Formations

While investors are likely to experience certain difficulties dealing with Waves 1, 2, and 3 of a sequence, the problems really begin to start when you come to Wave 4. When you get to Wave 5, your dealing with a time bomb that could have a faulty clock. Wave 4 is the part of the sequence that's usually subject to the most bizarre and arcane, weird, and wonderful corrections. Wave 5 can extend itself well beyond five waves, making a wave count extremely difficult. Extensions are also subject to what Elliott defines as retracements and double retracements, complicating the situation even further.

Elliott, in his writing, places a great deal of emphasis on fifth-wave extensions. A thorough understanding of extensions, extensions of extensions, retracements, and double retracements, is vital to your mastery of the Wave Principle and its profitable application.

At all times, the important problem is in attempting to pinpoint the terminal phase of Wave 5 in any cycle degree, for the corrective action which follows Wave 5 will be greater than any experienced during the preceding run of the cycle.

The normal behavior of Wave 5 has already been outlined. Over the shorter term (less than twelve months), Wave 5 should remain within the confines of a trend channel drawn on an arithmetic scale. Over the longer term, the confines would be established by the upper trend line on a logarithmic scale. Wave 5 should be shorter than Wave 3 and approximate to the dimensions of Wave 1 in time and size. You know all of that! Now for the exceptions that bend the rule . . . extensions, inter alia.

The first indications that appear of an extension developing in Wave 5 would be if the amplitude and/or time span of Waves 2 and 4 are subnormal. The possibility of an extended Wave 5 would be an extension occurring in either of the preceding impulse Waves 1 or 3. While extensions usually occur in Wave 5, they can occur in either Waves 1 or 3. They hardly ever occur in more than one impulse wave of a movement. Extensions usually only occur in new territory of the current cycle. Corrective Waves 2 and 4 can never be subject to extensions.

You should be reasonably certain when the market is in a major downward cycle or major upward cycle. This is ascertained by the nature of the impulse move. If the pattern structure reveals five downward waves and three upward waves, the cycle is clearly downward. Impulse Waves 1, 3, and 5 of the downward cycle could then be subject to extensions. The A, B, C upward corrective waves in a downward cycle would not be subject to extensions.

Figure 22 serves to show the nature of the behavior patterns when extensions occur in the various impulse waves.

On rare occasions, an extension of waves, all of approximately equal size, will occur as in Figure 23.

It is vitally important to recognize extensions when they happen, since serious mistakes in counting the wave formation could result if these extended waves go unnoticed. When an extended wave occurs, the move takes on a count of *nine* rather than the usual five. In the case of an extended first wave, one finds five waves in the first wave, with four waves of the same degree that follow. In the case of an extended third wave, the first two waves comprise the normal count. Wave 3 has a five-wave count to which waves 4 and 5 are added. When an extension occurs in the fifth wave, it is somewhat less troublesome. The five waves of the extension are simply added to the four waves preceding.

Only on the odd occasion has Elliott made reference to volume characteristics in helping to identify wave movements. In the case of an extension, one can gain corroboratory evidence from the volume figures. Volume tends to expand during an extension. In *The Wave Principle* Elliott states: "Volume tends to climb on a throwover, and when this throwover is by the

Figure 22
EXTENSIONS OF VARIOUS IMPULSE WAVES

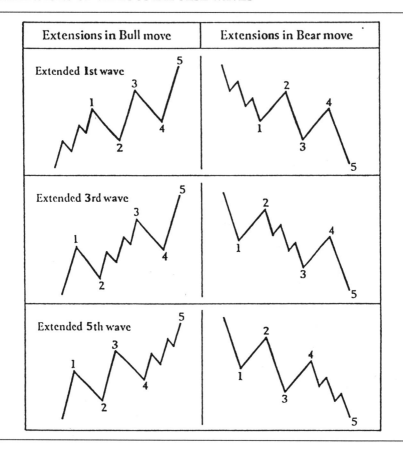

fifth Intermediate Wave of a Primary movement, volume should be very heavy."

Generally, an extension can be seen as either a five-wave pattern with an elongated wave, or a nine-wave pattern with approximately equal components, the latter formation being difficult to detect, but also quite rare.

Verification of a first-wave extension is relatively simple, once the third wave of the same cycle degree has been completed. The first sign that an extension may be taking place in a first wave would be when the wave breaks out of the trend channel on arithmetic scales. It is most likely that you would be using arithmetic scales at the beginning of a movement.

Figure 23
EQUAL WAVE EXTENSIONS

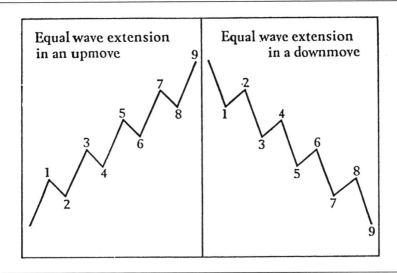

As the subsequent action unfolds, should Wave 3 fall appreciably short of the dimensions of the first wave, it is likely that an extended wave has developed in the first impulse move, precluding an extension of the fifth wave. One should then check the wave count very carefully. While such a reassessment of the components of the first wave may not appear to be of much forecasting value, remember: if a first wave becomes subject to an extension, the subsequent impulse moves are very likely not to extend. You can then act with greater confidence when a five-wave movement draws closer to the upper limits of a trend channel. If either the first wave or the third wave has been extended, we can forecast with the added knowledge that it is highly probable that the fifth wave will end at or below the upper trend line.

The extended wave pattern which comprises nine sub-waves of relatively equal dimensions is a rare occurrence. But, it is worth anticipating. This type of extension will usually occur in the third wave. It will rarely, if ever, occur in a fifth wave.

Extensions in a bull market are indicative of added strength in subsequent movements. When an extension occurs at the earlier stages, one can anticipate sub-normal corrective waves and a bull move likely to reach the

Figure 24
EXTENSIONS OF EXTENSIONS

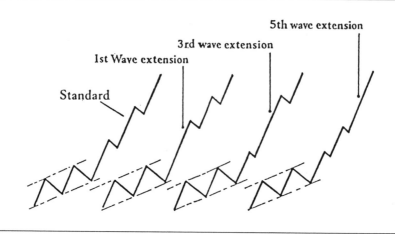

maximum target objectives. When extensions occur in downward impulse waves (these would be Waves 1, 3, or 5 of Wave A or Waves 1, 3, or 5 of Wave C), a generally weak market is anticipated. One would expect to see subsequent up waves of the next-higher degree experiencing repeated failures, falling short of the upper limits of the trend channel. One would not anticipate extensions taking place in any of the impulse moves of the upward waves, had such extensions occurred during the impulse moves in the downward waves.

Extensions of Extensions

The rules govern both extensions, and extensions of extensions, a not uncommon phenomenon when a fifth wave begins to extend and span upward. Figure 24 shows three different types of extensions along with the standard. The channels have been drawn to represent extensions of a previous fifth wave. Note the increase in the angle of incidence when an extension of an extension occurs. This is a normal phenomenon in extremely vigorous markets. The concept of extensions to wave movements applies to waves in all degrees.

Retracements and Double Retracements

When an extension occurs in the fifth wave of a movement, an extremely important phenomenon will occur. In view of the importance of this phenomenon and its persistence, recognition of fifth-wave extensions is paramount.

According to the basic tenets of the Wave Principle, most fifth-wave extensions are followed by a double retracement. Double retracements are reserved for extended fifth waves, never occurring during extensions that appear in first or third impulse moves.

An extension of the fifth wave is never the end of a cyclical movement. When an extension occurs in the fifth wave, rather than turning out the normal A-B-C down wave characterized by a completed five-wave progression under normal circumstances, an entirely different pattern is anticipated. The practical importance of this rule of double retracement is that it gives the analyst a clue as to what is likely to happen next.

In *The Wave Principle,* Elliott defines a retracement as "the travel of a described movement between two specified points which is covered again." A corrective down wave and subsequent resumption of the trend would therefore represent a double retracement.

Following an extended fifth wave, the first retracement will occur immediately in a succession of three down waves, ending approximately at the same level at which the extension began, which should also be in the vicinity of the second wave of the extension.

The second retracement will travel beyond the peak of the original extension. While the first retracement will occur immediately and in three waves, as often as not, it will take time for the second retracement to develop. When an extended fifth wave develops, there is an exceptionally high probability that the market will ultimately rise to a new high during the second retracement of the move. Figure 25 illustrates the behavior pattern.

Very often we find two extra waves formed by the double retracement that do not appear to have a place within the normal wave count. In the progression of a cycle, one should find three impulse waves going upward, interrupted by two downward corrective waves, totalling five. We should then find two downward waves, interrupted by one upward corrective wave, totalling three, and thus completing the eight-wave cycle. What happens to the two waves formed by the double retracement? How do they fit in?

Figure 25
DOUBLE RETRACEMENT

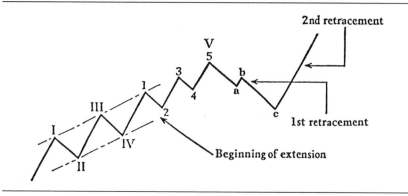

Elliott made it quite clear that these double retracements would later fit into conventional overall patterns. It certainly would not be a question of getting a couple of extra wave patterns, which could be conveniently added as a sort of hiccup between two sets of waves, for instance, to be disregarded with the wave count starting anew, and then treating the next set of waves as if the double retracement had no meaning. Conventional wave patterns were intended to remain.

The manner in which subsequent patterns develop from the double retracement is quite simple and is also a guide toward subsequent market behavior.

When a double retracement occurs following the fifth wave of either the first impulse move in a series or the third impulse move in a series, normal corrective action follows. In terms of the wave count, the first retracement (A, B, C) merely becomes Wave 2 (if following an extended first wave), or Wave 4 (if following an extension of the third wave). The second retracement merely reinstates the direction of the main trend, forming the initial stages of either the third or fifth wave, remaining a part of the conventional wave count. In effect, the double retracement following an extended first or third wave merely represents a corrective wave, plus part of a subsequent impulse wave.

Fail Safe

If you're very lucky, very, very lucky—don't expect to be so lucky—you may never have to deal with extensions, extensions of extensions, and double retracements. When you do have to deal with this phenomenon, you're going to have problems. I have problems. Elliott experienced the same interpretative problems. Problems are a way of life. Accept them. They're an investment reality. You can't have everything. Take your thumb out of your mouth and stop behaving like a spoiled child!

One way of coping with the problems of extensions and the difficulties they present is to anticipate their likely occurrence when an extension seems probable and come up with a battle plan. You're battling for your investment survival. You'll have to build a defense against the attack that will be launched by the bears at the final point of the fifth wave of the fifth wave. Elliott was fully aware of the problems through his own experiences: "A thorough understanding of extensions is very important. Warnings of this phenomenon have been sought without success and for certain reasons, it is probable none exist. However, losses can be avoided and profits obtained by learning the behavior of the market subsequent to their occurrence "(R.N. Elliott, *Confidential Letter*, December 14).

We can anticipate fifth-wave extensions—obviously, the most important—in several ways, which I will now outline:

1. Rarely, if ever, will more than one impulse wave of a cycle become extended. If either Wave 1 or Wave 3 has been subject to an extension, it is most unlikely that Wave 5 will be extended. In such an event, Wave 5 can be expected to be of normal duration and amplitude, ending in proximity to the top of a trend channel and with dimensions similar to that of Wave 1 while shorter than Wave 3.

2. If neither Wave 1 or Wave 3 of the cycle had become extended, then you must begin to investigate the various possibilities that might indicate that a fifth wave extension—and possible double retracement—is on the way.

3. If either Wave 2 or Wave 4—particularly Wave 4—is of sub-standard dimensions in either time or amplitude, an extension becomes an increasing possibility.

4. If Wave 2 and Wave 4—particularly Wave 4—is of sub-standard dimensions in time or amplitude, or both, while containing an incomplete

count or a failure, or both, then an extension becomes an even greater possibility.

5. If the economic environment is inflationary, the chances of an extended fifth wave—provided there has been no extension in either Wave 1 or Wave 3—would be greater than during a period of deflation or falling inflation.

6. If during the fifth minor wave of a standard five-wave count, the level of volume begins to expand rapidly and the momentum of the price action is accelerating, a fifth-wave extension becomes likely.

7. When confronted with an extended fifth wave, be aware of its properties. Fifth-wave extensions will be taking you into new territory in the existing cycle and have a strong tendency to be subject to a double retracement, as already explained.

8. Monitoring the structure of the double retracement is crucial. The extension itself will have four waves. The first wave constitutes a pullback from the peak of what originally appears as a standard Wave 5. The pullback will fall short of the lower limits of the trend channel. The market will then turn, which is when the extensions of the standard five-wave count actually begin. The first retracement will be a three-wave affair that does what its definition implies . . . it retraces the extensions, taking the market back to the starting point of the extension, but rarely below that starting point.

9. By way of definition, a retracement is simply a reaction whose amplitude is the equivalent of a previous market movement. A double retracement recoups the ground that was lost during the retracement, often involving a further extension, which will be subject to a similar double retracement.

It Gets Worse!

The treatment of a double retracement, following an extended fifth wave, can lead to mind-wrenching complications and often does. According to the very basic tenets of Elliott, when a five-wave movement of primary dimensions has been completed, we then expect a corrective phase—a bear market—that will purge the market of all of the excesses that were accumulated during the five-wave, complete bull market. This correction, or bear market, has a life of its own, independent of the previous movement, under normal circumstances.

Elliott's double-retracement refinement is in the category of another of those deviations from normal circumstances. The retracement element of the double retracement merely acts as a temporary interruption to the overriding trend, while the second retracement constitutes a resumption of that trend. Obviously, when the peak of the second retracement—which could follow extensions of extensions and a series of double retracements—is at hand, the entire second retracement must be given special treatment, along with the movement that preceded it, for the subsequent downswing is likely to be greater in amplitude than anything experienced during that particular trend up until the terminal peak.

The first retracement of a double retracement falls short of reaching full corrective status, equalling rather than exceeding the extension that preceded. When the second retracement acts as the precursor to a major bear market, both the first retracement and the second retracement take on an entirely different meaning. Normal corrections begin when the impulse wave ends, rather than constituting a part of the waves of the movement that is being corrected. At the terminal juncture of a bull market, a retracement and double retracement are part of the continuing bull market, while also part of the corrective bear market.

Welcome to Elliott's Irregular Top

In actuality, a double retracement, which follows an extended fifth wave, forms part of an *irregular top*. I will deal with this subject in greater detail as we continue, but for the time being an irregular top should be defined as an A-B-C correction where the Wave B rises to a level above the peak of the preceding Wave 5. Thus, when dealing with a double retracement, an ending part, the first retracement becomes Wave A rather than a complete A-B-C wave in itself. The second retracement is treated as Wave B rather than as the initial swing of a subsequent move. This is then followed by Wave C of five waves downward.

When we have an irregular top of this nature, comprising a sub-normal Wave A and stronger-than-usual Wave B, the Wave C is likely to take on quite dramatic proportions and be exceptionally fast-moving. The Great Crash in Wall Street actually behaved in this manner.

Figure 27 is that of the debacle known as the Great Crash, as represented by the movement of the Dow Jones Industrial Averages during the

Figure 26
ELLIOTT'S IRREGULAR TOP

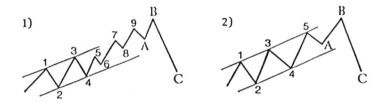

(1) An irregular correction A, B, C, following an extended Fifth Wave.
(2) An irregular correction A, B, C, following a normal Fifth Wave

"Irregular Correction'. When dealing with corrective waves generally, some broad observations should be noted. As a general proposition, waves along the main trend composed of 5 sub-waves (or 9 in the case of an extension) will prove to be far more easily identifiable than will be the corrective waves. Corrective waves, particularly in bull cycles, tend to develop irregularities and, as we have discovered, may not necessarily be 3-wave affairs or subject to the normal 5–3–5 count.

It follows then, if a wave cannot be sub-divided into five sub-waves according to Elliott's tenets, it therefore must be a corrective wave. In analysing the corrective waves, far more latitude is allowed than in the case of the more readily definable impulse waves, when making a count. By their very nature, impulse waves tend to be clean-cut affairs, as if these waves were generated by sudden impulse behaviour. Impulse waves are usually so well delineated that it is almost impossible for even the novice to misinterpret them. Like the perfect play in billiards – so easy that it keeps the duffer's interest up!

period November 1928 to July 1932. During my previous discussions of this period, many may have been confused by my reference to the orthodox top which began in 1928, presaging the collapse. Figure 27 illustrates this more clearly. The orthodox top of the 1921–28 bull market ended during November 1928, at which point the actual bear market started. Down wave A was actually the first wave of the bear market, although the Dow Jones

Figure 27
GREAT CRASH CHART

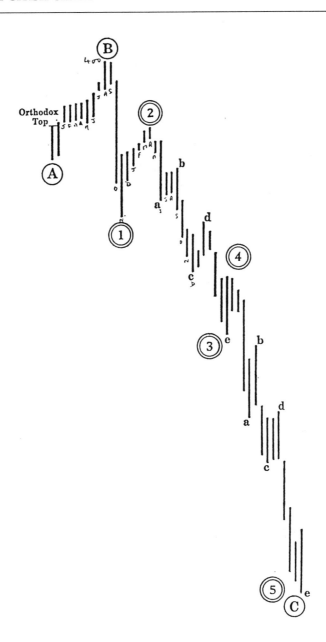

Industrials subsequently rose to a new high at B. Wave B represents the corrective wave in the bear market, which took place between November 1928 and September 1929, thus forming an irregular correction. Wave C was of extraordinary dimensions, encompassing the move from September 1929 to July 1932, thus completing the irregular correction. This move was certainly not illogical in view of the inflationary pressure built into the succeeding bull move, the sub-normal bear markets that characterized the entire 1921–1928 period, and the extended nature of the fifth wave, which terminated the entire bull swing. After that, corrective Waves A and B were also sub-normal. Despite the fact that one Harvard professor stated in 1929, "The stock market has reached a permanently high plateau," a severe bear market was on the cards and already under way.

11
Corrections

If you can keep your head when all about you
Are losing theirs . . . you'll be a man, my son!

—RUDYARD KIPLING

IF

Rudyard Kipling, in his poem, was referring to attitudes during a time of war. His sentiments are no less applicable to the battle for investment survival in the world's markets. Like in any war, you're in combat against many seasoned veterans. A number have sophisticated weaponry. Yet, an even larger number are fighting today's battle with the weapons of the last war. A still-large number of your adversaries are financially unwashed and financially unwashable, acting in unanimity. At the end of a bull market and at the beginning of a bull market, the period when the fifth-wave-of-the-fifth-wave develops, is when the majority of your opposing forces will be making complete and utter fools of themselves. With the aid of the Wave Principle, if you can keep your head and use it well, you can be a richer man . . . my son!

The main thrust of my efforts so far has been to help you analyze the behavior of impulse waves, those waves that trend in the direction of the overriding primary trend. I have only briefly touched on periods of irregularity, which seem to act in contradiction to Elliott's basic tenets. To many inexperienced stock market operators—along with those addicted to the concept of moving averages, head-and-shoulder patterns, triple tops, double bottoms, rounding saucers, and flying boxcars—what I have presented so far may seem like an exhausting and mind-boggling exercise. That's only because it is!

Those who feel they have not fully mastered the Wave Principle, as presented so far, should not worry. You're not a dunce! You're not a mental defective! You can read and think and make money. Relax! Take time off to re-read the first eight chapters and try again! Have another slice!

At the risk of being paralyzingly boring, a trait which has always come easy to me, I am now going to recapitulate the basics of Elliott's theories before introducing any more exhaustive details of mind-boggling complexity that are an inherent imperative of the Wave Principle. No matter how mind-wrenching you think what lies ahead is going to be, it will be more soul-destroying than that. But you WILL master the Wave Principle. I have wa-a-a-ys of MAKING you master the Wave Principle.

Let's recapitulate, O.K.?

Back to Basics . . . Again

A complete market cycle consists of eight waves. If you find a chart that goes back to the time of the Industrial Revolution, tracing the grand super cycle, you'll see that the overall trend has been growth. That hasn't changed. It might change soon. But, it hasn't changed yet.

The first five waves of a cycle represents the *growth phase* of the cycle. The final three waves of the cycle are the downward or *corrective waves*. These corrective waves may retrace the entire growth phase of the cycle being corrected, but will rarely, if ever, dip below the peak of the first wave of the cycle of the next-higher degree. There remains a continuing pattern of net growth over the course of two cycles, one of a lesser degree than the other.

The growth phase of the cycle is made up of five waves, three of which are upward waves and two of which are downward waves. During the growth phase, the up waves, or *impulse waves* of the cycle, can be broken down into waves of a lesser degree. Those will have five components. The corrective waves of a cycle only have three components, rather than five, when broken down to a cycle of a lesser degree. The corrective phase of a cycle occurs after three impulse waves—separated by two corrective waves—have been completed.

The corrective phase of a complete cycle will have three waves. The growth phase of the cycle with which most are familiar is a *bull market*. The corrective phase of a bull market is a *bear market*. During a bull market the primary trend is up. In a bear market, the primary trend is down. A bull market has five waves, comprising three impulse waves in an upward direction, which are interrupted by two corrective waves in a downward direction. During the bear market, which is the corrective phase of a bull market, involving cycles of the same degree, there will be three waves in the primary trend rather than five—two downward waves interrupted by one corrective upward wave.

For the purpose of identification, the five waves of the upward phase of a bull-market cycle are labelled I, II, III, IV, V. The three waves of the bear market are labelled, A, B, and C. There are always five sub-waves in an impulse wave and three sub-waves in a corrective wave. Impulse waves are those that travel in the direction of the primary trend. When the primary trend is downward, as in a bear market, when impulse Wave A and impulse Wave C are broken down to waves of the next-lesser degree, each will normally have five waves. The one upward corrective wave of a bear market, Wave B, will have three sub-waves when broken down to the cycle of the next-lower degree, since it is a corrective wave, rather than an impulse wave, even though it is moving in an upward direction.

The components of corrective waves II and IV of the growth phase of a cycle are often labelled *a, b,* and *c* for purposes of identification, while the components of impulse waves I, III, and V are labelled 1, 2, 3, 4, and 5. If waves *a* and *c* of waves II and IV are broken down to waves of the next-lower degree, these will be found to have five components. If Wave *b* of Waves II and IV are broken down to waves of the next lower degree, they will be found to have three components.

The eight-wave complete primary cycle, when broken down to waves of the next-lower degree, will have twenty-one waves in the upward phase of the cycle and thirteen waves in the downward phase of the cycle, for a total count of thirty-four waves. Figure 28 shows a complete idealized cycle, with a breakdown of all components to the next-lower degree.

The numbers 3, 5, 8, 13, 21, and 34 are integers of the Fibonacci Summation Series. The use of this series can be useful in confirming the number of waves in a cycle, impulse wave or corrective phase, when the count seems obscure. Important turning points in the cycle occur when the number of waves in accord with one of the Fibonacci Summation Series integers. The Fibonacci Summation Series can also be used to anticipate when and at what level trend changes are likely to occur in the future.

Impulse waves have certain characteristics, whose identification can assist in confirming the position of the market within a cycle while also having forecasting value. Impulse Wave III of a cycle will always be longer in time and larger in amplitude than impulse Wave I. If impulse Wave III

Figure 28

BASIC FIVE-WAVE PATTERN WITH A-B-C CORRECTION

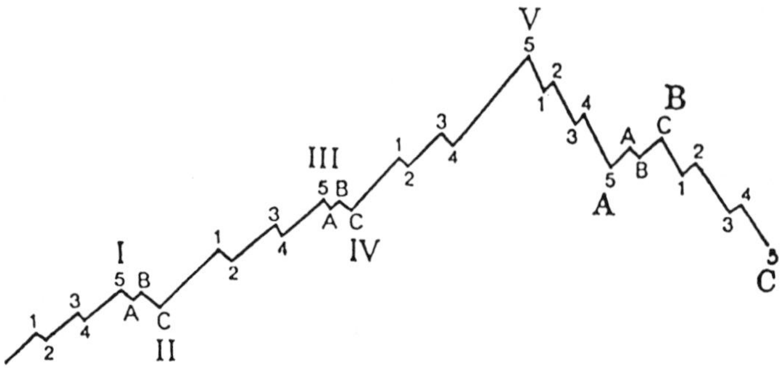

appears shorter than impulse Wave I, a counting error is likely to have occurred.

Impulse Wave V will often contain dimensions similar to impulse Wave I. Impulse Wave V, in an unextended form, will be either smaller in size or shorter in duration than impulse Wave III. Impulse Wave V, in an unextended form, will rarely be longer in duration and larger in size than impulse Wave III.

All impulse waves can become subject to extensions and double retracements. Extensions will take the number of sub-waves in an impulse wave beyond the count of five. When an extension occurs in one impulse wave, it is unlikely to occur in any other of the same cycle degree. Although extensions can occur in Waves I, III, and V, they usually occur in Wave V. An extension in Wave V often becomes subject to a double retracement and an irregular top. Wave A of the corrective A-B-C wave becomes part of the extension and double retracement, while Wave B rises to a level above the previous Wave V. The ensuing bear market then takes on the appearance of having only one wave, which is Wave C .

Corrective Waves II and IV also have characteristics which can assist in wave-count confirmation, while having forecasting value. One of the most important of Elliott's tenets is that the bottom of Wave IV never falls below the top of Wave I in the growth phase. If Wave IV does appear to fall below the peak of Wave I, a counting error is likely to have occurred.

Corrective waves alternate in their characteristics during the course of a cycle. Normally, corrective Wave II is short and sharp, respectively. Corrective Wave IV is usually more shallow and protracted in time. If corrective Wave II is shallow and extended in time, then corrective Wave IV is likely to be short and sharp.

In a bull market, the upward impulse waves will have a count of five sub-waves and the downward corrective waves a count of three sub-waves. When the downward corrective wave, during what is perceived to be a continuing bull market, suddenly takes on a count of five waves, it is likely that the bull market has ended and a bear market has begun. Likewise, during a bear market, if the upward corrective wave, which ordinarily has three sub-waves, develops a count of five waves, it is likely that the bear market has ended and a new bull market has begun. Waves that contain five sub-waves are directional and indicate the main movement of the waves of a higher degree.

It is necessary to maintain charts that show waves of various different degrees at all times. For those operating in the US stock market, a chart showing the price action since the beginning of the super cycle will prove extremely useful for cross-referencing. It is important to maintain charts of monthly, weekly, daily, and hourly price action in any market that you are following, with as much previous price data as possible. Formations that may not seem clear on the detailed price-action charts, such as the hourly or daily charts, can often become abundantly clear on the less-detailed weekly and monthly charts.

Arithmetic charts should be used for plotting short-term price activity on a cyclical basis for movements of, say, six months or less. Arithmetic charts must be used in conjunction with range charts, drawn on a logarithmic scale for longer-term price movements and channelling purposes. Cyclical charts based on closing prices or the average range over a week or month are not recommended.

Using the principles of trend channelling is an aid to confirming cycle placement and the wave count. Trend channels also have forecasting value.

Is all of that clear? Su-u-u-u-u-re it is! Now we start on the real ball-breaking or ovary-straining—whichever the case may be—details.

Corrective Waves . . . Consistently Inconsistent

When dealing with impulse waves, there is really only one major deviation from the basic Elliott count and the basic tenets that could provide difficulties. The deviation from the basic principle involves the tendency of one of the impulse waves to become extended and develop a greater number of waves than the five-wave norm, producing a count of nine, sometimes more, since there can also be extensions of extensions.

The other difficulty in dealing with impulse waves involves the tendency for Wave V extensions to become subject to a double retracement, where the final waves of the impulse wave are also part of a corrective wave.

Aside from these deviations from the basic formation, impulse waves are relatively easy to deal with, compared with the corrective waves. Just as the secondary correction noted by Charles Dow in his works is the most deceptive aspect of market behavior, so, too, are the corrective waves II and IV in the basic five-wave structure peculiar to the Wave Principle.

When dealing with the corrective waves of a cycle, the refinements developed by Elliott result in further deviations from the basic format. There will be many occasions when the corrective phase of a cycle will produce what appear to be inconsistencies in the basic Wave Principle. Periods of deviant-behavior patterns, as noted and categorized by Elliott, are an inherent aspect of the Wave Principle and should be considered as such. When these refinements are mastered and assimilated, it will be readily seen how these deviations from the basic format give the Wave Principle its inherent flexibility, making it much more adaptable to market behavior in real time and in the real world.

In the basic format, every corrective phase of a cycle will be composed of three waves. There is no deviation from that tenet, in the same manner as all major movements have five waves. Where difficulties will at times arise is when an attempt is made to break the waves down for the purpose of isolating the smaller-component sub-waves. Yet, always bear in mind that there remains consistency in corrective patterns regardless of their shape, size, duration, or direction. During a major or minor upward movement, the corrective waves take the form of a downward, or sideways movement. In a major or minor downward movement, the corrective waves will produce an upward sideways movement.

The only exception to the basic tenets is in the case of an irregular correction, where two waves of the correction also comprise the upward movement in a major uptrend. At the same time, the completion of an irregular correction will have the final effect of being a downward movement, correcting an uptrend and an upward movement when it is correcting a downtrend.

The corrective formations that are to be introduced will be categorized as belonging to the corrective phase of either a bull market or a bear market for the sake of simplicity. Corrective formations in a market where the overriding trend is downward will be referred to as being *inverted.* Therefore, whenever the expression "inverted" appears, this is with reference to the upward corrective formation in a downward movement.

Corrective formations fall into three general categories, which are the *zig-zag,* the *flat,* and the *irregular* correction. It is often difficult to forecast the exact nature of the type of formation that will occur at the end of an impulse wave, duration, and extent. The tendencies already outlined may be of some assistance; e.g., if corrective Wave II is a zig-zag, it then becomes likely that the formation of corrective Wave IV will be a flat.

Irregular corrections may appear after either of the impulse waves, but usually only appear after a Wave V has been completed. Inverted irregular corrections are very rare. If impulse Wave I has been subject to an irregular correction, an irregular correction is most unlikely to appear in either Waves III or V. If an irregular correction has appeared in either Wave I or III, then an irregular correction would be most unlikely to occur in Wave V. There is usually one irregular correction in cycles of the same degree.

If an irregular correction has neither appeared in Wave I nor Wave III, the use of trend channels can be an aid in anticipating the likelihood of an extension, double retracement, comprising part of the irregular correction that may follow a completed Wave V.

The proper assessment of corrective waves is vital for the information they will provide regarding the prospective strength or weakness of the impulse wave that follows. Accurate categorization of corrective waves is one of the most important aspects of the Wave Principle in a strategic context.

Figure 29 shows the idealized shape of the three categories of corrective waves, which are particularly peculiar to the smaller waves, especially when plotting hourly movements on your charts. When these corrective formations are found within cycles of higher degrees, the individual components will begin to take on movements that appear to vary from the normal wave structure in terms of the number of sub-waves. It should be remembered that the general outline of the formation will be the same regardless of the wave degree. It will only be the number of inner components that vary.

Figure 29
CORRECTIVE PHASES IN SMALLER WAVES

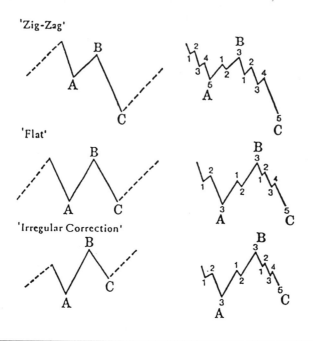

Figure 30
5-3-5 ZIG-ZAG BREAKDOWN

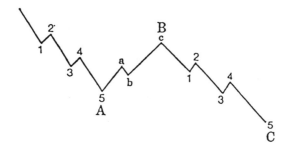

The Zig-zag Formation

The simplest form of all of the corrective waves is the zig-zag, its name adequately describing its shape. This particular formation provides an ideal model to which other corrective formations can be related. The zig-zag in its simplest form consists of a downward drive that corrects an existing uptrend, interrupted by a rally. The size of the rally is limited to the Golden Ratio integer, .61815. The Wave B rally of the A-B-C zig-zag should therefore never exceed sixty-two percent of the amplitude of Wave A. Wave C of the zig-zag, in its idealized form, would be of the same approximate dimensions of a Wave A in size and duration.

After the completion of the fifth and final wave of a major bull market, spanning a period of, say, two to three years, the corrective down wave will begin. If this corrective down wave takes the form of a zig-zag, it can then be broken down into its intermediate and minor cycles. The idealized formation of the breakdown would appear as in Figure 30.

As can be seen from the idealized diagram, the breakdown of waves to the cycle of the next-lower degree has a 5-3-5 count. The intermediate trends, Wave A and Wave C, are downward, while Wave B is an intermediate uptrend, assuming the formation is acting to retrace a bull market of normal dimensions.

Wave A of the formation has taken on the characteristics of an impulse wave since it is directional, moving in the same direction as the overriding trend. Wave A has five sub-wave components, as would be the characteristics of any directional impulse wave.

Wave B of the movement is counter to the overriding trend. This Wave B is therefore corrective, rather than directional. Wave B is acting to correct the ground covered by Wave A. As a corrective wave, Wave B has three components, a, b, and c of the cycle of the next-lower degree. Wave B has taken the form of an inverted zig-zag. If we were to break up the a, b, and c wave components of Wave B to the cycle of the next-lower degree, which does not appear on the diagram, we would have a 5-3-5 count, the basic count of all sub-waves of a corrective wave.

However, the sub-waves of minor waves do not always subdivide in this way, or, if they do, the time element may be so small that the divisions may not be readily apparent. The Stockmaster, a device available for tracking every single change of the Dow Jones Industrial Averages, will provide complete price data for all wave formations. Since this machine reports every single change in the movement of the DJIA, in theory, every single wave can be studied down to the very smallest degree. Similar information is not available for other markets. When dealing with waves involving a very short time frame, in many cases valuable price data may have been omitted or may not be available. It will become necessary to use considerable license when attempting to analyze waves of sub-minor, minuette, and sub-minuette categories. I do not recommend the use of the Wave Principle for very short-term, intra-day trading. The Wave Principle is best employed for anticipating important short-term, medium-term, and long-term terminal junctures.

Application of the Zig-zag

When the zig-zag formation has been identified, its special characteristics can assist the investor in anticipating at what level the particular correction is likely to come to an end, as early as the completion of first and second waves of Wave A. It is possible to obtain a projection of the likely extent of the total A-B-C correction by using the tenets of the Wave Principle introduced thus far; e.g., Wave 3 of an impulse wave should be limited to 1.6185 percent of the dimensions of Wave I; Wave V should approximate the dimensions of Wave I; corrective waves are limited to .6185 percent of impulse waves; and there are rarely extensions to be found in the impulse waves of an overriding downtrend. The projections that can be obtained through the deployment of these tenets can also be cross-referenced by the tenets applicable to all corrective waves.

There are two rules that will help you to approximate the maximum extent of a corrective action, whether it be a zig-zag, flat, or irregular correction. While these rules apply to all corrective waves, they will prove the most useful after a zig-zag has been identified.

Maximum Corrective Action

There are two rules that will help us to determine the maximum extent of any corrective action, even before the waves have been completed:

1. If the zig-zag is Wave 4 of the cycle, the maximum extent of the corrective action will be down to the peak of Wave 1 of the same cycle. At this point I would remind the reader that assessing maximum extent is not intended to suggest that the move will, in fact, reach its maximum extent. The corrective wave may reach its maximum extent, but, then

Figure 31
EXPECTANCIES IN AMPLITUDE AND TIME SPANS

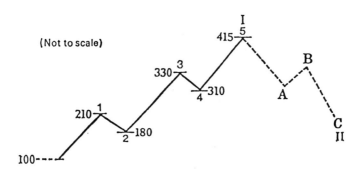

again, it may not. Should the move be approaching its level of maximum extent, the probabilities for success are highly favorable. Until such time as the move reaches its maximum-extent level, the probabilities for an important turn are not quite as favorable, but this does not mean that an end to the corrective phase cannot occur well above the maximum-extent level that is forecast.

2. If the zig-zag is Wave 2 of the cycle, the maximum extent of the down move will be down to Wave 1 of the cycle of the next-lower degree. When the first five waves of a new bull move are completed, a down wave of longer time and greater size than either of the two corrective waves in the five-wave movement will appear. This wave will become Wave 2 of the next-higher degree. Therefore, we can establish a minimum and maximum expectancy for the succeeding corrective movement. The minimum expectancy would be equal to the maximum time period of either Wave 2 or Wave 4 of the preceding movement. The minimum amplitude will also be equal to the maximum amplitude of either Wave 2 or Wave 4 of the succeeding movement. Let us use the five-wave sequence shown in Figure 31 as an example.

In Figure 31, we have a sequence of five waves showing their time span and size. When attempting to establish the minimum expectancy for the size of Wave II (A-B-C corrective zigzag), we determine the maximum size of either Wave 2 or Wave 4. In this case the maximum size was Wave 2 involving a downswing of 30 points. The minimum time of the down move can be established by determining the maximum length in time of either Wave 2 or Wave 4. In this respect, Wave 4 was the longer wave in time, involving a downswing lasting three months. Thus, we can establish the minimum expectancy of Wave II, which will act to correct the five-wave movement, involving a minimum fall of 30 points over a minimum period of three months. Simply, the basic tenet of Elliott states that the corrective wave following five completed waves of a cycle must be greater in time and amplitude than any of the previous corrective waves of the cycle, which, when completed, will become a wave in the cycle of the next higher degree.

When determining the maximum extent of the subsequent Wave II, we merely establish where the peak of the first impulse wave of the next-lower degree of Wave I occurred. In the above instance, such a peak occurred at 210. In order to establish the maximum length in time of the move, we revert to the Golden Ratio of the Fibonacci Summation Series. The time span of the corrective wave should not be greater than 0.618 of the time span of the wave which it is correcting. In Figure 31, the total five-wave formation spanned twenty-three months. The maximum expectancy for the corrective move would thus be approximately fourteen months.

As you can see, even before we begin the corrective phase of the cycle, we can obtain some rough guidelines as to what can be expected in terms of the subsequent magnitude of the coming bear phase. In the example diagram, we established a minimum expectation of the next down move as being not less than 30 points, spanning a period of not less than three months, and having a maximum expectancy of fourteen months, spanning no more than 205 points.

Strategic Deployment

At this stage, many who attempt to make predictions with their charts will dismiss the idea as suffering a broader margin of error. This is because most fail to recognize that the margin of error implicit in most chart work is either much broader or totally irrelevant, the latter being the thesis of students of modern capital market theory. When dealing with factors which tend to anticipate events before they occur rather than following them as they occur, movements of minimum and maximum expectancy, which provide empirical evidence of resolution to the extent which Elliott has provided, can be of immense benefit to the investor in terms of overall strategy. In the preceding example, investors would have liquidated their holdings upon the completion of the five-wave movement and would not consider any repurchases until the down move had lasted at least three months and involved a minimum downswing of 30 points. Should the down move go into its thirteenth month and involve a swing of, say, 190 points, investors would then start picking the shares they intended to buy for the succeeding upswing, in anticipation of a big bull move soon to develop.

Naturally, the question will arise, "What does one do in the intervening eleven months?" Should the market turn upward after the fourth month and one waited for a further nine months to take action, a massive move could have been completed. The answer to that question comes from the inherent behavior pattern of the zig-zag.

By the time the down move has reached the minimum expected, based on the calculations that were made by analyzing the structure of the five-wave up move, we will, no doubt, have a great deal more data to help us. For instance, once Waves 1 and 2 of Wave A of the zig-zag have developed, we can employ the channelling technique described previously. We could then determine the probable size and timing of Wave A, from which we can obtain a further probability as to the extent of both Wave B and Wave C. In the development of a zig-zag, Wave B will be shorter in time and amplitude than Wave A, while Wave C will be in proportion to Wave A, both in time and size.

When Waves 1 and 2 of corrective Wave A have been completed, we would carry out the following procedure:

1. A channel will be constructed in accordance with the principles outlined: guidelines will then be established for the duration and amplitude of the completed five waves, which will comprise Wave A of the zig-zag. We can then establish a minimum amplitudinal expectancy for Wave B.

2. The expectancy can be established by assessing the maximum duration and amplitude of Waves 2 and 4 of the five waves that make up Wave A, as established by the channel. Remember Elliott's rule regarding extensions. Extensions are unlikely to occur in corrective waves. Therefore, neither Wave A, Wave B, nor Wave C are likely to be subject to any extended movements.

3. Expectations for Wave B can be established by treating the bottom of Wave 1 as the maximum point of corrective action, and multiplying the time span of Wave A by the Golden Ratio of 0.618 will determine the maximum time it will take to complete the move.

4. Once a probable minimum and maximum time and size expectation has been calculated for Wave B, one merely adds the expected size of Wave A's peak to the peak of Wave B to get an approximate idea of what the total A-B-C correction is likely to involve. The time span can be calculated similarly. The time span of Wave C should be proportionate to that of Wave A.

5. A further refinement is brought into play when we near the turn of the pattern. Once Waves A and B have been completed and followed by four waves of Wave C, we can pinpoint the exact ending of the down move by using a further tenet of Elliott's. Regardless of the nature of the corrective action, there is an extraordinarily high probability that Wave 5 of Wave C will be equal to Wave I of that same Wave C. By adding the size of Wave I of Wave C to the peak of Wave 4, we will thus come up with the exact bottom of the A-B-C move.

Dealing with the Flat

Like the zig-zag, the corrective wave which carries the *flat* label takes its name from its appearance, that of a horizontal formation interrupting the overriding trend, bordered by relatively fixed margins at the top and at the bottom of the formation.

When dealing with the zig-zag, there is the first downward thrust that sets the stage for the rest of the pattern. The initial downward thrust is interrupted by a rally, which normally has finite dimensions. Wave B of the rally will travel no further than the trough of Wave 1 of the sub-wave and will being limited to .6185 percent of the amplitude of Wave A. The second downward drive of the zig-zag, Wave C, will take on dimensions similar to that of Wave A in time and size.

The flat has totally different characteristics. Although the flat will have three basic waves like any other corrective formation, Wave B of the flat will often rally back to the beginning of the corrective pattern, which would be the peak of the preceding impulse wave. The flat is sometimes found in corrective Wave II, but most often in corrective Wave IV. A flat can follow

Figure 32
FLAT COMPONENT WAVES

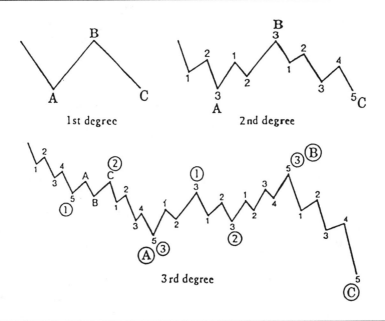

1st degree   2nd degree

3rd degree

impulse Wave I and impulse Wave III. There have been occasions when a flat has followed impulse Wave V. Those occasions are extremely rare.

All three waves of a flat will have similar amplitude, although the two troughs of the flat—or two peaks, in the case of an inverted flat—are unlikely to be in close proximity. The most important distinction between the flat and other corrective formations is in the number and sequence of the subwaves. Broadly, the flat will appear precisely as described. When broken down, it seems to take on a life of its own. Instead of comprising five sub-waves downward, three upward, and five downward like the zig-zag, the flat will normally have a count of three sub-waves in Wave A, three sub-waves in Wave B and five sub-waves in Wave C. Figure 32 is an example of the flat broken down into waves of two lower degrees.

Flats are rarely perfectly horizontal affairs, as the idealized diagram might imply. At all times we are dealing with rough, visual approximations. In either an upward movement or a downward movement, the flat is likely to be sloping upward or downward, sometimes in the opposite direction. The flat might also have some fairly jagged edges in real-time movements.

Essentially, what characterizes the flat is the close proximity of Wave B of the formation to the peak (or trough, if inverted) of the five-sub-wave impulse move which it is correcting, normally Wave III. Another factor is the reasonably close proximity of the end of Wave C to the terminal points of Wave A.

Obviously, since Wave A of the flat has only three components rather than the normal five, there can be considerable interpretative confusion. There are observations that can be made which will help limit the confusion, particularly an awareness that the corrective action that is approaching is likely to take on the formation of a flat.

Once the first three waves of a five-wave pattern have been completed, assuming Wave II of those three waves has been identified as a zig-zag, Elliott's theory of alternation alerts you to the strong possibility that approaching Wave IV will be a flat. Rather than expecting Wave A of oncoming Wave IV to have five sub-waves, you will be ready for a three-wave count preceding Wave B.

Of course, when dealing with a flat, you will have to modify some of your forecasting techniques. Since the complete count of the sub-waves of Wave A of the flat will only be three waves, you will not be able to employ the channeling technique that is designed for a five-wave formation, as is the case with Waves A and C of the zig-zag. When attempting to project the dimensions of Wave A of a flat, you must deal with the movements of the next degree lower, treating Wave A of the flat as a zig-zag in the wave of the next-lower degree, where the channelling technique can be employed for both the individual components of Wave A and Wave B of the flat. Wave C can be treated normally, as if it were part of an ordinary zig-zag, since it will not necessitate its breakdown to waves of a lesser degree.

If you break the flat down into components of two degrees lower, we find Wave A consists of a zig-zag, which in turn consists of a downward movement having five waves, an upward movement having three waves and a downward movement of five waves. Wave B of the flat takes the form of an inverted zig-zag, which, broken down, will have five upward waves of the next-lower degree, three downward waves of the next-lower degree, and five upward waves of the next-lower degree. Wave C of the flat will have the same components as any other Wave C, i.e., three waves down interrupted by two waves up. When broken down, the normal 5-3-5-3-5 count will tie in with the breakdown of Waves A and B as in Figure 33.

Figure 33
BREAKDOWN OF THE FLAT

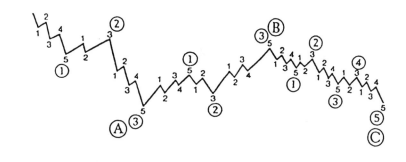

When Waves 1 and 2 of Wave 1 of Wave A have been completed, we then draw our channel in the same manner as we would do for any zig-zag. This channel will then give us the approximate terminal level for Wave 1 of Wave A of the flat. We next use the same procedure outlined with respect to plotting the terminal ending for Wave B and Wave C of a zig-zag to give us waves 2 and 3 of the flat, which, in turn, provide the terminal point of Wave A of the flat. Once the terminal point of Wave A of the flat has been calculated, the rest is comparatively simple, for both Wave B and Wave C of the flat are similar to the same dimensions of Wave A.

There are several aids that will help when dealing with the flat. The first aspect one must consider is the minimum expectancy of the projected corrective move. Basically, the flat is composed of a downward zig-zag, followed by an upward zig-zag, then a normal five-wave downward move. Should a relatively shallow downward zig-zag have been completed in less time than we would normally expect for the completion of a zig-zag, it is likely that such a downward move is only part of a much larger corrective pattern, not complete in itself. One would then be on the alert for the possible development of a flat. Naturally, should such a downward move take place in a Wave 4, the previous corrective Wave 2 having been a zig-zag, the more reason to be on the alert for the flat.

At times, Wave C of a flat will take on added dimensions. This is another tenet dealt with in detail under Elliott's Theory of Alternation. One will be warned of such an occurrence when the first wave of Wave C falls below Wave 2 of Wave B, yet is significantly higher than the beginning

Figure 34
ELONGATED WAVE C

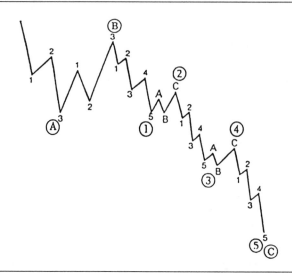

of Wave B, as in Figure 34. (Note: For purposes of illustration, Wave C has been broken down into one degree lower than Wave A and Wave B.)

When this occurs, one must revise the projection downward. Originally, it would have been anticipated that Wave C of the flat would have ended at or about the level of Wave A. When the first wave of Wave C penetrated the bottom of Wave 2 of Wave B, we readjust our minimum expectation for this Wave C in the same manner as when attempting to anticipate the terminal point of Wave C in dealing with the zig-zag.

Further, when attempting to forecast the bottom of Wave C of a flat, one assumes Wave 3 will be of greater dimensions than Wave 1, Wave 5 will approximate Wave 1. Thus, we multiply Wave I by three, then subtract the anticipated maximum expectancy of the corrective moves, as previously outlined. The result will give us the expected dimension of Wave C, when the first wave of such a Wave C is greater than anticipated. One can use the channelling technique or any of the other methods which enable one to forecast the end point of a five-wave movement. Elliott makes special note of this phenomenon in *Nature's Law:* "Whether or not Wave C of an inverted flat is elongated or not, it still remains corrective."

Dealing with Irregular Corrections

You should not be a stranger to irregular corrections, since I have already dealt with this subject in my treatment of impulse waves. The interpretative problem of dealing with an irregular correction is that Wave A and the wave of the correction form part of an extended impulse wave.

In the case of the zig-zag, the peak of Wave B will never retrace more than the first four waves of the pattern. In the case of the flat, Wave B will retrace the whole of Wave A of the correction, but not much more. When dealing with an "irregular" correction, Wave B will retrace all of the ground of Wave A of the formation.

Flats usually appear at the end of Wave III of a cycle, in the form of corrective Wave IV. Irregular corrections usually appear after the Wave V of a cycle and represent the corrective formation of the entire cycle. When Wave B of a corrective movement exceeds the fifth wave of the cycle that it is correcting, this is defined as an *irregular correction* under Elliott's treatment of corrective waves. The terminal point of the fifth wave of the cycle is considered the orthodox top of the primary bull market. Wave B of the corrective formation is defined as an *irregular top* for purposes of definition.

The wave count of an irregular correction is precisely the same as that of the flat. The irregular correction has the classic three-wave count. Wave A of an irregular correction, when broken down to waves of the next-lower degree, has a three-wave count, unlike the zig-zag, but exactly like the flat.

Figure 35

NORMAL FIVE WAVE BULL MARKET WITH IRREGULAR CORRECTION

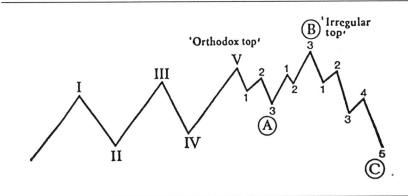

Wave A of an irregular correction has two sub-waves interrupted by a rally. Wave B of the formation has two sub-waves interrupted by a decline. Wave C consists of three downward waves, each interrupted by two upward waves, which is the normal characteristics for all waves C of a corrective formation. I am, of course, referring to corrective waves in an uptrend, rather than inverted corrective waves. The same principles apply to inverted corrective waves.

Figure 35 shows a normal five-wave upward progression which is terminated by an irregular correction. Note the position of the orthodox top and the irregular top. Waves A, B, and C all constitute the correction, although Waves A and B are seemingly a component of the bull market, since the terminal point of Wave B would represent a new all-time high in the bull market.

Actually, the irregular correction is far easier to deal with than the flat, because of its frequent occurrence at the end of the extended fifth wave of a five-wave movement. When occurring at the end of a fifth wave of a five-wave movement, the dimensions of Wave A can be simply targeted, since Wave A represents the first retracement of the double retracement that follows the extension. Since the first retracement of a double retracement only covers the ground of the extended portion of Wave V, the distance Wave A of the irregular extension is going to cover, under these circumstances, can be readily ascertained.

We can establish a minimum expectation for Wave B of the irregular correction, since we know the extended Wave V is going to be doubly retraced. Wave B of the irregular correction must at least reach the peak of Wave V in its extended form. The expectations for Wave B can also be established by projecting the sub-waves of Wave B. Wave C of the sub-wave of Wave B in an irregular correction is likely to have the same dimensions as Wave A of the same degree, sub-wave B limited to .6185 of the ground covered by sub-wave A.

When Wave V becomes extended, it is not always followed by an irregular correction, and irregular corrections do not only follow an extended Wave V. At times, an extended Wave V may be followed by a simple zig-zag. The time factor should be the final arbiter in this respect. When the first downward reaction to an extended Wave V takes place over a period of time, which is less than that which one normally expects of a corrective Wave A in a cycle of the same degree, but greater than that of the time frame of the Waves A of Waves II and IV of the five-wave cycle, it is highly likely that an irregular correction is in the course of development.

Should the first retracement following an extended Wave V become protracted in time, involving a period which is appreciably longer than any of the corrective Waves II and IV in their entirety, it then becomes likely the first retracement following that extended Wave V will turn into a zig-zag. The second retracement, Wave B, although running counter to the overriding downtrend, will constitute a normal wave in the downtrend, rather than Wave B of a double retracement, and therefore fall considerably short of the peak of extended Wave V.

Irregular corrections will also occur following unextended five-wave upward and downward movements. In the case of an irregular correction following an unextended Wave V, Wave B simply becomes elongated and stretches to a level above the unextended Wave V. No double retracement of an extended Wave V is involved. The Wave B that reaches a level above the previous unextended Wave V can be identified as such, since it will only have three sub-waves like all waves B. If Wave B were part of the overriding uptrend, it would have five or more waves.

Rules for forecasting the likely minimum and maximum extent of irregular corrections are the same as those which apply to the zig-zag and the flat, excepting those items which are peculiar to an irregular correction when it follows an extended Wave V. The forecasting rule applicable under such a development has already been noted.

Further Observations for Corrective Waves

The identification and study of corrective movements can have outstanding forecasting value in terms of assisting the investor in determining the type of action which is likely to follow when the corrective wave is completed. An impulse wave that follows a corrective zig-zag, assuming the zig-zag is of normal dimensions, will also be of normal-cycle dimensions with respect to its relationship to the impulse wave preceding. For example, if Wave IV of a formation is a zig-zag, then it becomes likely that Wave V will be unextended, taking on the amplitude and time frame of Wave I of the cycle.

If the zig-zag falls short of its normal dimensions, having a Wave B that is smaller in amplitude and shorter in time that the idealized model, while Wave C of the zig-zag is shorter that Wave A, possibly failing to reach the lower parameters of a trend channel, the impulse wave that follows is likely to be much stronger than usual, reaching optimal dimensions within the relationships of the Wave Principle.

In the course of an uptrend, the upward movement that follows the completion of a flat will be far stronger than the upward movement that follows a zig-zag. When Wave IV takes the form of a flat during a bull market, that bull market is likely to end in quite a blaze of glory. The longer in time and wider in amplitude the flat, the stronger the move that is likely to follow.

When a corrective Wave II or corrective Wave IV in the form of an irregular correction appears, the strongest markets of all are indicated for the ensuing impulse waves. If corrective Wave IV takes the shape of an irregular correction and there has been no extension in either Wave I or Wave III, it then becomes almost certain that Wave V will become extended, stretching to nine waves and possibly more.

The basic principles that apply to the corrective waves in a bull market also apply to the corrective waves in a bear market, but in reverse. If the corrective waves in a bear market show above-average strength, the downward moves that follow will be less severe than normal bear-market behavior would indicate. If the corrective moves in a bear market are notably weak, then the further downward drives that follow the completion of the corrective waves will be of greater severity than usual.

A zig-zag that undershoots its normative dimensions in a bull market is a signal that subsequent movements will be strong. When a zig-zag undershoots its normative dimensions in a bear market, the indications are that the subsequent impulse move in the bear market will be severe. A flat in a bull market indicates above-average strength. A flat in a bear market indicates greater-than-average weakness.

Irregular corrections in bear markets are sometimes seen, but these are very rare formations in a bear market. In a bear market, the best way to determine how much selling pressure the bears are going to exert is to estimate how much punch the bulls have during the rallying action.

As a general proposition, waves travelling along the main trend composed of five waves (or nine, in the case of an extension), will prove to be far more readily identifiable than will be corrective waves. Corrective waves are easier to deal with in a bear-market cycle than in a bull-market cycle. During a bear market, corrective waves are subject to far fewer deviations and irregularities. Corrective waves during a bull market are subject to a far greater number of irregularities. As you will soon discover, corrective waves in a bull market may not necessarily be three-wave affairs. You have already discovered that the normal 5-3-5 sub-wave count does not always apply. In the case of both the flat and the zig-zag, the count is 3-3-5.

Normally, it follows that if a wave count cannot be sub-divided into five sub-waves, according to Elliott's tenets it therefore must be a corrective wave. The investor must be certain that every effort is made to differentiate impulse waves from corrective waves. In analyzing the corrective waves, far more latitude must be allowed than in the case of the more readily definable impulse waves when counting the waves. By their very nature, impulse waves tend to be clean-cut efforts, as if these waves were generated by sudden, impulsive behavior. Impulse waves are usually so well delineated that it is almost impossible for even the novice to misinterpret them . . . by hindsight!

12
Complex Corrections

It is somewhat like a rough road map. With Elliott, you don't feel like you are in the middle of a jungle.

—R.J. Hill

Tactics, strategy, and forecasting would be a relatively simple matter if the only type of corrective action involved Elliott's Zig-zag. In fact, forecasting the end of the fifth wave and the extent of the corrective waves would not be all that difficult if corrective action was limited to only the zig-zags, flats, and irregular corrections. These corrective waves have commonality. The rules governing the structure of Wave B and Wave C of all three types of corrections are exactly the same. The difference between the zig-zag and the other two types of correction rest primarily with Wave A. Wave A of a zig-zag has five sub-waves, whereas Wave A of the flat and the irregular correction have three sub-waves.

Unfortunately, life and the Wave Principle are never so simple. In addition to the three basic corrective formations already outlined, Elliott has also observed what he defines as *complex corrections* and *mixed complex corrections,* where a number of the guidelines set down for the basic forms of corrective action are violated. Elliott went into great detail in an attempt to categorize every single price movement in a market cycle, in order to produce the greatest possible degree of accuracy when using his method. Many Elliott practitioners feel the amount of detail Elliott called for was unnecessary. There are many examples of contemporary interpretations utilizing the Wave Principle which seem to side-step and ignore some of Elliott's more-detailed refinements. I feel this is an extremely dangerous practice. Every effort should be made at categorizing all types of corrective action as it occurs, if only to cross-reference the broad guidelines that may have previously been forecast. Cross-referencing is extremely important during the fifth impulse wave of a primary bull market and the fifth wave of Wave C of a primary bear market.

Those who are now readying themselves for deployment of the Wave Principle in their decision-making process should not be overly dismayed by the more-complex corrective formations. The majority of the basic principles governing basic corrective action apply to the complex corrections. The deviations to the basic rules primarily appear in the count of the component sub-waves of the correction in typical A-B-C form. The rules governing minimum and maximum size, along with minimum and maximum durations, apply to all types of corrective waves, zig-zags, flats, and irregulars, whether they be simple, complex, or mixed complex.

Unlike dealing with an impulse wave, when dealing with the early stages of a corrective wave, it will always be extremely difficult to anticipate the form that the corrective wave is going to take, given the number of possible variations. Yet the investor can still be comforted by the knowledge that, regardless of the irregularities of the corrective action, it will remain subject to an A-B-C, count and its maximum extent in time and duration will be governed by the basic principles that have already been outlined.

Several of the complex corrections had neither appeared in Elliott's first work, *The Wave Principle,* nor in the series of articles appearing in *The Financial World,* published several years later. The treat-ment of complex corrections does not make its appearance until Elliott's magnum opus, *Nature's Law,* which was published in 1946 and completed shortly before Elliott's death.

The publication of *Nature's Law* seems to have coincided with the termination of Elliott's *Interpretative Letters.* One wonders, had Elliott lived, whether there would have been further refinements to the Wave Principle, or if additional refinements had been taken with him to the grave. This we will never know. What we do know is that Elliott's accomplishments were remarkable on the basis of what he had achieved with the Wave Principle up until the time of his death.

Double Threes and Triple Threes

In *Nature's Law,* when dealing with the subject of corrective waves, Elliott introduces the concept of what he defines as *double threes* and *triple threes*. Essentially, these double threes and triple threes are nothing more than zig-zags, flats and irregular corrections in a deviant form, due to the unusual multiplicity of the sub-waves.

A. Hamilton Bolton, in his writings, seems to have altered the terminology, referring to double and triple zig-zags, along with double and triple flats, in order to give a clearer definition to these sub-categories. I prefer the additional categorization introduced by A. Hamilton Bolton for descriptive purposes and will use Bolton's categorization rather than Elliott's for purposes of simplicity. This contribution made by A. Hamilton Bolton, albeit a minor one, is the only improvement to the Wave Principle ever introduced by one of his disciples which I consider to be of any value, predictive or otherwise.

With Elliott's introduction of double threes and triple threes we have another variation of the zig-zag, the *double zig-zag*. We also have an additional variation on the inverted zig-zag, which is the *double inverted zig-zag*.

Neither Elliott nor A. Hamilton Bolton ever made reference to the possibility of a triple zig-zag or a triple inverted zig-zag. It must therefore be assumed that such a formation had never been observed by either. Elliott's concept of the double three would appear to be only applicable to the zig-zag, but not that of the triple three. The triple three seems to have been a formation reserved strictly for the flat.

The Double Zig-zag and the Inverted Double Zig-zag

When the number of waves in a simple zig-zag begins to become compounded, taking on the structure of a double zig-zag—the same holding true for the inverted zig-zag—that zig-zag takes on a totally different characteristic. The normal, A-B-C zig-zag has a sub-wave count of 5-3-5. The double zig-zag incorporates two zig-zags in Wave A and two zig-zags in Wave C, giving a count of seven. Wave A will break down into three waves instead of five, the two simple zig-zags interrupting another zig-zag in the opposite direction. Wave B of a double zig-zag is of the traditional nature. Wave C of a double zig-zag is like Wave A, breaking down into two simple zig-zags, which are interrupted by a zig-zag in the opposite direction of the preceding five sub-waves.

Figure 36

SINGLE ZIG-ZAG AND DOUBLE ZIG-ZAG

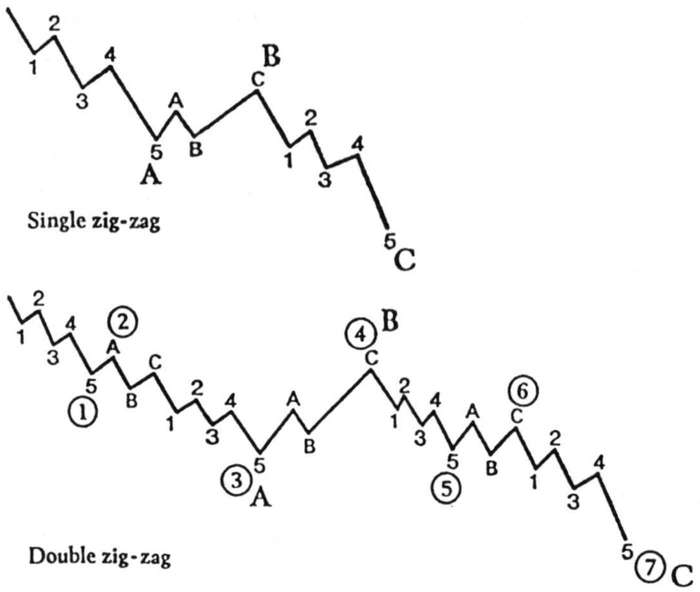

Single zig-zag

Double zig-zag

Double Flats and Triple Flats

A *double flat* is broken down in the same manner as a double zig-zag, in both the regular and inverted form. The double flat also has seven sub-waves like the double zig-zag. Unlike the double zig-zag, but like flats in general, the seven waves are all of near-equal dimensions. The simple flat has three waves of equal size, broken down into a count of 3-3-5; the double flat will have seven waves of equal size, broken down into a sub-wave count involving an A Wave comprising two simple zig-zags, interrupted by another simple zig-zag in the opposite direction of the preceding five sub-waves. Wave B of the double flat is of normal structure. Wave C of the double flat is similar to Wave A.

The *triple flat,* as the corrective wave in an uptrend and the *inverted triple flat,* as the corresponding corrective wave in a downtrend, takes on even greater dimensions than that of the double flat by extending four more waves. In some respects, the triple flat is easier to deal with than the double flat, since we are getting closer to the normative 5-3-5 count once

Figure 37
DOUBLE FLAT

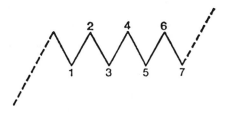

Figure 38
TRIPLE FLAT

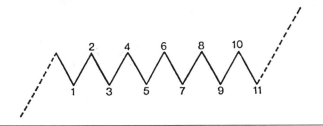

again. A breakdown of the eleven waves of a triple flat will contain three zig-zags, interrupted by two zig-zags in the opposite direction, in which the first waves constitute Wave A. Wave B will be of the standard structure, representing Wave 6. Wave C will once more contain five sub-waves, consisting of three zig-zags in the direction of the overriding trend and two counter to the overriding trend, as in Wave A of the triple flat and triple inverted flat.

Mixed Corrective Formations

Elliott discovered that the concept of double threes and triple threes often led to mixed formations. In other words, when a double three or a triple three begins to take shape, a corrective formation that began as a double zig-zag might end as a double flat would end. Wave A of such a formation would involve two zig-zags, interrupted by a zig-zag moving in the opposite direction of the overriding trend. Wave B would be standard.

Wave C might then involve the same type of configuration that constitutes Wave C of a double flat, incorporating two zig-zags in the direction of the overriding trend and one in the opposite direction.

Mixed corrections can also begin in the shape of a double flat and end as a double zig-zag would end, in a mirror image of what has been described when a mixed correction begins as a double zig-zag.

Mixed corrections can become quite confusing when attempting to arrive at an accurate wave count. It is useful to remember that whether you have a count of three waves, seven waves, or eleven waves, when the corrective wave is acting to correct an uptrend, the last of the sub-waves will be in a downward direction. When the corrective wave is inverted, acting to correct a downtrend, the last of the sub-waves will be in an upward direction. Corrective waves will always have a count of three, seven, or eleven waves of the same degree.

Figures 39 and 40 show a mixed correction and an inverted mixed correction. In Figure 39, Wave A begins as a double zig-zag, while Wave B resembles Wave B of a standard zig-zag, and Wave C that of a triple flat.

Figure 39

INVERTED MIXED TRIPLE THREE CORRECTING A DOWNTREND

Correcting a downtrend

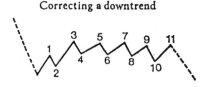

Figure 40

MIXED TRIPLE THREE CORRECTING AN UPTREND

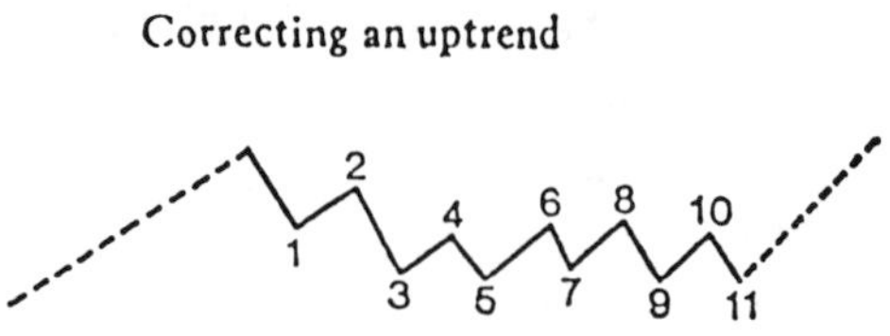

Correcting an uptrend

Figure 41

INVERTED MIXED DOUBLE IRREGULAR CORRECTION

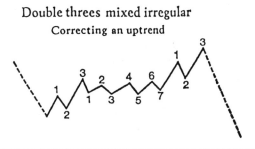

Double threes mixed irregular
Correcting an uptrend

In Figure 40, Wave A is again the typical inverted double zig-zag, Wave B that of a standard inverted flat, and Wave C that of an inverted double flat.

Mixed corrections are normally of the triple, three variety, rather than double-three, involving eleven waves rather than seven. The double-three, seven-wave count, has been reserved for mixed irregular corrections. Obviously, it would be foolish to assume that zig-zags and flats were subject to mutations while the irregular correction remained, immune to such hybrid development.

Elliott never observed a triple mixed irregular correction, but does make reference to the inverted mixed double irregular correction. There is also no reference to a mixed double irregular correction, a double irregular correction, or a triple irregular correction. Although these may not have ever been observed, it would be unwise to assume they are not a distinct possibility. Permutations of those examples which have not been observed are not included. By now, I hope to have provided a sufficient understanding of the Wave Principle to enable the reader to construct these other hybrid formations himself, for future reference.

Figure 41 shows an inverted mixed double irregular correction, as it would appear in idealized form, acting to correct a downtrend.

The double zig-zags in normal and inverted forms, along with certain elements of the mixed formations, seem to involve an exception to the general principle that the third wave of a corrective movement, Wave C, up or down, will always end with a five–subwave-count. It is the general rule of this five–sub-wave ending that gives the analyst the all-important clue as to when, and at what level, the corrective wave is going to end.

With this broad range of corrective formations, it can be extremely difficult for the analyst to be certain of the current position of a market within the cyclical framework, or to be able to anticipate future developments. However, observations reveal that formations that fall in the double, three, or triple three category, along with the complex mixed formations, will rarely, if ever, be seen in waves of large degrees, but only in smaller formations of minor and sub-minor dimensions.

It was Elliott's objective to include every possible type of wave permutation, categorize it, and analyze it as part of his Wave Principle. He would appear to have succeeded in this respect, in a manner uncommon to any other form of analysis dealing only with price movements. Elliott does not state the expected frequency of the more bizarre and complex price permutations. He does place a rarity value on the triple flat, while at the same time inferring that most of the more-complex formations are common to the flat.

In my second book on the Wave Principle, *Supertiming,* I expressed the view that perhaps Elliott was attempting to take his work too far, adding to the complexity of these corrective waves, and asked whether the additional work involved was worth the effort. Since I ventured that view fifteen years ago, I have completely revised my opinion, humbled by the clues to future market behavior that a serious study of these more, complex corrective formations eventually provided.

Diagonal Triangles and Horizontal Triangles

Technical analysts will refer to triangles in a variety of ways. They have been called bunched-top formations, coils, flags, pennants, and wedges. The terminology is interchangeable. The important element is that the triangle is representative of a very special cyclical phenomenon and appears with considerable frequency in most price formations.

Elliott made some extremely important contributions to the analysis of triangular formations in a price structure. In his early writings, Elliott endorsed the theory of conventional chart analysis, agreeing that symmetrical triangles were usually formations implying a continuation of whatever trend was persistent prior to the development of the formation. Elliott, upon further observation, re-interpreted his treatment of triangles in his later writing. This was especially evident in his *Interpretative Letters,* where he placed considerable emphasis on triangular formations.

Elliott's most important contribution to the study of triangular formation was the empirical evidence he had accumulated to show that triangular formations were almost invariably a phenomenon that followed impulse Wave III. Triangles were peculiar to Wave IV of a formation, taking the shape of that final consolidation prior to the end of an important trend.

Elliott originated the idea that triangles were composed of five waves themselves, pointing out that it is possible for triangles to make a *breakout* in the wrong direction, apparently, yet follow up quite quickly with a recovery and fulfillment of the promise of the entry trend.

On the one hand, triangles constitute a further deviation from Elliott's basic tenets, being a corrective wave having five sub-wave components, rather than three sub-wave components, as is normal for a corrective wave. Yet, this anomaly can certainly be tolerated and need not cause an interpretative problem, since triangles are so easily identified. The shape of a triangle is readily recognizable. Triangles only occur in the larger formations. Triangles are also limited to Wave IV formations with very rare exceptions. A triangle will never be seen in impulse Waves I, III, or V. The triangle will rarely occur as a Wave II. The possibility of making a counting error by failing to recognize a triangle, or of making an error by incorrectly interpreting the components of a triangle, are slight. The appearance of a triangle in the wave formation is often a welcome sight that helps the analyst verify his course when there are counting problems in the previous formation.

Engaging in the mental gymnastics necessary for the interpretation of complex corrections in the form of double threes and triple threes, in their mixed and inverted forms, can be time-consuming and soul-destroying. A concentrated detailed study of triangular formations, the principles involved, and their probable occurrence will certainly prove to be worth the effort. The empirical evidence supporting the probable resolution of a triangle is exceptionally reliable.

As Elliott explains in his original *Wave Principle*: "Wave movements occasionally taper off to a point, or broaden out from a point, in the form of a triangle. These triangular formations are important since they indicate the direction the market will take at the conclusion or approximate apex of the triangle."

In Elliott's *Wave Principle,* he referred to triangles as being of both the contracting and expanding type. This would seem to pose a logistical problem, since an expanding triangle could not have an apex, only an upper and lower trend line that expanded outwards. The following figures are early examples which Elliott cited as expanding and contracting triangles.

Figure 42

CONTRACTING TRIANGLE   **EXPANDING TRIANGLE**

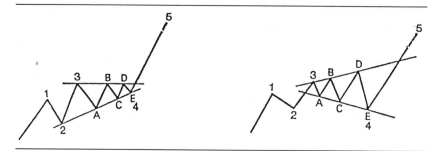

Figure 43

CONTRACTING TRIANGLE IN AN UPTREND AND DOWNTREND

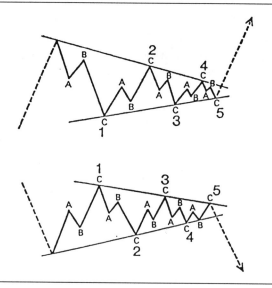

In his later writings, Elliott abandoned all reference to expanding triangles, placing these formations in an alternate category covered by other principles that deal with corrections. Elliott concluded that the only type of triangle that was worthy of special treatment and detailed analysis was the contracting type. Figure 43 shows two types of contracting triangles, those acting to correct an uptrend and a downtrend. The triangle acting to correct an uptrend would typically appear as Wave IV of that uptrend. The triangle which is acting to correct the downtrend is the type that would be found in Wave 4 of Wave A of a zig-zag, or Wave 4 of Wave C of a zig-zag.

As can be seen in Figure 43, the triangle contains five sub-waves, which consist of five three-wave zig-zags when broken down to the cycle of the next-lower degree. The count of the inner components of a triangle would therefore be 3-3-3-3-3, each set of three waves contracting in size.

Elliott segregates triangles into two classes, the *horizontal triangle* and the *diagonal triangle,* claiming the development of a horizontal triangle represents "hesitation on the part of the main price movement." Here it would seem Elliott is stating the obvious. Since the triangle is a corrective wave, it could only serve as a hesitation of the main price movement, which would be resumed when the correction is complete.

As would be expected of all corrective movements, at the conclusion of the horizontal triangle, when the apex is broken, the market will resume the original trend—upward or downward—that it was pursuing prior to the triangular hesitation. Horizontal triangles have the same significance as flats. The major difference between a horizontal triangle and a flat is that the horizontal triangle is much easier to analyze and deal with.

Elliott divided his horizontal triangles into four classes. The *ascending horizontal triangle* has a flat top but rising bottom. The *descending horizontal triangle* has a descending top but a flat bottom. The *symmetrical horizontal triangle* has a rising bottom and descending top. In his early writings, Elliott also included what he called a *reverse symmetrical horizontal triangle.* This appears as an expanding triangle having an ascending top and ascending bottom. As mentioned, Elliott abandoned the expanding triangle in his later works. The inclusion of the expanding triangle at this stage is for purely academic interest, having no analytical significance.

Figure 44 shows idealized diagrams of the four types of triangles categorized by Elliott.

Diagonal Triangles

In the ascending horizontal triangles and the descending horizontal triangles, one of the trends is horizontal. In the symmetrical horizontal triangle, although neither the bottom of the trend channel nor the top of the trend channel will be horizontal, the convergence will be in a horizontal direction.

Figure 44
1) ASCENDING HORIZONTAL TRIANGLE
2) DESCENDING HORIZONTAL TRIANGLE
3) SYMMETRICAL HORIZONTAL TRIANGLE
4) REVERSE SYMMETRICAL HORIZONTAL TRIANGLE

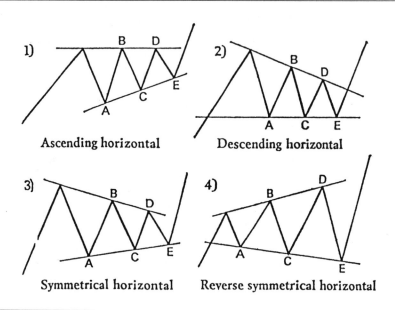

Ascending horizontal   Descending horizontal

Symmetrical horizontal   Reverse symmetrical horizontal

In the diagonal triangle, both trends will be pointing upward in the case of the ascending diagonal triangle. Both trends will be pointing downward in the case of the descending diagonal triangle. The ascending diagonal triangle and the descending diagonal triangle have the same structure as all other triangles. Both will consist of five sub-waves. Each of the five sub-waves will consist of three sub-waves of the next-lower degree. The amplitude of the first wave of the triangle is greater than that of the third wave. The amplitude of the third wave is greater than that of the fifth wave.

Overlaps between the fourth wave and the first wave of the diagonal triangle occur with considerable frequency, as is the observation for all triangles. These overlaps are not necessarily obligatory, but are the only known exception to Elliott's rule that says the end of Wave IV must never fall below or rise above the peak or trough of Wave I.

Figure 45

ASCENDING DIAGONAL   DESCENDING
TRIANGLE   DIAGONAL TRIANGLE

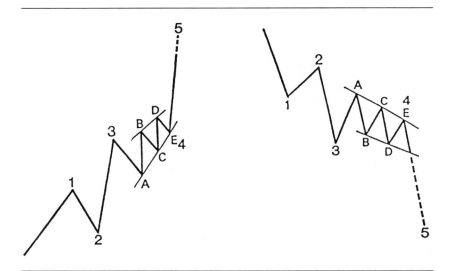

If any of these qualifying tenets are violated, the formation will fall into a category other than that of a triangle.

Diagonal triangles, while appearing as Wave IV formations, will quite frequently be the type of triangle that appears when impulse Wave V becomes subject to an extension. An early warning of the likelihood of a diagonal triangle developing as the extension of Wave V would be an exceptionally strong Wave III that covers considerable distance in a short period of time but fails to become extended.

Diagonal triangles are also frequently found in the Wave IV position of Wave C of an A-B-C correction. They are less frequent in the Wave IV position of Wave A of an A-B-C correction.

There are five types of triangles: three horizontal and two diagonal. Figure 45 shows an idealized version of an ascending diagonal triangle and a descending diagonal triangle.

Triangular formations, although falling in the category of a complex correction, are among the least-difficult formations to deal with and analyze. In recent years, considerable confusion has been added to the analysis of triangles, in the context of the Wave Principle, by certain practitioners who claim triangles can be found in Wave B of A-B-C corrections and also can be found as impulse waves as well as corrective waves. One such practitioner also claims to have observed a triangle where the sub-waves of the triangle contain a breakdown into five waves of the next-lower degree, rather than three. According to this particular practitioner, triangles of this type are found in Wave A positions and are always followed by a Wave B.

These innovative versions of Elliott's Wave Principle were probably developed to simplify the task of counting and place formations into categories which may have previously defied categorization. In the long run, practices of this type will often compound counting errors rather than simplify counting. The Wave Principle is about the most flexible of all technical tools. Within this flexibility there are rules and phenomena that Elliott had observed, which provide a stochastic rigidity to some degree. By adding to the flexibility and arriving at a point where any formation can appear anywhere, we are approaching randomness to a degree that could render the Wave Principle useless.

I would be the last to disagree that markets can do anything they like, any time they like. In fact, in my writing, I continually advise investors that this is a fact of market life which is an inalienable truth. Yet, in spite of this, there will remain form. Elliott believed he had discovered this form. The empirical evidence strongly suggests that he has come closer than anyone else to discovering a basic form in the psychological input of markets. It would be unwise to tamper with what has produced such outstanding results to date.

Elliott asserts that triangles occur primarily in Wave 4 formations. At no time had there appeared in Elliott's writing, up to the time of his death, any reference to a triangle as a Wave B structure or as an impulse wave, the only exception being the observation of a triangle developing in the form of an extended fifth wave. Although Wave I and Wave III can also become extended, such extensions have not been triangular. Perhaps, if Elliott had lived longer and observed more, he might have changed his mind; then again, he might not have. I prefer the Scotch verdict. If there is an indication that a triangle may have developed in Wave B of an A-B-C correction, or impulse Wave I, or impulse Wave III, be wary. You may find yourself victim of a counting error.

Whether triangles are horizontal or diagonal, they will usually be found in Wave IV formations and contain five waves, each of which will have three sub-waves. Where a triangle appears in a formation other than a Wave IV, or has less than five waves—or more than five waves—it is unlikely to be a triangle, as defined by Elliott within the context of the

Wave Principle observed by Elliott. In these circumstances, what appears as a triangle may be components of a much larger formation, which would fall into a different corrective wave category or a combination of waves of two different degrees.

Elliott points out that the most important aspect to be noted in both horizontal triangles and diagonal triangles is where they begin. Wave B of the triangle must be *fixed.* It is Wave B of the triangle that will dictate the subsequent direction of the market's movement. In order to fix Wave B—establishing its peak and trough—one must be able to identify Wave A and the beginning of Wave C in terms of their divergence from other formations.

Identifying Wave A is simple enough. Wave A will normally begin at the terminal juncture of Wave III and be followed by a wave that is more powerful than would be expected of Wave B of a zig-zag, but less powerful than Wave B of a flat. Wave A will have three sub-waves instead of the usual five. You will have plenty of input to help alert you to the possibility that a triangle is in the course of development. You can then fix the parameters of Wave B accordingly.

For all intents and purposes, the practitioner using the Wave Principle can treat the triangle in its various forms as usually a Wave IV phenomenon, rarely appearing in any other segment of the cycle. Figure 46 is an idealized diagram showing a horizontal symmetrical triangle as it would

Figure 46

| HORIZONTAL SYMMETRICAL | HORIZONTAL SYMMETRICAL |
| TRIANGLE IN A DOWNTREND | TRIANGLE IN AN UPTREND |

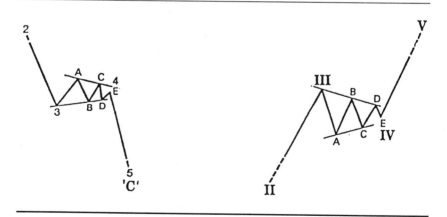

appear in either Wave 4 of Wave A, or Wave 4 of Wave C in a zig-zag or a flat in a downtrend. The diagram also shows the horizontal symmetrical triangle as Wave IV of a rising trend.

In the example that shows the horizontal symmetrical triangle as Wave 4 of Wave C, the direction of Wave B is downward. At the conclusion of Wave E of the triangle, the market, which has been hesitating, will then resume the original decline. Wave 5 of Wave C begins at the terminal juncture of Wave E of the triangle.

In the example that shows the horizontal symmetrical triangle appearing as a corrective Wave IV of an upward movement, one would assume Wave C of the corrective series hit bottom at Wave II and was followed by a five-wave impulse drive, peaking at Wave III. What follows is a wave having three sub-waves which would constitute Wave A of the triangle. The triangular hesitation is completed at the end of Wave E, which coincides with the terminal juncture of Wave IV and the beginning of Wave V.

Wave V Extension Triangles

The most common type of triangle is the horizontal variety, which appears in the Wave IV position of an overriding uptrend on the Wave 4 position of Wave A, or Wave C in a downtrend. Elliott makes special reference to the occurrence of a triangular formation in the development

Figure 47
DIAGONAL TRIANGLE IN EXTENDED WAVE V

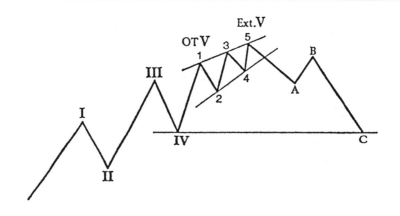

of the fifth wave of a primary movement. When one observes the development of an upward or downward diagonal triangle, the formation can be treated as having the most reliable forecasting value when it appears as the fifth wave of an important upward or downward movement, rather than in Wave IV position. According to Elliott, an exceptionally sharp movement follows the completion of a diagonal triangle in the extended Wave V position.

Figure 47 is an idealized version of a diagonal triangle in the extended Wave V position of an uptrend.

Several observations can be made about this formation. Note the manner in which the orthodox top, labelled *OT,* falls short of typical Wave V expectations. In the nomenclature of the Wave Principle, this tendency is referred to as a *failure,* which has a special predictive value. I plan to deal with failure in greater detail as we progress.

Following the failure, the Wave V then develops an extension, which, unlike the standard extension, contains truncated waves. This could occur as a result of a sudden positive news item, or other similar extraneous items, causing a trend which was in the process of weakening to suddenly develop temporary strength. Volume characteristics play an important role in the proper identification of this triangular formation. Peak volume levels are likely to be reached at the orthodox top of Wave V. Although the market may be making ascending peaks at waves 3 and 5 of the triangle, the direction of volume is likely to disagree with the direction of the price movement.

As can be noted, Wave 2 of the triangular formation is in a downward direction, along with Wave 4, while Waves 3 and 5 are in an upward direction. The entire impulse wave formation—Waves I–V—becomes subject to a correction on the completion of sub-wave 5 of the triangle, when the market reverses direction. Normally, part of the corrective phase that follows an extended Wave V incorporates a double retracement. When the extended Wave V takes the form of a diagonal triangle, that extended Wave V takes on properties that are at variance with normal extended Wave V patterns.

The formation of a diagonal triangle as an extended Wave V is indicative of a market that had been developing underlying weakness prior to the development of the pattern. This diagonal triangle is a sign that a major up-move is coming to an end and that the early stages of the bear market to follow are likely to be extraordinarily violent. The diagonal triangle serves to add to the excesses that are an intrinsic aspect of the final stages of a bull market. Rather than anticipating a double retracement as the outcome of the extended Wave V, which would (a) pull back to the level at which the extended Wave V began representing Wave A of the corrective phase, and (b) produce a Wave B of an A-B-C correction that would recover the ground lost and subsequently rise to a level exceeding the peak of the extended Wave V, we look for a totally different outcome when a diagonal triangle appears as a Wave V extension.

Following a normal extended Wave V formation, Wave C inflicts all of the bear market damage, since Wave B of that particular formation will take the market to a new high, albeit on greatly reduced volume. The diagonal triangle—which is characteristic of hesitation in price action, with its inherent implications—precludes the development of a B Wave that rises to a level above the peak of the extended Wave V, as is the case with the normal irregular correction that follows the standard extended Wave V. The A-B-C correction that follows the completion of a diagonal triangle, when it occurs in the form of a Wave V extension, acts to correct the entire structure, taking the market back to the base of the triangular formation as illustrated in the idealized diagram.

Triangles in Small Formations

Regardless of the size of the triangle or the time frame covered, all the waves of a triangle must be part of a movement in the same direction, either upward, downward or sideways. If the triangular pattern appears mixed, quite simply, you are not dealing with a triangle—you're dealing with a different type of complex correction, where a different set of rules apply.

When a triangle appears as part of a large formation, the overriding trend spanning some six to twelve months or longer, the triangle should be

Figure 48
A PARTIALLY DEVELOPED TRIANGLE

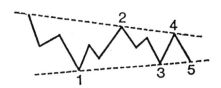

Figure 49
UNDEVELOPED SMALL FORMATION TRIANGLE

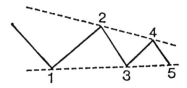

well defined and take on a fully developed appearance. Each of the five waves will be well delineated, showing the three component parts, as in the previous illustrations. However, when the formation takes place over shorter periods, the triangle may not appear as fully developed, particularly the fourth and fifth waves. Waves 1, 2, and 3 may take on the normal appearance of having three components, but the detail required for the fully developed fourth and fifth wave of a small triangle may not be available. Triangles developing over short periods of time as sub-waves may sometimes take on an appearance which looks like the idealized illustration in Figure 48.

In the very small formations where triangles have developed, spanning a few hours, a day, or a week, the waves of the triangle may simply appear as single movements. The three-wave sub-waves of the five waves of the triangle may not be visible in any of the waves at all. The only guide the user of the Wave Principle might have under such circumstances would be the outline of the triangle; that is, the tangent that may be drawn against the peaks and troughs of the components waves. The idealized version of the symmetrical horizontal triangle shows how this may appear in a small formation.

In practice, all triangles precede a very powerful thrust in the direction of Wave 2 of the triangle when completed. Before taking action in anticipation of the thrust, the trader must await the completion of Wave 5 of the triangle in order to be certain that a triangle has actually been formed. Here Elliott offers an important clue: "When the range (weekly or daily) in a triangle embraces the entire width of the triangle, the end has about arrived. Confirmation should be required in wave number five."

In general, small formations are going to be far more difficult to deal with than larger formations. Far better results are likely to be achieved when analyzing triangles in the larger formations, where all of the details are apparent. The old rule, "When in doubt stay out!" applies to triangles to an even greater extent than other formations.

The Psychology of the Triangle

It was Elliott's assertion that natural law of the universe and harmony in the world were an implicit aspect of the behavior of markets in which there was mass participation. Man, as part of this, operates on principles of human behavior that have recurring patterns. These patterns of greed, fear, or caution are exhibited by waves of optimism and pessimism, with varying degrees between the two extremes; each subsequent wave of optimism or pessimism is related to all previous waves. This causes a rhythm, or orderly sequence, in markets, according to Elliott.

With this thought in mind, it will always be helpful for those who deploy the Wave Principle to try to equate the various price formations to the activity of actual investors in the marketplace.

When a price movement fluctuates in a progressively narrower range, as in a triangle, it is, in effect, winding up like the spring of a mechanical toy or a watch. The tighter the spring is wound, the more energy it will store. Just as the wound spring will eventually release the energy needed to move the toy or start the watch, the coiling action of a price mechanism will propel price movements. In the toy or the watch, the energy is mechanical. In the market, the energy builds on the increasing tensions and uncertainties experienced by buyers and sellers. Suddenly, like an orgasmic experience, the tension is released and the latent force explodes, breaking the apex of the triangle.

As explained, triangles are formations which act as a price hesitation in the overriding trend. The trend that was in motion before the formation of the triangle continues in the same direction after the triangle is completed. The only time the formation of a triangle will act as a precursor to the reversal of a trend will be when it appears in the form of an extended Wave V.

When a triangle develops as Wave 4 of Wave A in a bear market, the first upward drive of the triangle will give you a rally in a bear market. The highest level of the triangle, which would be at the peak of the first of the five waves, would occur when buying power dries up and profit-taking ensues. At that point, a measure of uncertainty will overtake the bulls who thought the rally in a bear market was the beginning of a new bull market. The sell-off from the Wave 1 peak will produce Wave 2 of the triangle.

The rally which follows Wave 2 of the triangle will not carry the same conviction as the bear market rally which constitutes Wave 1. The sell-off that followed the first wave will have left many with the suspicion that the bear market might not be over just yet. The rally following Wave 2 (Wave 3) will be shorter in time and dimension than Wave 1. The declining Wave 4 of the triangle will serve to increase the anxiety among the bulls even more. The small rally that constitutes Wave 5 of the triangle will increase anxiety among the bears in the same manner, but not to the same extent.

In character with the triangular formations will be the tendency for the volume of trading activity to have steadily diminished, as buyers and sellers in the marketplace have become increasingly uncertain of the future direction of the market while the triangle was spinning out its pattern. At the apex of the triangle, buying and selling reach equilibrium. At that stage, it takes very little selling pressure or buying power to tip the balance and trigger a strong wave of self-feeding trend-following. This gives us Elliott's *thrust,* a phenomenon which is common to the resolution of all triangular formations.

When a triangle starts to develop, there is a tendency for supply and demand to be moving in the direction of temporary equilibrium, representing nothing more than a pause in the long-range trend of the price structure. A weighting of sixty percent has been given to the probability that once a triangle is resolved, the trend which preceded the triangle will continue. This would be the case when triangles develop as the Wave 4 of Wave A of Wave C of an A-B-C correction, or as corrective Wave IV of an upward movement. On the basis of deductive logic, we could therefore assume that on the other forty percent of occasions, triangles will develop as a Wave V extension, presaging a major reversal.

General Observations on Complex Corrections

Robert Balan, author of the *Elliott Wave Principle Applied to Foreign Exchange Markets,* observed that the market spends about seventy percent of the time in a corrective phase and thirty percent of the time moving in impulse waves of the same degree. This observation is not only true of foreign exchange markets, but all other mass markets as well. Balan's comments would appear to be thoroughly consistent with the tendency for equity markets to spend more time in a rallying phase. The major difference between the action of a bull market and a bear market is that during a bear market, the declines are quick and dirty, while the rising periods are slow and labored. When dealing with the corrective phase of a market, these tendencies should be kept at the forefront of your mental energies.

Since the market is likely to spend seventy percent of the time in a corrective phase, it is extremely important to place considerable emphasis on corrective formations and their possible, and probable, resolutions in space and time. You must use the appropriate tools with the same care and attention a surgeon would use in selecting the right scalpel. When dealing with corrective phases, you will be dealing primarily with relatively short time frames. You will therefore want to use arithmetic charts for the analysis of corrective sub-waves rather than logarithmic or semi-logarithmic charts. You must also conduct your analysis on cyclical charts rather than line-and-bar or point and figure charts. The latter will obscure a great deal of the price information that you're going to need. Line-and-bar charts and point and figure charts should only be consulted as a cross-reference for the larger formations.

It will prove helpful to maintain every-price-movement charts as well as hourly, daily, and weekly range charts, where possible. When dealing with the US equity market, it is possible to obtain every movement in the Dow Jones Industrial Averages. The object is to determine the precise number of waves at the early stages of a correction, in order to anticipate the type of correction you're going to run into. If Wave A of a correction has five sub-waves, you can then begin to plan for the 5-3-5 count of a zig-zag. If there is a sharp rally after the first sub-wave of Wave A, then you will want to prepare yourself for a flat or an irregular correction and the prospective movements such a correction would entail.

Highly sensitive charts will be a great aid in helping you count the wave formations. You're going to need all the help you can get. This is particularly true of small triangular formations and the mixed complex corrections

Figure 50
HOURLY RANGE   **DAILY RANGE**

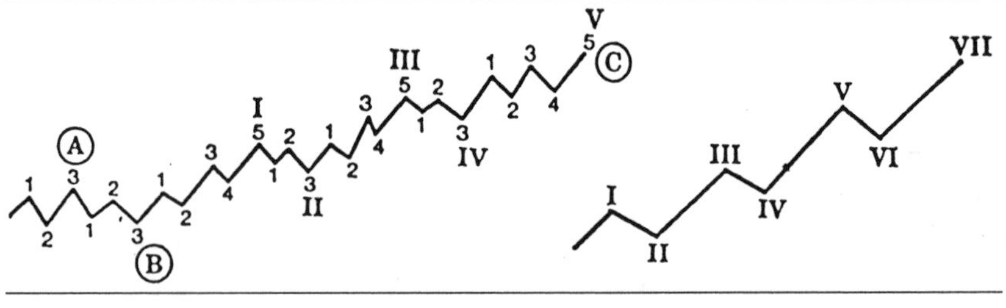

Figure 51

DOUBLE ZIG-ZAG	HOURLY RANGE	DAILY RANGE

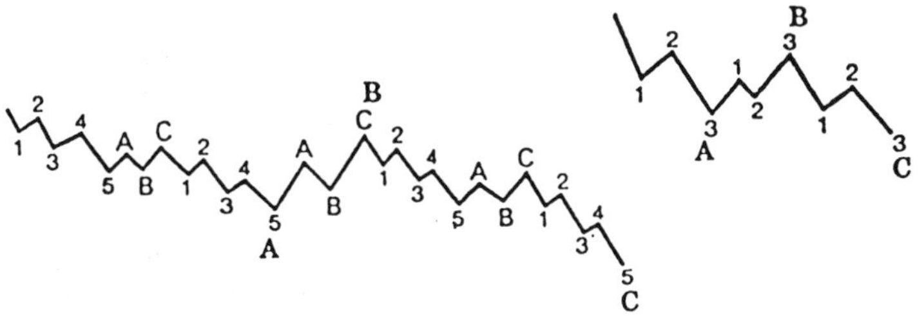

involving double threes, double fives, triple threes, and triple fives. I have produced an idealized version of an inverted irregular correction, which has taken on complex dimensions incorporating an elongated Wave C, as it might appear in the Wave 4 position of Wave A of a zig-zag. This type of Wave C in an inverted complex irregular correction is not an uncommon occurrence.

The chart on the left side of Figure 50 gives the hourly range of the price movement, while the chart on the right only shows the daily range of the price movement. In the daily range chart, the precise composition of the first upward wave cannot be seen. The analyst could very easily wrongly assume that the first wave of the formation was composed of five waves. The daily range of this inverted irregular correction would appear as being composed of seven waves and subject to incorrect interpretation and identification. When the waves are broken down into their hourly movements, it can be seen that the entire movement rests within the framework of a typical complex correction having three waves, each sub-wave having a 3-3-5 count.

Similar formations occur with the complex zig-zag patterns. A zig-zag may not have an elongated wave, as in the case of an irregular correction. But zig-zags do tend to enlarge and double, so to speak. Figure 51 shows an idealised version of how a double zig-zag might appear as the Wave II in a rising market on both the hourly chart and on a daily range chart.

In the hourly range chart, we see the perfect complex double zig-zag in every detail. The formation is unmistakable. There is very little room for a counting error when dealing with a structure that has been so perfectly formed. But, when we take this formation, eliminating the details as it would appear on a daily range chart, the formation becomes very difficult to analyze. The pattern certainly appears incomplete, having three waves down, three waves up, and three waves down. The analyst might be on the look-out for a triangle, since the wave count would only seem to be applicable to a triangle. This double zig-zag is illustrated as it would appear as a Wave II. Triangles are nearly always found in Wave IV positions. The use of every-price-movement charts or hourly charts can be of immeasurable assistance in the correct identification of formations, while acting to reduce the chances of counting errors, particularly when dealing with the complex corrective formations.

One of the most disconcerting aspects of dealing with corrective movements is that it is nearly impossible to determine whether or not a formation that begins as a simple correction is going to become enlarged and turn into a complex correction. While it is difficult to estimate the final size and shape of a correction until it is complete, the task is not impossible. There are certain guidelines that will help.

The general rules which apply to the Wave Principle, are always available to help you establish maximum and minimum price parameters, whether you're dealing with an impulse wave or a complex correction. In the majority of situations, corrective action, regardless of its nature, will be completed somewhere within the boundaries of these minimum and maximum price objectives. Of course, these minimum and maximum price objectives can, at times, be far apart.

The best way to attempt to anticipate the possible nature and extent of a corrective move, is by estimating the minimum and maximum price objectives of that move in accordance with its relationship to the existing cycle degree. For example, if the five-wave downward movement develops after the completion of a Wave III and that five-wave formation falls significantly short of what would be expected of Wave A of a Wave IV, you will then be on the alert that such a five-wave downward movement was likely to develop into a double zig-zag. If you review the principles of the wave relationship, you should be able to develop similar aids to help you establish minimum- and maximum-price parameters within the area of corrective action.

Once you have established a probable minimum- and maximum-price objective, you can then begin thinking about when the corrective formation is likely to end. The combination of minimum- and maximum-price parameters, along with the probable time frames, should give you a reasonable indication of what to expect, regardless of how complex the corrective wave becomes.

Time Frame Cross-referencing

The Golden Ratio is a superb aid in time frame cross-referencing. Waves relate to each other in accordance with the Golden Ratio in both time and amplitude. If you are analyzing a Wave II formation, which appears to give you the full 5-3-5 count, but the time the formation has taken to develop is appreciably less than would be called for if the sum of 61.8 percent were subtracted from the number of hours or days of Wave I, there is a strong likelihood that what you interpreted as a 5-3-5, A-B-C zig-zag will subsequently become a flat, irregular correction, mixed complex correction, double three, triple three, or even possibly a triangle.

The time factor should be given quite considerable weight when attempting to anticipate the possible duration of complex corrective wave formations. The analyst may find the development of a double three falls short of the normal time-frame expectation for that particular formation. He would then be alerted to expect the continuing development of the formation into a triple three. A calculation of the prospective time frame of a pattern in accordance with the 61.8-percent ratio formula will help you deal with the other complex wave formations.

The erratic behavior of corrective wave patterns means that it is vital for you to maintain and consult highly sensitive charts on at least an hourly basis, plotting each move of the market in order to dissect and measure the time frame of each and every wave. But, a word of warning: the minor movements should not be allowed to cloud your judgement of the overriding trend.

When involved with the minor movements of complex corrective waves, the newcomer to the Wave Principle will experience considerable difficulty in counting and classifying the waves. If you do get the feeling of being lost in the maze of minor movements, step back and consider the big picture in the waves of the higher degree in order to get your bearings once again. Ultimately, the patterns will be resolved, while the impulse waves will clarify the position. In application, your best results with the Wave Principle will come on your medium- and long-term trades, not as a short-term trader. You really want to use the Wave Principle for the purpose of exploiting the big swings in the market. The techniques I am advocating are intended to help you anticipate when the big swings are likely to occur.

Figure 52
BULL AND BEAR MARKET FORMATIONS

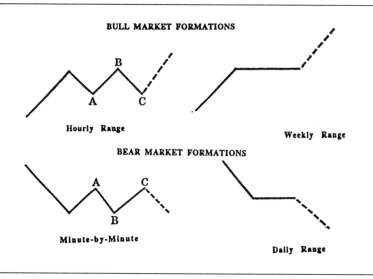

BULL MARKET FORMATIONS

Hourly Range

Weekly Range

BEAR MARKET FORMATIONS

Minute-by-Minute

Daily Range

Another Credo

It should be recognized that in real time, a corrective wave, whether it be complex or simple, need not necessarily take the form of a downswing in a rising market or an upswing in a falling market. The corrective wave in an exceptionally strong market can often take the form of a sideways movement or even a movement that is sloping gently upward.

A correction takes place when there is a strict departure from the momentum of the previous five-wave pattern. Should an irregular correction develop and this correction get plotted on a less-sensitive daily or weekly chart, the sub-waves will lose definition. The irregular correction will then assume the appearance of an upswing. A flat will give the appearance of merely a sideways movement on an insensitive chart.

Sideways movements and gently sloping upward movements in a rising market of exceptional strength, that show a strict departure from the movement of impulse Waves I and II and that also occur at the completion of a five-wave movement—or nine-wave movement, if the fifth wave becomes extended—always adhere to the same infrastructure. They have three important waves—excepting the triangle—and are all corrective by nature.

The following are idealized versions of the manner in which the elimination of detail seems to alter the characteristics of a pattern. Figure 52 is intended to illustrate the manner in which the flat, positioned as Wave IV of an uptrend, might appear on an hourly chart as opposed to its appearance on a weekly cyclical chart.

The second diagram shows the manner in which a flat, positioned as Wave IV of a Wave C, might appear on a minute-by-minute range chart compared with a daily cyclical chart.

The Predictive Value of Corrective Waves

Although you may have difficulty determining the nature of the corrective wave while it is in the course of formation, when it's complete, it's fairly simple to observe. When a corrective wave finally does run its course—in most cases, terminated with the end of the fifth wave of a Wave C (i.e., when correcting an uptrend, but inverted when correcting a downtrend), the analyst is offered many clues as to what will follow.

As I have already outlined, a corrective wave that takes the form of a triangle will produce a very strong thrust when the apex of the triangle is violated following the end of the fifth wave. In practice, the investor could then afford to take greater-than-average risk when considering exposure to a market upon the completion of a triangle. The same holds true after the completion of a sideways movement of double threes or triple threes, but to a slightly lesser degree.

The simple flat will also be the precursor to a stronger-than-usual movement after completion, but of a lesser degree than would be the case following completion of a complex flat, in the form of a double three or triple three. A flat, after completion, will always give the next impulse wave of a bull market or bear market added strength or weakness, respectively. Should the flat make its appearance as Wave II, the momentum of impulse Wave III will be as strong, if not stronger, than Wave I, while the amplitude will be considerably greater. If the flat appears as Wave IV, then the bull market is likely to come to an uproarious ending, stronger in momentum and amplitude than either impulse Wave I or impulse Wave III. A Wave V followed by a Wave IV flat is also likely to become extended if no previous extension had occurred in either impulse Wave I or impulse Wave III.

Yet, of all the corrections that presage violent market action, the irregular correction, when it appears following the end of a bull market, is the most menacing. The worst bear market of the last two-hundred years, including the Crash of 1929, occurred when Wave V of the bull market was followed by an irregular correction.

When acting as a Wave II or a Wave IV, the irregular correction is the harbinger of a market whose strength and dynamism will mount during the impulse wave that follows. Any move that follows an irregular correction should prove to be exceptionally strong and reliable in a rising market. The corrective action of the sub-waves will be shallower than normal. The impulse waves in the sub-wave category will be strong and protracted in time and size. Additional strength can be expected if the terminal juncture of Wave C of an irregular correction is at a level which is higher than the peak of sub-wave 4 of Wave A.

A zig-zag is the type of corrective action that will be witnessed most frequently. When a zig-zag occurs as a corrective wave, the momentum, duration, and amplitude of the impulse waves to follow are normal. When a zig-zag occurs in a Wave II, the momentum of Wave III will be slower than Wave I, although of greater duration and amplitude. When a zig-zag appears as Wave IV, Wave V will be of about equal dimensions to Wave I in time, momentum, and amplitude. If Wave IV takes the form of a zig-zag, Wave V extensions rarely occur.

The Final Word

The flexibility inherent in the Wave Principle allows for continuing development of corrective waves and impulse waves beyond restrictive definable norms, permitting the inclusion of various fundamental developments in real time. However, there is no disruption in the sequence or form, such as would happen in the outbreak of war, turning an inverse head-and-shoulders bottom into the continuation pattern in a bear market. On that occasion, the much-loved head-and-shoulders pattern would have given a false signal. This cannot happen with the Wave Principle. The Wave Principle does not give signals or perform in any manner resembling the unflagging vigor of a boy scout waving the semaphore flag.

We may watch a Wave II developing in a normal manner, then suddenly find that a news development triggers a rally. The Wave Principle will automatically adjust itself to accommodate this rally, altering the structural development of the general formation in accordance with the input of new fundamental data. A zig-zag might become a flat or mixed complex correction, for new data has been introduced that will strengthen the trend. We then simply adjust our forecast for what the probable minimum- and maximum-price parameters of the flat are likely to be. The wave will remain corrective. The input of new data will not change that.

In the same manner, we may be getting closer to what we have targeted as the probable end of a bear market at the fifth wave of a Wave C. Without warning, an upheaval might occur, like the military coup in the Soviet Union. The fifth wave of that Wave C is then likely to become extended. We then make a readjustment in our forecast in order to accommodate the exten- sion of Wave 5 of Wave C, while anticipating the double retracement and irregular correction that is likely to be a consequence of the extended Wave 5. The primary trend will remain unaltered. Here, there is a discipline which no other method of price fluctuation analysis has ever been able to provide. It is the lack of this type of discipline that has been ruinous for so many investors.

Elliott, in his development of the Wave Principle, despite its complexity, left no stone unturned. Analysts who have used the Wave Principle have commented, "Elliott begins where most other technical methods end." I feel this comment is well justified, if, for no other reason, than his strictly pragmatic approach to the behavior of markets, a phenomenon which very few who are involved fully comprehend.

In order to appreciate and exploit the movement of markets, the individual must first accept the limitations of available forecasting techniques and devise a method of working within these limitations, avoiding inflexible judgement and the search, or expectation, of absolutes at all cost. Elliott understood these, the truth of markets, to a far greater degree than any other analyst of his era. Such an understanding is fundamental to efficient security analysis and successful investment and is also endemic to the effective use of the Wave Principle.

This chapter concludes my treatment of the most mind-wrenching elements of the Wave Principle, Elliott's categorization and formulation of corrective waves. We have seen how the impulse waves are easily definable, while the corrective waves can take many shapes and forms. The most troublesome aspect of the corrective phase of a market movement is that there is no way of telling what type of correction will ultimately develop following the initial move. We can begin with a simple zig-zag, anticipating the bottom of the zig-zag in accordance with the tenets learned, then discover the zig-zag has become a double zig-zag or part of a mixed complex maze of uncertainty. We may find that replaying action develops after three waves of an anticipated five wave, Wave A of the zig-zag. We switch our stance and begin making adjustments for the possibility of a flat, only to find we end up with a triangle. In short, it is very difficult to determine exactly what kind of stock market movement you're dealing with until it's over, when the market is in a corrective phase, which is seventy percent of the time.

With the Wave Principle, we look through a glass darkly. I still think that's better than looking at your reflection in a carnival mirror.

13
The Ultimate in Finesse

> If the doors of perception were cleansed, everything would appear to man as it is, infinite.
>
> —William Blake

My grandfather spent most of his life rising through the ranks of a lumber company in the United States. He retired at the age of fifty-five and began to play the stock market with some of the wealth he had accumulated. He seemed to be fairly good at it, at a time when an investor could be good at it.

When I was a small boy, my grandfather would often take me to the brokerage office he dealt with. I was fascinated by the whole affair and deeply impressed with my grandfather's activities. From quite an early age, I had in the back of my mind that someday I would become a part of this industry.

In 1956, I felt my boyhood dream had come true. I joined a New York brokerage firm and was on my way to becoming a "customer's man," which is what the Street used to call stock peddlers in those days. I became quite streetwise fairly quickly. I became thoroughly disillusioned just as quickly.

I began my career on Wall Street harboring the wide-eyed, bushy-tailed notion that I was entering a profession where I would be encouraged to perform a useful and meaningful service for people by rendering constructive investment advice. I soon discovered there was no room on Wall Street for that kind of schoolboy idealism. Wall Street is a business. Like any other business, it has a product. My function was to sell the products in a manner which was in the best interest of the firm who employed me. The interests of the firm's clients was only an ancillary consideration, and not a particularly important one.

"If this is what stockbroking is all about, I would rather shovel shit for a living!" Those were my parting remarks when I resigned from the firm and from the field of stockbroking . . . forever! This is not intended as a condemnation of Wall Street in any way whatsoever, even though it may sound that way. The great fathers on Wall Street will seemingly offer clients the prayer rug at the temple of investment. Although the players end up with nothing more than the equivalent of a set of knee pads at the world's biggest floating crap game, the players like it that way. Wall Street plays the game for the players and the players play the players. If the players wanted it a different way, Wall Street would play it a different way!

After leaving the stockbrokerage business, I spent a considerable amount of time reflecting on the successes and failures of my clients. My tenure as a "customer's man" provided me with an education that I never could have acquired any other way. I had at least become an insider in a game where millions spent their lives and fortunes as outsiders.

I remember sitting in a plane one afternoon, half-drowsy, watching my customers parade through my mind as if I were counting sheep: the winners and the losers, the smart and the dumb, the jolly and the miserable. I tried to recall the reasons why some of them lost and some of them won. I finally concluded the most prominent reason was a non-reason: pure, blind chance.

For every reasonable client who diligently tried to protect himself against loss and came out a winner, there was another reasonable client who diligently tried to protect himself against loss...and lost, and there was always a complete fool who failed to protect himself against loss and didn't lose.

The securities industry will never admit this, and probably won't like to hear it said. But, it is a fact, and you can be certain of that: the securities industry is like a massive global conspiracy. Like any conspiracy, the stock market is not what it appears to be. If it portrayed itself as it actually were, no doubt it would cease to exist. As an investor, it is not possible to accumulate stock profits by participating in the illusion as it is perceived. For the average investor, investing is a game of chance, nothing more, nothing less.

Wall Street . . . The Other Las Vegas

Unfortunately, it's a game of chance that's rigged in favor of "the house" to an extent that would never, ever be permitted in Reno or Las

Vegas, where you always know the odds you're playing against. Yet, like other games of chance, whenever there's a winner, his exploits are hoisted to the top of the flagpole for all to see, giving the impression that anybody can do it; the ship you have been waiting to come in is just entering the harbor; the pot of gold at the end of the rainbow is sitting there for the asking. Wall Street knows that it is a very simple matter to convince investors of the things they want to be convinced of to start with . . . like bull markets rising in perpetuity.

If you ever saw the investment portfolio of your stockbroker or investment adviser, you would probably run a mile. I had a stockbroker in London who had a degree in economics and is a self-styled expert on the US bond market. He would issue the most elaborate pontifications on Federal Reserve policy, and, with utter confidence, issue proclamations about what the US bond market was going to do. Being a conservative chap, his own money was safely tucked away in deposit accounts. He refused to go anywhere near the stock market or the bond market.

By contrast, I was doing business with another stockbroker who, while commenting on a wide range of stocks, had placed his entire pension fund in the stock of a company who employed his wife. It is assumed that he assumed he was privy to inside information. The inside information proved to be no less valuable than the bulk of all so-called information. The company evaporated, along with the pension fund of the stockbroker.

When you go to a gambling casino, you do not expect the croupier to tell you what numbers are coming up next on the roulette wheel, or what the next card is going to be on the blackjack table. You expect the croupier to simply make certain your bet is properly placed and pay you efficiently, and in the correct amount, when you win. I use a stockbroker in the same manner as any gambler would use a croupier. I have never, at any time, acted upon the advice of a stockbroker.

The investment advisory business is even more fantasy-prone than the business of stockbroking. Aside from providing sales literature in the form of investment advice, a stockbroker does have an important administrative function, which is necessary for investors. With the investment advisory industry you have pure, undiluted fantasy. The modus operandi for the investment advisory industry is similar to that of the securities industry in general, where the objective is to convince people of what they want to be convinced of to start with. Children want to believe there is a Santa Claus, and adults want to believe there is someone with a touchstone somewhere that will unlock the secret of making vast and effortless profits in the speculative arena without risk.

On Gurus and Systems

From time to time, investors will be presented with a new guru, method, idea, technique, or system which will supposedly offer the answer to the age-old, insoluble problem of achieving consistent profits in markets. Many investors will embrace these gurus, methods, ideas, techniques, and systems with unquestioning fervor, such is their desire to believe.

Investors seem to prefer to turn a blind eye to the actual achievements of those who prefer these wondrous methods. I can assure you, the success record of advisers is nowhere near as awe-inspiring as their methods. In London, one of the better-known chart analysts, who made regular contributions to one of Britain's major financial publications, managed to acquire the sum of $600 by the age of sixty. After working with his charts for more than forty years and perfecting his "chart method," he decided to invest the sum of $600 in the market, using his method. In the UK stock market, it is possible to speculate with relatively small amounts of money. Normally, with prudence and caution, and a sane money management technique, the average speculator could last six months with $600 before being wiped out. The expert chart analyst, with his refined technique, was wiped out inside of three weeks. He never did manage to scrape together enough money to play the market again.

In recent years, a partnership was formed between two self-styled experts on the trading techniques of W.D. Gann. Each believed the other was the possessor of special secrets that W.D. Gann had discovered, that neither were yet to unearth. Each believed that once these secrets were revealed, they would both be the beneficiary of the complete method that had enabled W.D. Gann to accumulate the trading fortunes that were claimed. Each believed the other had already accumulated considerable wealth in markets, based on the amount of their individual knowledge of W.D. Gann's technique up until then.

The two individuals were very secretive about the amount of W.D. Gann's material that had been acquired. Yet, both agreed to form a partnership for the purpose of promoting Gann's work in the United States and throughout Europe, teaching the techniques of W.D. Gann in the hope that secrets would be revealed that neither had ever gained access to, up until that time.

They decided to charge several thousand dollars for this special course on the trading techniques of W.D. Gann, which was to be held in hotel rooms in various major cities. In the process of selling this teaching program, the claims that were being made by the two individuals regarding their individual prowess were extraordinary. They were so extraordinary they were sickening. One of the individuals was well known to me. I only managed a very brief acquaintance with the second. During that brief acquaintance, I offered a wager. "I would like you to call five market turns. You can choose any market you like. The turns you call can be any time you like within the next year. I will give you five-to-one odds. To win, you only have to be right on two out of the five turns you choose. You only lose if you are wrong on four out of the five."

That was the terms of my wager. What prompted me to make this wager was the insistence, by this individual, that he could call market turns with one-hundred-percent accuracy at all times, using the methods of W. D. Gann. I found that type of bravado an insult to my intelligence, particularly since I had the impression that this individual had as much market acumen as a mentally arrested dishwasher.

The big hitter was willing to bet the British pound equivalent of $200 at the time, leaving me on the hook for $1,000. I was not worried. Within three months, four out of the five turns he had called were wrong. By the end of the year, all five were wrong. The partnership was disbanded. The two partners began arguing with each other. Neither had ever learned the complete secrets of W.D. Gann. I have yet to see the slightest bit of evidence to indicate that either had ever made a profitable trade using W. D. Gann's techniques. If I said that both now lived a very modest existence, that would be an overstatement. I was never able to collect the wager that I had won. I don't think too much of people who refuse to honor their commitments.

The techniques of W.D. Gann have become quite fashionable over the past few years and have served as a very useful promotional cosmetic for a number of investment advisers. Whether or not any of those who are using the methods of W.D. Gann have access to all of the "secrets" is not known to me. The man who probably has all or most of these "secrets" is John Gann, the son of William D. Gann, a New York stockbroker. John Gann had absolutely no use at all for the techniques of his father. He spent his entire investment career as a fundamental analyst. When he was asked to accept the Technician of the Year award posthumously on behalf of his father, he never appeared at the award dinner held by the New York Society of Technical Analysts. I hope you get the message!

With more than a quarter of a century in the securities industry behind me, these little vignettes are only a small sample of the stories I could tell you about the smoke-and-mirror fantasies that are peculiar to this extremely bizarre form of endeavor. The game goes on. It never seems to change. The systems and methods come and go. The gurus rise and fall.

In days gone by, the Price Earnings Ratio was thought to offer the panacea for all analytical problems the final answer to the investment maidens' prayer. After that it was discounted cash flow, then multiple regression analysis, cycles, the Hatch system, the Coppock system, Random Walk, modern portfolio theory, the efficient market hypothesis, the buy-low–sell-high method, the buy-high–sell-higher method, the buy-and-hold strategy, the high-yield strategy, the hedge strategy, the beta factor, the alpha factor, serial correlation, the relative strength factor, some complementary to each other, others in direct opposition of each other, etc., etc., ad infinitum, ad nauseam.

The number of systems and methods that have gained popularity and then fallen from favor is only exceeded by the gurus whose popularity has meteored and plummeted in parallel. In the old days, the men who you would most like to be seated next to at the dinner table were market wizards, Roger Babson and Jesse Livermore. Livermore wiped himself out after falling from favor. He subsequently blew his brains out in the toilet of the Sherry Netherlands Hotel. His suicide note said he considered his life to have been a total failure.

In later years, Jim Dines and George Lindsay held the mantle of leading guru. Lindsay called a wrong turn on gold and jumped out of a window to his death. Jim Dines was more fortunate. He, too, called a wrong turn on gold, but got the message that things were not going well when his followers showed up at his Carnegie Hall investment lecture disguised as empty seats.

Joe Granville was top of the heap in analytical circles not too long ago. He then turned bearish when he should have been bullish. His piano-playing performances, during the course of his lecture, did little to assuage his followers who sold at the wrong time. Granville has since joined the ranks of fallen idols.

Another of the gurus to achieve superstar status in recent years was Robert Prechter. Prechter is of particular interest, since many believe him to be the messiah of the Wave Principle. Prechter, like the other burning lights that were candles which were blown out, called a turn incorrectly and was bearish when he should have been bullish. He has since been relegated to relative obscurity compared with his superstar era in 1984. At a 1985 investment conference in New Orleans, one of the analysts who was speaking addressed his audience and said, "You know what? Prechter keeps all his own money in mutual funds." The analyst then lunged into the crowd and retrieved Robert Prechter, who happened to be passing by at the time. Prechter, after cautiously mentioning that his Elliott Wave Theory advice was intended only for risk-taking professional traders, confirmed that what was said was true. I've had correspondence with Robert Prechter. I've never been too happy about the Robert Prechter version of the Elliott Wave Principle. Apparently, he's never really been all that enamored with it either.

Casting Pearls Before Swine

The systems and methods appear and disappear. The gurus rise like comets and burn themselves out like meteorites. With the arrival of every new guru and the appearance of each new method or system, investors in large numbers will accept the latest fad or fashion as finally offering the touchstone for unlimited wealth, only to find bitter disappointment before long. So each method and each guru in turn is discarded and new ones sought . . . and the new ones duly make their appearance . . . but the results are always the same.

Why? Well, it is certainly not because the methods and systems are without purpose and the gurus are inept bums. Jesse Livermore made fortunes in markets. Roger Babson, James Dines, George Lindsay, Joe Granville, and Robert Prechter are all skilled investment analysts with many long years of experience, whose talents are a credit to an industry where mediocrity and hypocrisy have become the norm. These men, each and every one of them, have cast pearls before swine and been criticized because the pearls did not turn out to be blue-white flawless diamonds. The methods and systems that have been introduced and developed are the product of the most brilliant minds in the world, which have been skillfully utilized by successful professional investors.

The basic problem for those outside the profession is one of totally unrealistic expectations that have been perpetuated by the securities industry at large. The dilemma arises as the consequence of a lack of understanding of the securities industry and markets on the part of the financially unwashed investor, who is the end user of the techniques that have been made available. Investors en masse have been programmed in such a manner that they believe there is no need to acknowledge, or accept, the same type of forecasting in markets that confront the medical profession when a physician attempts to make a prognosis. The industry encourages investors to continue their futile pursuit of a totally infallible approach to markets that will guarantee profits. And there remain those handful of unscrupulous individuals, always ready, willing, and able to imply such guarantees are available . . . at a price, with a disclaimer. As long as markets exist, such an approach will never exist. This is a reality of the marketplace that must be accepted.

What does all of this have to do with the Wave Principle? you might ask. Knowing what you don't know; recognizing how the world works; acknowledging the vested-interest objectives of most members of the securities industry; and gaining an awareness of the behavior of markets, along with the factors that influence markets over very short and very long periods, is quintessential for the proper application of the Wave Principle.

Twenty-five years ago, during 1966, after mustering all of the self-righteous indignation I could possibly muster, I was determined to set the record straight and tell it like it is. I then began formulating the editorial policy for an investment publication. The objective of my publication, *Investors Bulletin,* was to make certain, at all times, that focus was directed toward the real world of investment, behind the veil of vested-interest, conceptually distorting disinformation. In so doing, I naturally assumed I would end up with a very unique publication, divorced from the competition. I never expected to win any popularity contests, but that was never my goal, nor an aspiration I had ever found necessary.

Since I began publishing *Investors Bulletin* in 1967, I have pursued an editorial policy that has been designed to concentrate on the psychological and fundamental essentials, which I considered mandatory for dealing in markets rather than focusing on tips, recommendations, and prediction. I have always subscribed to the philosophy, "If you give a man a fish, you feed him for a day. If you teach him how to fish, you feed him for a lifetime." I rarely use the Wave Principle for the purpose of making predictions in my publications. You may have noted the conspicuous omission in this book of applications of the Wave Principle based on my personal interpretations. This has been a deliberate policy on my part.

Over the years, I have continued to study the Wave Principle and apply its tenets to my market activities. I continue to assert that the Wave Principle offers solutions and answers to investment problems that reach beyond any other technical method ever developed. At times, my studies have taken me down blind alleys. On other occasions I have been rewarded with startling new revelations. During the thirty-five years I have worked with the Wave Principle, I have abandoned a number of aids and developed new ones, in order to reach the ultimate finesse in its application.

Turning to the conceptual once again, if you want to get the right answers, you have to ask the right questions. There are a few more peripheral elements of the Wave Principle that can give you some very useful answers . . . if you ask the right questions.

Elliott's Theory of Alternation

There is no doubt that the Wave Principle will often lead you into a maze of confusion, particularly when you begin analyzing the infrastructure of corrective waves. When this occurs, you must stand back and look at the big picture. Of all of the aids I have recommended, I consider this to be the most useful.

In spite of the array of formations and variations of corrective-wave and impulse-wave movements that I have outlined, in a broad sense, you have only one in eight possibilities. I can narrow that down even further. Identification of the current position in an uptrend offers you only one of four possibilities. Identification of your position in the impulse waves of a downtrend—which is essentially corrective—offers you only one in four possibilities.

I have now taken you from the simplistic to the complex and back to the simplistic once again. Figure 53 will show you what I mean.

A breakdown of the impulse waves and corrective waves in the illustrations would be classified as follows, regarding the two different trends. Figure 53 is for illustrative purposes only. For the sake of simplicity, I have not broken the zig-zags down into subwaves.

Figure 53
VARIATIONS IN IMPULSE-WAVE CHARACTERISTICS
UPTREND   **DOWNTREND**

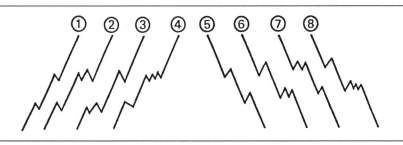

Uptrend

1. This is a typical five-wave pattern. Corrective waves II and IV are of the zig-zag variety.

2. This is a typical unextended five-wave pattern. Wave II is a zig-zag. Wave IV is an irregular correction.

3. This is also a typical five-wave pattern. Neither is Wave V is extended, nor are the other two impulse waves. Wave II is a flat. Wave IV is a zig-zag.

4. In this normal five-wave pattern, Wave II is a zig-zag and Wave IV is a triangle.

While there are four basic possibilities in the formation of an uptrend, from what we have learned so far, these are subject to probabilistic ranking. The most likely of the four possibilities would be the formation where Wave II is a zig-zag and Wave IV is a flat. Zig-zags are common to Wave II formations and triangles common to Wave IV formations. The second most likely would be the formation where Wave II is a zig-zag and Wave IV an irregular correction. Irregular corrections are also common to Wave IV patterns, although sometimes appearing in a Wave II. Without a knowledge of Elliott's Theory of Alternation, you may feel that the least likely formation to appear would be one where Wave II is a flat and Wave IV is a zig-zag. Actually, this is not the case. Elliott's Theory of Alternation indicates that a formation where Wave II and Wave IV are both zig-zags is a far less likely occurrence than a formation where Wave II is a flat and Wave IV is a zig-zag, even though zig-zags are common to Wave II formations and flats common to Wave IV formations.

Downtrend

1. In this normal, unextended five-wave pattern, Wave II is an inverted zig-zag and Wave IV is also an inverted zig-zag.

2. Once more, we find a normal five-wave pattern. Wave II is an inverted zig-zag. Wave IV is an inverted irregular correction.

3. This normal five-wave corrective pattern, where none of the impulse waves have been extended, shows corrective Wave II as an inverted flat and corrective Wave IV as an inverted zig-zag.

4. Finally, we have a normal five-wave pattern, where Wave II is an inverted zig-zag and Wave IV is a triangle.

The same probabilistic ranking can be applied to the corrective waves of the impulse waves of a downtrend, as has been applied to those in an uptrend. With the exception of those formations where both corrective waves are zig-zags—and therefore low probability formations—we find the nature of corrective waves actually alternating. Elliott's Theory of Alternation is yet a further refinement of the Wave Principle. Here we have another aid toward wave categorization, designed to help you anticipate the nature of prospective corrective action and the likely behavior of the price movement during the coming phase of the cycle.

Elliott's Theory of Alternation has a number of basic applications, the most obvious being the manner in which five-wave formations alternate with three-wave formations when a bear market follows a bull market and corrective action follows impulse wave action. According to R.N. Elliott, form, balance, symmetry, and alternation are a "law of nature" and are inviolate. Leaves on the branches of trees appear first on one side of the main stem and then on the opposite side, alternating their position. Alternation occurs in galaxies, flowers, sea shells, and bumps in pineapples, and was fundamental to Niels Bohr's discovery of the process of cognition. Alternation, in the geo-political science, was an inherent feature of Oswald Spengler's findings in *Decline of the West*. Kepler tried to describe the distances between two planets as a system in which bodies are alternately inscribed and circumscribed in spheres. There is an endless list of examples that can be offered by nature and the sciences which support the principle of alternation. But, the object of this exercise is the pattern of alternation as it is reflected in human activity. With human activity, we have continuous alternation with little alteration.

Autumn follows summer, night follows day, famine follows feast, bear markets follow bull markets, and yang follows yin. Bull markets and bear markets alternate. A bull market is composed of five waves and a bear market of three waves. Five and three alternate—this same rule governs all the degrees, from the most minute to the most grandiose over time.

Within the five-wave upward movement, Waves I, III, and V are in an upward direction, and waves II and IV are in a downward direction. Within three waves of a downward movement, the first wave is downward, the second wave is upward, and the third wave is downward. The first wave of a downward movement will have Waves 1, 3, and 5 travelling in a downward direction, while Waves 2 and 4 travel in an upward direction. Up alternates with down. Odd numbers alternate with even numbers.

All of this may seem perfectly obvious. What may not be quite so obvious are the somewhat subtle implications of Elliott's Theory of Alternation, as applied to the movement of corrective waves in the manner he set down in *Nature's Law,* viz: "Waves 2 and 4 are corrective. These two waves alternate in pattern. If Wave 2 is a 'simple' wave, Wave 4 will be complex, or vice versa. A 'simple correction' in the smaller degree is often composed of merely one downswing. If the 2-Wave gives this appearance, the 4-Wave will involve at least three waves downward or sideways."

In the larger degree, such as complete bull and bear markets of a cycle degree, the corrective waves will naturally be correspondingly larger. Preparation for the final downswing will often be an extremely tedious affair. Initially, one will find a downward movement coming from the completed five-wave bull market. This will comprise the first wave of Wave A, which will normally be anticipated as a subsequent A-B-C correction. When broken down, if this Wave A turns out to be a zig-zag, then Wave B will turn out to be a flat inverted. If Wave A is a flat, Wave B is likely to be an inverted zig-zag. In any event, regardless of the structure of Waves A and B, Wave C will comprise five waves.

Thus, in the same manner as Waves 2 and 4 alternate, Waves A and B in corrective waves of larger formations also alternate. Waves 2 and 4 will take turns in complexity, as will Waves A and B.

Irregular corrections also alternate. As explained in Chapter Nine, an irregular correction takes place when Wave B reaches a higher level than the previous peak of the five-wave pattern. Major bull market peaks alternate between orthodox tops and irregular tops, Elliott cites the peak of the 1916 bull market in the United States as having an irregular top. In 1919, the top was regular. In 1929, the top was irregular. In 1937, the top was regular again. Each time the Dow Jones Industrial Averages rose to a new peak, the type of peak alternated with the previous peak.

Alternation is also expected to take place in the length of waves, and, in particular, the extent of corrective action. Logically, corrective Wave 2 should be shorter in time and/or amplitude than corrective Wave 4. If we refer to the January 1975–June 1976 bull market movement, which produced four waves, this phenomenon is clearly demonstrable. Corrective Wave 2 lasted approximately nine weeks, between June and August of 1975, resulting in a zig-zag, which took twenty-eight percent from the value of the FT30 between the June peak and the August trough. The pattern was a perfect zig-zag having five downwaves, three upwaves, and five down-waves.

One would have thus anticipated a much more complex Wave 4, probably extended in direction, but shallower in amplitude. What occurred was a mixed complex triple three with an elongated Wave C—in the broad category—a flat. It ran the full extent of the maximum expectancy for Wave 4, terminating at precisely 61.8 percent of the duration of the preceding Wave 3. It encompassed its full amplitudinal dimensions, terminating at the top of Wave I of the move. However, the amplitude was only fifteen percent, as compared with twenty-eight percent in the case of Wave 2. Elliott's Theory of Alternation developed with clockwork precision in that particular instance . . . and many others.

Elliott's Theory of Alternation goes a long way in helping one anticipate the likely formation of subsequent corrective waves, the most elusive aspect of the Wave Principle. Given a simple corrective Wave 2, we are then on the alert for a troublesome Wave 4. Given a Wave 2 which falls short of the maximum time span, we are then placed on the alert that Wave 4 is likely to run its full time span.

Should an irregular correction develop in a Wave 2, Wave 4 will have a normal top. Bull market peaks and bear market troughs will thus alternate in the development of orthodox or irregular tops and bottoms.

Hamilton Bolton adds a succinct touch to Elliott's Theory of Alternation: "The writer is NOT convinced that alternation is INEVITABLE in types of waves in larger formations, but there are frequent enough cases of alternation to suggest that one should look for it, rather than the contrary."

I would like to add that the lack of inevitability in most of Elliott's tenets, provides the Wave Principle with the type of flexibility which is necessary for dealing with capital market movements. Seeking absolute inevitability in any form of analytical principle is bound to lead to totally unsatisfactory results. As the casino operator asked the gambler who insisted he had found a system for beating the roulette wheel, "Your system may be great, but can you teach it to the roulette wheel?"

Avoiding Counting Errors

Elliott seemed at all times to be acutely aware of the problems Wave Principle users may have, if a counting error occurs. He repeatedly stressed the rules governing the behavior of the different waves in order that counting errors can be avoided, to the point of nearly becoming dogmatic.

In *Nature's Law,* Elliott proposes the hypothesis: "The three impulse waves, 1, 3 and 5 are seldom of the same length. One of the three is usually considerably longer than either of the other two. It is important to note that Wave 3 is never shorter than both Wave I and Wave 5. For example, when Wave 3 is shorter than either Wave 1 or Wave 5, as in the graph below, the correct method of counting is as follows:"

While Elliott states that Wave 3 can never be shorter than both waves 1 and 5, he goes on to say that if Wave 3 appears to be shorter than either Wave 1 or 5, it is necessary to re-classify the count. The underdeveloped Wave 3 actually extends the corrective Wave 2. Whereas, it may have originally appeared that Wave 2 was a complete correction in itself, Wave 3, which is shorter than both Wave 1 and Wave 5 is actually Wave B of an irregular correction. What was originally thought to be Wave 4 becomes Wave C. Instead of completing the pattern with a five-wave count, Wave 5 becomes Wave 3. Abbreviated Wave 3 actually borrows two waves from the succeeding movement.

In Figure 54, another fundamental infraction has occurred, which confirms that the original count was erroneous. That is, Wave 4 overlaps Wave 1. The fact that a Wave 4 should never overlap the peak of Wave 1 is one of the prime Elliott tenets. Both in *Nature's Law, The Wave Principle,* and the works of others who have used and observed the Wave Principle, no deviations or exceptions are permitted with regard to the rule of impulse wave relationship; i.e., waves 1 and 5 should be shorter than Wave 3. Wave 3 can, at times, be shorter than waves 1 or 5, but never shorter than both. The maximum extent of Wave 4 will be to the peak of the

Figure 54

INCORRECT COUNT **CORRECT WAVE COUNT** **CORRECT COUNT**

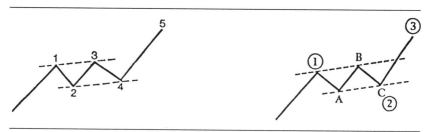

preceding Wave 1. With all of Elliott's exceptions, additions, refinements, etc., these simple basic impulse wave relationships remain constant.

Thus, should Wave 4 dip below the peak of Wave 1, one knows that an error in counting has taken place, and therefore a complete recount is necessary. The same would hold true if we find a pattern of development where Wave 3 is shorter than both Wave 1 and Wave 5.

A particularly grey area of Elliott's work, when dealing with counting errors, appears to be the relationship between the time frame of corrective waves and its relationship to impulse waves within the cycle of the same degree. Of course, the size of a corrective wave must, by its very nature, be smaller than that of an impulse wave in terms of amplitude. Normally, one would expect a corrective wave to be shorter in time and amplitude than the impulse wave it is correcting. In most of Elliott's idealized examples that show the relationships of the waves, both in *Nature's Law* and *The Wave Principle*—and in my idealized versions—the shape of corrective waves would seem to confirm the view that most corrective waves are smaller in size and shorter in time than the impulse waves they act to correct.

This is highly misleading. When Elliott referred to the size of a corrective wave in relation to an impulse wave, this reference was solely with regard to amplitude and not time. When Elliott goes on to apply his principles to actual stock market behavior, there are several examples where the time frame of corrective waves seem to span periods which extend beyond what one would consider to be a normal relationship with the preceding impulse wave.

While the duration of corrective Wave II and corrective Wave IV may not normally be longer than impulse waves I, III, and V, extended time frames in the corrective waves do occur with considerable frequency. Acting upon the assumption that a corrective wave will be completed within a time frame which is shorter than the impulse wave it is completing will invariably lead to dangerous counting errors.

There is a tendency for waves that are of the zig-zag variety to be shorter in both duration and amplitude, compared with the impulse waves they are correcting. In the case of flats, triangles, and irregular corrections, simple, complex, and inverted, it will be found that the duration of these waves often exceeds the duration of the impulse waves that are being corrected. This is particularly true in the case of an irregular correction.

Where Elliott has used the appearance of an irregular correction to demonstrate a common counting error in his illustrations, it is clear that the inference is one of an amplitudinal relationship. While Elliott makes no reference to time-frame relationships, in the previous illustration taken from Elliott's work, if a time scale were placed underneath his examples, the fact that Wave 2 appears to take two waves from the succeeding impulse wave means that the actual time span of the irregular correction extends well beyond the time span of Wave 1. It can readily be seen that the corrective Wave 2, when involving an irregular correction, will be far longer in duration than Wave 1, which is the impulse wave being corrected.

Never be misled by the time span of a corrective wave. Elliott allows very little flexibility when it comes to the relative size of waves within the broad context of the Wave Principle. Yet, there is considerable latitude when it comes to anticipating the duration of a wave.

If one refers to Elliott's classification of the super cycle in the United States from 1857 to 1928 in Part IV of the Appendix, it becomes clear that in the Wave Principle, the size of the waves takes precedence over time in Elliott's illustrations.

Super Cycle Classification, 1857–1928

Cycle Wave I	1857–1864	(7 years)
Cycle Wave II	1864–1877	(13 years)
Cycle Wave III	1877–1881	(4 years)
Cycle Wave IV	1881–1896	(15 years)
Cycle Wave V	1896–1928	(32 years)

In Elliott's own analysis of this super cycle wave, it can be seen quite clearly that both corrective waves exceeded the preceding impulse waves by vast time spans, and Wave III is shorter in time than both Waves I and V. However, Wave III was smaller in amplitude than Wave V, but greater in amplitude than Wave I on the logarithmic scale. Obviously, considerable latitude is allowable for time-frame relationships between corrective waves and the impulse waves they are correcting. There is no allowable deviation from size relationships.

This point is extremely important, for the most serious errors in counting are likely to occur when dealing with irregular corrections. Unless one pays strict attention to the size of the Wave 3, Wave B of an irregular correction could be interpreted as Wave 3. The actual Wave 3 would become a Wave 5. We would be anticipating a full A-B-C bear market, if an irregular correction was counted incorrectly. All we would normally expect would be the subsequent development of Wave 4 and Wave 5 when counting correctly.

Failures

Failures are not what they sound like. When a failure occurs, this does not mean an error has arisen in the method, or that a mistake has been made. A *failure* occurs when an impulse wave weakens and falls short of its normal objective.

In Figure 55, it would appear that the fifth wave has failed to develop and a bull market took place, made up of three upward waves followed by five waves downward. There are two things wrong with that interpretation. First, a bull market would never be composed of three waves—it is always five; and second, a corrective bear market wave would comprise three waves rather than five. What has actually occurred has been a failure in the fifth wave, the subsequent decline stealing two waves from the advance. The correct count is shown on the diagram below. A breakdown of the pattern to the next-lower degree will help you resolve the problem of whether Wave B was a Wave 5 or not.

Figure 55
FAILURES

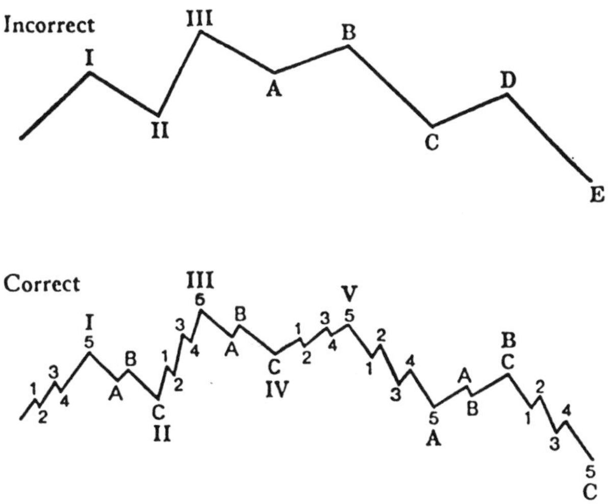

Elliott's discussion of failures was limited to only a small mention in the 1938 edition of *The Wave Principle*. In *Nature's Law,* published in 1946, no mention at all was made of this phenomenon. A.J. Frost, in the 1967 *Supplement to the Bank Credit Analyst,* does take the matter of failures a bit further.

Although Elliott's claim was that failures are rare, Frost states that failures are not uncommon and gives warning to the analyst of impending strength or weakness, depending on whether the failure occurs in a bull or bear cycle. According to Frost, a failure occurs when the fifth wave in a bull cycle fails to penetrate the top of the third wave in the cycle. In a bear cycle, the failure occurs when the fifth wave of Wave C fails to penetrate the low of Wave 3 in Wave C. Empirical evidence supports these ideas.

Failures have often been ignored by students of the Wave Principle. This was probably due to Elliott's brief coverage of the matter and its complete omission from *Nature's Law.*

Hamilton Bolton, writing extensively on the Wave Principle for more than fifteen years, also neglected the aspect of failures. Nevertheless, recognition of the failure is vital, for the Wave Principle can become a muddle unless one is constantly on the look-out for the possibility of a failure developing in the fifth wave of a movement. In the same manner as erroneous counting can drastically change the possibilities of future wave progressions, so, too, can the non-recognition of a failure. Left undetected, a fifth-wave failure will turn a five-wave count into a three-wave count. This would mean Wave 4 of the corrective wave looks like Wave 2 of the next-higher degree. This would compound itself until the count becomes baffling and totally undecipherable. In view of its readily recognizable appearance, the failure should rank among the more important tenets of Elliott's Wave Principle.

Thrusts

Thrusts occur predominantly after the completion of a triangle or horizontal movement. All during the movement, a contraction in volume takes place, reflecting investor indecision and reluctance. Suddenly, some investors tip the balance, and all others follow the lead in a powerful move which is called a *thrust*. In essence, a thrust is a dynamic move which follows a period of hesitation or consolidation, which, in technical terms, is likely to be one of accumulation preceding a mark-up phase. The very nature of a thrust is one of greater-than-ordinary power; therefore, corrections within the thrust are likely to be of sub-normal duration and size. Since a thrust follows corrective action, it is obvious that thrusts only occur as impulse waves, primarily impulse Wave 5, since the triangle or horizontal is most likely to be Wave 4.

Thrusts can also occur following an irregular correction, where Wave C produces an upward zig-zag. A thrust can also follow a flat. Elliott claimed a thrust would follow naturally from a triangle, and that triangles and flats had similar technical implications with regard to the subsequent strength of succeeding impulse waves. The reasoning is fairly clear. Both of the aforementioned patterns are likely to be of sub-normal fullness, indicative of a market which is gathering strength. Should corrective action only be shallow in either Wave 2 or Wave 4, encompassing only sub-normal corrective action, it stands to reason that a warning of strong ensuing action is being flashed. Corrective action will take the form of a normal zig-zag at least fifty percent of the time, within the context of the varying cycle degrees. The rest of the corrective action will show a variety of flats, triangles, horizontals, irregular corrections, and upward zig-zags. In the case of the irregular correction and the upward zig-zag, the signal that a thrust is likely to follow will be an abbreviated Wave C. Wave C will end above the trough of Wave A (assuming an upward impulse set of waves), and the bigger the gap, the greater the power of the ensuing thrust. All bets would be off for the thrust if Wave C fell below the trough of Wave A in either case.

The Use of Volume

It would seem from Elliott's writings that his inclusion of volume as applicable to the Wave Principle was progressive and had never been fully developed. Elliott hardly mentioned volume characteristics in his early writing. It wasn't until he began publishing his *Interpretative Letters* that volume was mentioned with any frequency. Even then, there is little indication that Elliott believed volume trends would develop along the same lines as alternating corrective and impulse waves.

While Elliott applied the Wave Principle to a large number of time series, he never seemed to apply the Wave Principle to the movement of volume. I can also assume that such an application was deemed to reflect double-counting in the mind of Elliott in terms of the manner in which volume relationships could be synchronized with wave relationships.

Elliott's reference to volume would seem to be wholly in an ancillary context. Elliott makes reference to the pattern of trading volume in the discussion of corrective waves, particularly triangles, flats, and irregular corrections, in both their simple and complex form, normal and inverted. As a general rule, Elliott claimed the level of volume had a tendency to gradually diminish during the life of a corrective phase. Elliott's observation was that when the level of volume reached a comparatively low level within a corrective phase, that particular corrective phase was coming to an end.

This tendency for volume levels to diminish during the life of a corrective phase has considerable interpretative value. An awareness of this phenomenon can be extremely helpful when dealing with irregular corrections and extensions. By closely monitoring the movement of volume, the analyst can anticipate the prospective development of an extended wave before it becomes fully extended. This is especially important when dealing with an extended Wave V.

As mentioned previously, an extended fifth wave will take on four additional waves, producing a count of nine waves. When seven of the nine waves are completed, the pattern becomes highly vulnerable to a counting error. At the completion of the seventh wave, it becomes difficult to determine with precision whether or not the two additional waves following the five-wave count are actually two waves of what will be a four-wave extension, or Waves A and B of an irregular correction.

Figure 56 shows the two possible interpretations of the same formation. When the market turns downward after the completion of seven waves, that could mean a sharp fall in the form of a large Wave C, or a minor decline followed by a new bull market high.

Figure 56
IRREGULAR CORRECTION   **WAVE FOUR EXTENSION**

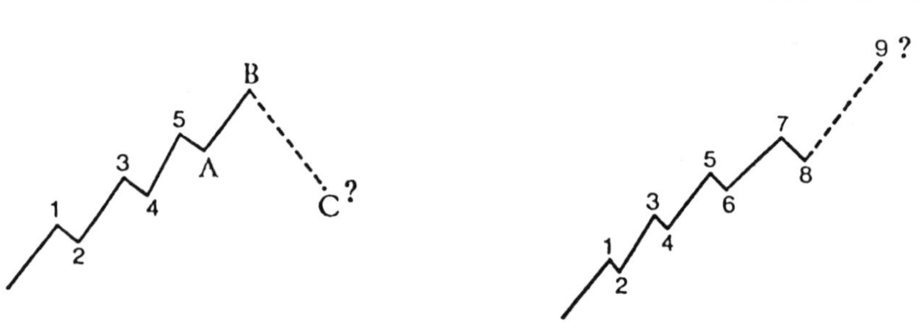

While a breakdown of the waves to a smaller degree can help establish the position and help to differentiate the subsequent possibilities, quite often, volume characteristics will act as an excellent arbiter. If the level of volume at the end of the seventh wave was lower than at the end of the fifth wave, it then becomes likely that an irregular correction is in the course of development and that the seventh wave is Wave B, to be followed by Wave C, which could take the market all the way back to the peak of Wave 1.

During the course of an extended fifth wave that develops four more waves, volume at the peak of the seventh wave is likely to be even higher than at the peak of Wave 5. In a bull market, the peak level of volume is likely to be reached at the end of the ninth wave. In the preceding illustration, if the level of volume on the seventh wave exceeds that of the fifth wave, the maximum extent of any correction would be back to the peak of the first of the next-lower degree of Wave 7, which would be at a level which is higher than the peak of Wave 5. The minor correction would then be followed by another new high for the market and for volume levels. It can readily be seen that a monitoring of volume levels can be an invaluable guide in these circumstances.

According to Elliott, there is a relatively consistent relationship between the pattern of volume, the characteristics of the impulse waves, and corrective waves of an uptrend. Any deviation from these characteristics should be regarded with suspicion.

During the course of a major five-wave uptrend, volume will tend to gradually increase during the course of the first wave of the cycle, contract during the second wave of the cycle, expand during the third wave of the cycle, contract again during the fourth wave, and be reaching new cycle highs during the fifth and final wave. Further highs will be recorded if the fifth wave becomes extended.

As the five-wave cycle progresses, the volume recorded during Wave 2 should be far less than that which was seen during Wave 1. The volume levels recorded during Wave 3 should be greater than those of Wave 1. Volume levels during Wave 4 should be less than those recorded during Wave 3, but greater than that of Wave 2. The volume of Wave 5 should be the highest of the cycle, although not significantly greater than that of Wave 3. There have been occasions, although rare, when the volume during Wave 5 has been greater than Wave 3. Figure 57 shows the typical relationship between the trend volume and a five-wave upward trend.

The illustration demonstrates the manner in which volume levels should be expected to continue to advance during Waves 1 and 3, but become

Figure 57

THE PATTERN OF VOLUME IN A BULL MARKET

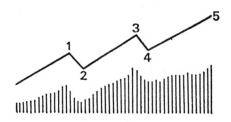

somewhat labored during the course of Wave 5. Also note that although the level of volume should contract during Wave 4 of the sequence, even at the terminal point of Wave 4, volume is still comparatively high.

In general, during the course of an ongoing bull market, volume and price should agree in their general direction. When the market rises, the level of volume should also rise. When the market falls, the level of volume should contract. As long as the level of volume continues to expand, and there is no divergence between price and volume, one can assume a further advance in the price action is likely.

When the fifth and final wave is reached, volume divergences will begin to appear. If the level of volume continues to rise while the price action suddenly turns lethargic, you are being warned that an important reversal is in the offing. When the price action starts to advance, but volume does not, the upward move is nearing an end.

Volume characteristics during a bear market differ markedly with the relationship between price and volume during a bull market. During a bear market, price and volume will move in opposite directions. When the market rises during the temporary rallying phase in a bear market, volume will tend to contract. During the declining phases, volume will tend to expand.

During the course of the bear market, although volume will continue to expand as the market falls and contract as the market rises, in general, the level of volume will diminish. Heavy volume will characterize Wave 1 of Wave A of the bear market. The volume recorded during Wave 5 of Wave A is likely to be far less than that of Wave 1. The level of volume during Wave B of the bear market will be less than was recorded during Wave A. Wave 1 of Wave C will show volume at higher levels than that of Wave B, but at levels much lower than either Wave 1 or Wave 5 of Wave A.

Additional Observations on Volume

A bull market will often end with a massive buying stampede in what has been described as a bullish climax, involving orgasmic behavior throughout the length and breadth of the investment community. Screams of "Buy! Buy! Buy!", "Give it to me! Give it to me! Give it to me!", "I want it! I want it! I want it!", can be heard in a chorus of exquisite delight, as investors en masse come to the conclusion that the stock market will rise in perpetuity.

While these orgasmic rampages at the end of a bull market are not as common as the investment community has been led to believe, there is also a popular fallacy suggesting bear markets end with the shattering threat of financial castration and certain emasculation, where all investors withdraw at the same time with the same fervor as on entry. This is not really so. The fallacy probably developed from observations of abnormally vicious C Waves, that are characteristic of bear markets that follow an irregular correction. The Wave C that followed the Crash of 1929 was probably the most devastating on record. The Wave C following the irregular correction of 1972 in London, spanning two-and-one-half years, was another especially savage affair.

To suggest that a selling climax has been under way for nearly three years in these markets, from 1929 to 1932 and from 1972 to 1974, respectively would not be a particularly useful or helpful analysis. The bottom of Wave C in both cases did end in a panic accompanied by an earth-shattering dumping of stocks. That happened long before those bear markets came to an end. At the bottom of the bear market in the United States in 1932, and at the bottom of the bear market in the United Kingdom during 1975, there was only a whisper when the last private investor who intended to sell sold the last share he had to sell. The level of volume was at rock bottom, along with the market.

Elliott adds a note of caution about markets, when the level of volume is extremely low: ". . . when markets are abnormally 'thin,' the usual volume signals are sometimes deceptive."

In my own experience, I have made certain observations in the area of volume characteristics, which can be usefully applied in a supplemental manner to the Wave Principle as a confirmatory aid. The Wave Principle in itself is intended to be a graphic illustration of human behavior, attempting to isolate the non-random elements of human behavior. There can be no denying that the number of stocks or commodity contracts purchased by individuals, as a group, at any given time, is an element of human behavior that will have non-random characteristics.

At any given point in time, markets are either under distribution or accumulation, which involves non-random trend persistency of a stochastic nature. Shifts in supply or demand characteristics, as expressed by changes in volume trends, can often give warnings of current or approaching trend reversals.

A rise in volume levels is a normal expectation following a break above the upper parameters of a triangle or a flat; following a period of low activity; when a market breaks above an historic high; or when corrective action has been completed or is drawing toward completion. Heavy volume under any other conditions is likely to indicate a reversal of the prevailing trend.

When volume expands as the price action declines, this is characteristic of a liquidating market. The downtrend is likely to continue until there is a reversal in the volume relationship. An approaching end to the downtrend is indicated when the level of volume begins to contract as the market falls and expands on rallying action.

An abnormal increase in volume after a trend has been in progress for some time indicates the end, or the approaching end, of that particular impulse wave, or corrective phase.

When the price action becomes labored after a sharp rally, while volume contracts significantly, a trend reversal is indicated.

When volume begins to contract during secondary rallying action, a continuation of the downtrend is indicated.

A sharp one-day rally on low volume indicates short covering. The price levels achieved are unlikely to be maintained.

Following a day when there is exceptionally high volume, be on the alert for the possibility that either a buying climax or a selling climax has occurred. If volume refuses to expand within three days of the suspected climax, the climax will have been confirmed.

If the general volume trend has been in the direction of the price trend, but then begins to reverse, a downtrend is indicated. If the general volume trend has been in the opposite direction of the price trend, but gradually begins to move with the price trend, an uptrend is indicated.

The treatment of volume is fairly simple and logical. Increased volume means increased activity, decreased volume means a decrease in activity. Increased volume in an uptrend means buying with greater vigor. Increased volume in a downtrend reflects selling with greater vigor. There is an element of non-randomness in volume trends, which has anticipatory value and cannot be ignored.

Analyzing volume trends at historic highs can be extremely useful. Areas around important historic highs can lead to trend reversals more often than not. If a break through an old peak occurs in a slow and deliberate fashion, accompanied by gently rising volume, the chances are that a series of new all-time highs will follow that could carry on for a considerable period in time and space.

A move through an historic peak is unlikely to be sustained if volume is exceptionally heavy while the price movement is narrow. Similarly, a sharp move through an historic high is unlikely to be sustained if volume levels on the day of the move are low.

The breaking of the apex of a triangle on heavy volume is significant, indicating the corrective pattern has been completed. A break of a triangle on low volume is not significant, indicating the pattern is likely to extend.

The breaking of the resistance level of a flat on high volume is significant. If a break occurs on low volume, it becomes likely that the price action will return to the confines of the flat. If simple, the flat is then likely to become complex.

During a rising impulse wave, it is a sign of weakness if volume continues to expand while the price action begins to narrow. Under these circumstances, supply can be seen to be gradually exceeding demand. If the level of volume continues to rise while thrusts become increasingly powerful, this is a sign of strength, since demand under such conditions will be exceeding supply.

Approaching the end of a corrective phase, it will be a sign of strength when volume begins to increase while the price action narrows. This type of action will often be the precursor to a final low-volume Wave 5 of Wave C before the next upswing.

During the course of a rising impulse wave, high volume after the movement has been under way for a period will mean a temporary cessation of the movement. This need not necessarily mean the onset of corrective action or a serious trend reversal. High volume at the mature stages of an upward drive is indicative of a pocket of supply that must be absorbed before the movement can be resumed.

Heavy volume is constructive, provided there is a continuation in the trend of the price movement and the price movement does not re-enter a corrective flat or a triangle following a bulge in volume levels. If there is a re-entry into a congestion range following a high-volume upward thrust, this would follow distribution and be a sign of weakness.

Ancillary Considerations

It can be readily seen from Elliott's *Interpretative Letters* that he monitored a prodigious amount of data and applied his Wave Principle to this data. There are several references to the wave count for the Dow Jones Rail Average and for the US Corporate Bond Index. Elliott also applied his Wave Principle to the Federal Reserve Production Index and the Utility Averages. In one of his *Interpretative Letters*, Elliott constructs a wave count of the Ratio of Yield of High Grade Bonds to that of Common Stocks. In another, there is a wave analysis of the New York Times Combined 50 Industrials and Rails along with a wave analysis of the Herald Tribune Corporate Bond Index.

In *Interpretative Letter No 17*, August 25, 1941, Elliott wrote as follows: "Triangle Wave 3 ran from March 10, 1937, to March 31, 1938, and also formed Wave "C" of the flat counting from November 1928. This picture is confirmed by the corporate bond index, a graph of which is shown on page 4. Since the Treatise was written, I discovered that corporate bonds (particularly second grade rails) exert a dominating influence over equities and this feature has been mentioned several times in advisory letters".

Elliott also kept a running wave count of not only the Dow Jones Rail Averages, but also of secondary rail averages. Although Elliott never attempted to apply the Wave Principle to individual shares, in one of his *Interpretative Letters* he produces a wave analysis of US Steel. His basic preoccupation was the application of the Wave Principle to the current and prospective movement of the Dow Jones Industrial Averages. No doubt the monitoring of other indices were to act in a confirmatory fashion, assisting in the validation of whatever wave count may have appeared in the stock averages. Elliott conducted wave analysis of US Steel, in his day, in the same manner as one might currently wish to construct a wave analysis of IBM, or the long US Treasury. This would be based on the assumption that, as goes IBM and long US Treasury, so, too, will move the DJIA and the US bond market. If the wave count for IBM confirms the wave count of the Dow Jones Industrial Averages, the probability of a correct count is enhanced accordingly. A wave count of IBM might help to clarify a somewhat obscure formation that appears in the DJIA.

There are also references to Elliott's application of the Wave Principle to both industrial groupings and commodity groups, obviously for the same purpose as aforementioned. In *Interpretative Letter No. 14,* Elliott also applied wave analysis to the London Industrial Share Index. In that letter he wrote: "Graph (U) shows the London Industrials from June 26 to October 8 (61.1 to 82.5) in five waves which confirms my advice of July 9 to Forecast subscribers to the effect that the bear market low had passed. In 1932 and 1937 London reversed one and two months respectively, ahead of New York on this basis, New York should have bottomed in July or August."

In *Interpretive Letter No. 10,* Elliott furnished a wave analysis of what he describes as a "Private Average," in addition to a separate wave analysis of the Second Grade Corporate Bond Index, which he followed in addition to the High Grade Corporate Bond Index. In a report marked "Confidential" dated September 6, 1939, Elliott produced the illustration (Figure 58) which is a wave analysis of the Composite Market Sentiment Index, High Grade Bond Index, Business Cycle Index, Second Grade Bond Index, London Industrials Index, and the Dow Jones Industrial Average all synchronized.

In addition to that which has already been mentioned, Elliott conducted a regular wave analysis of US Government Bonds, the Dow Jones Composite Index of 40 Bonds, the Dow Jones 65 Stock Composite Index, the price of seats on the New York Stock Exchange, and probably several others which he had failed to mention. Elliott also monitored a great deal of fundamental statistical and economic data to which a wave analysis would not be applicable.

Those who feel that after mastering the Wave Principle—if they ever master it—can then simply begin calling turns, engaging in a bit of stock picking which is consistent with those turns, are going to be in for a very rude awakening.

It has been the tendency of those who have attempted to exploit the Wave Principle editorially to ignore the tremendous amount of effort, along with the plethora of ancillary factors utilized by Elliott. An impression has been given that the Wave Principle is an end in itself. This is not what Elliott had intended. Nor is it the manner in which he utilized his technique.

Throughout his writing, there are references to many fundamental

Figure 58

STATUS OF OPPOSING FORCES AS OF AUGUST 26, 1939

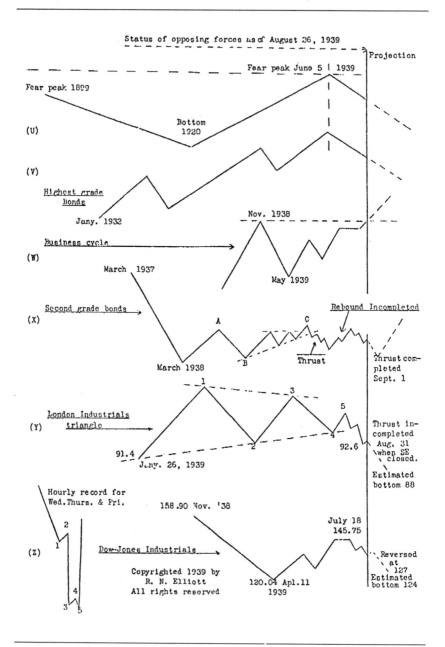

influences which he regularly monitored; e.g., federal debt, new corporate financing, trends in unemployment, trends in inflation, the Ratio of Yield of High Grade Corporate Bonds to the Yield of Equities, etc. Elliott never used the Wave Principle in a mechanical way as a substitute for knowledge, or as a quick and easy way to trade the markets, undeflected by thought and discipline, as certain of his practitioners have attempted.

While there are those practitioners who use the Wave Principle as a cosmetic, implying the method needs no other supportive data, there are others who do use a considerable amount of supportive data, which is inconsistent with the basic philosophy inherent in the tenets of the Wave Principle. I have been guilty of this practice myself. Using mechanical data which is not a direct reflection of human activity, or data which fails to accurately portray human activity, will produce conflicting and random results rather than act in a confirmatory manner.

In my original work, *The Elliott Wave Principle as Applied to the UK Stock Market,* and in my second book, *Supertiming,* I focused on the use of moving averages as being capable of smoothing out the erratic minor waves and helping to delineate the wave pattern, simplifying categorization. I experimented with eighty-hour moving averages, fifty-five-hour moving averages, and ten-day moving averages. I have since abandoned the use of all moving averages as confirmatory indicators, having discovered the commonality with the Wave Principle to be highly unsatisfactory. I really should have been warned: Elliott was perfectly capable of producing moving averages himself. If there were benefit to be gained, I am sure Elliott would have used them.

During the thirty-five years I have worked with the Wave Principle, I seem to have gone in a complete circle. A good deal of the past three-and-a-half decades was spent attempting to find ancillary devices to assist in confirming the position of a market cycle under the tenets of the Wave Principle. Aside from the use of moving averages, I have attempted to employ various technical indicators and certain computerized techniques. In my original work on the Wave Principle, written fifteen years ago, I made reference to several supplementary technical indicators, which I thought might be useful additions at the time. These were the Advance/Decline Index, the Index of Accumulation and Distribution, and the Momentum Index, along with a running total of net new highs and net new lows. I have since abandoned most of these, having discovered that the combination of basic fundamental statistical analysis and economic analysis; a study of in-depth market psychology; the basic tenets of the Wave

Principle; and a bit of personal introspection have given me the most satisfactory results.

I have found the basic tools used by so-called technical analysts, along with traditional chart techniques, more misleading and contradictory than helpful. Using traditional chart techniques is like trying to make a thermometer do the work of a barometer. A thermometer tells you what the temperature is. A barometer tells you what the temperature is likely to be.

Virtually the entire array of technical tools which have come into vogue are merely measures of existing market strength or weakness, which technicians have adopted as having predictive value, based on the simplistic hypothesis of "A trend in motion will stay in motion . . . until it changes." I find this approach over-simplistic and intellectually unsatisfactory. I doubt if any self-respecting climatologist would be willing to base his life study on the simplistic assumption that the trend of his thermometer will remain in motion until it changes.

The Wave Principle has been designed for the sole purpose of anticipating future price changes and projecting those future price changes in time and amplitude, based on a hypothesis that reaches far beyond the naive notion that a line that has already been drawn can tell you something about the shape, length, and size of the line undrawn. It should therefore be clear that the use of most technical indicators will be inconsistent with the objectives of the Wave Principle.

During the period that I have been using the Wave Principle, I have increased my reliance on volume statistics while attempting to use the Wave Principle in a manner which is as closely related as possible to the way Elliott was using it when he was alive. In the course of my experimentations, there is only one technique that I discovered, which seems to be a useful addition. This is a formula devised by Dr. Ralph Heiser of Switzerland, which is sometimes known as the Zero Balance technique and is used to calculate and assign a plus or minus value to a formation. When the balance line moves above a previously recorded market peak, the market is considered overbought. When the balance line moves below the previous lows, or principle low, the market is considered to be oversold. The technique is intended to be used as a directional indicator, serving to quantify the existing trend while acting as an aid in the anticipation of near-term possible changes in the trend.

It is first necessary to look backward from where the market may now be, so as to identify the important pivotal points. The pivot points should be

Figure 59
ZERO BALANCE EXAMPLE

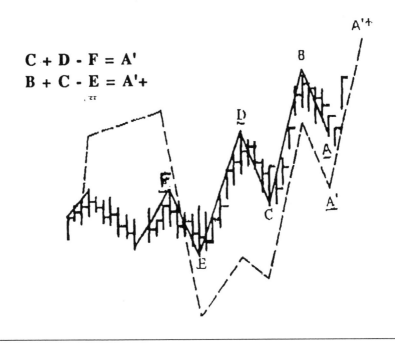

$$C + D - F = A'$$
$$B + C - E = A'+$$

labelled *A, B, C, D, E,* and *F,* as in Figure 59. The boundaries of the formation should be clearly defined.

The first step is to take the price level at pivot point C and add it to the price level of pivot point D. From the sum (C+D), subtract the price level of pivot point F. The result will be A'. (C + D - F = A'). If A' is at a level which is higher than A, then the trend is up. If A' is lower than A, then the trend is downward.

The second step is to take the price level at pivot point B and add it to the price level of pivot point C. From the sum (B+C), subtract the price level at pivot point E. The result is the possible target for A'+ (B + C -- E = A'+), as outlined in Figure 59. When these target levels—as they often do—are consistent with the other methods that can be used to make price projections with the Wave Principle, there is a high probability of occurrence.

14
Investing with
the Wave Principle

Only those objects should engage our attention, to the sure and
indubitable knowledge of which our mental powers seem to be
adequate.

—RENE DESCARTES

Although having little knowledge of the Wave Principle, Descartes was
probably quite influential in advancing the K.I.S.S. principle: "Keep it
simple, stupid!" When in doubt stay out! If you don't understand it, leave it
alone! As inane as these old cliches may sound, they should form the basis
of a conditioned response to your application of the Wave Principle in your
day-to-day market activities.

Descartes' approach to any problem began with the deliberate assumption that he knew nothing whatever about the basic elements of the
problem. That was his high point of departure. He completed his personal
unlearning process before he approached the problem. Unfortunately,
there are many investors who may have to spend years unlearning what
they think they know about the stock market before they are able to solve
the problem of how to accumulate wealth and avoid loss, as Descartes
would have done.

The first step in the unlearning process is knowing what you don't
know. A recognition of your personal imbecility potential, and that of
others, is a basic prerequisite for operating in markets. Humility won't cost
you a cent, but it could give you the psychological foundation from which
you can reap vast rewards. Descartes assumed he knew nothing about
anything and that most of the knowledge he had accumulated was probably
misleading and counter-productive. In markets, there is no need to as-

sume. You know that most of the dogma, pseudo-science, information, and opinions you have accumulated over the years are invariably irrelevant, erroneous, misleading, and counter-productive. We can all learn from Descartes.

While you're in the process of refining your conceptual approach to markets in a manner that would be compatible with your application of Elliott's Wave Principle, it would be useful for you to consider the works and words of this brilliant, skeptical seeker of truth. The way you think will determine your approach to markets. Your approach to markets will undoubtedly influence your application of the Wave Principle when you're operating with real money, in real time, instead of pretty squiggles on graph paper.

Descartes, Elliott, and Markets

Descartes was born at La Haye, in Touraine on March 31, 1596. His early education was at the Jesuit School at La Fleche, where he attended from 1606 to 1615. After the full curriculum of languages and humane letters, logic, ethics, mathematics, physics, and metaphysics, Descartes later declared, "I found myself embarrassed with so many doubts and errors, that it seemed to me that the effort to instruct myself had no effect, other than the increasing discovery of my own ignorance." In Descartes' increasing discovery of his ignorance—which we could all do well to discover in ourselves — mathematics alone appeared to be an exception, ". . . because of the certainty of its demonstrations and the evidence of its reasoning," he commented.

Descartes completed his formal education at the University of Pointers in 1616 and spent the remainder of his youth travelling, "resolved no longer to seek any other science that the knowledge of myself, or of the great book of the world." You may now begin to see why I am certain that Descartes, and others like him, would have made brilliant and unbeatable market operators. Single-mindedness is not a beneficial virtue in markets, or in life. An abundance of self-knowledge is the most valuable asset you could ever acquire.

Descartes dated his work in the field of philosophy—the paintings, literature, and music of the mind—as beginning in 1619. Early in that year, after his studies of algebra and geometry had yielded what he considered an "entirely new science," he wrote, "My project is unbelievably ambitious, but I cannot help feeling that I am sighting I know not what light in the chaos of present-day geometry, and I trust that it will help in dispelling that most opaque darkness." The mathematics of Leonardo de Pisa was well known to Descartes, establishing the basis for a large number of Descartes equations, as can be seen through various references.

Descartes derived an income from a family inheritance that was sufficient to make him financially independent throughout his life. There were only a few rudimentary stock markets in existence during Descartes' life in the seventeenth century. Although there are indications that he may have visited the Stock Exchange in Amsterdam, he is not known to have ever risked any of his money through participation.

Yet, Descartes was active in what amounted to just about the same thing as dealing on the stock exchange. He gambled with dice and playing cards. He studied the mathematics of gambling in his youth, recognizing the basic and essential mathematics of game theory, concentrating on those games in which non-randomness was observed. He had no time for games of natural selection, like roulette, unless the odds could be shifted in his favor. He rejected all of the gambling cliches and folk wisdom of the time, until he was able to verify and quantify all of the aspects to his own satisfaction, accepting nothing at face value. He independently arrived at what he considered to be the requisite paradigms of winning and losing. After satisfying himself that the methods he planned to use offered a reasonable chance of yielding results, he then went to Paris and won a small fortune. In one year, he won enough money with his gaming techniques that, by combining his newly accumulated fortune with that of his family inheritance, he was able to live most of his remaining life in comfort, without the need or desire to earn any more.

Descartes was operating with "cool money." It was money that he was not afraid to lose. Losing never induced despair or desolation, nor did winning evoke euphoria or exaltation. For Descartes, wealth was never an objective in itself. He considered wealth to be the incidental means that were required in order to embark on what he considered to be more worthy and personally rewarding goals.

Descartes simply wanted to spend his life as a free man, a slave neither to persons nor things—just ambling around, observing, studying, learning, teaching, and thinking of this and that. To his close admirers, he loudly, publicly announced that he was beginning his philosophy by totally cleaning out his mind, by doubting everything he had ever been told or had ever casually accepted as true, which included the existence of God and himself. "As comedians put on a mask to hide their timidity," he said, "so I go forward masked, preparing to mount the stage of the world, which up to now I have known only as a spectator."

During the nine years following Descartes' dedication to the philosophical approach he had adopted in 1619, he lived quietly as a "gentil-homme" while preparing to apply his newly discovered method to all knowledge. When satisfied that his mind had been sufficiently divested of all the inconsequential, irrelevant trivia and minutiae that act as impediments to most of our endeavors, particularly those of investors, Descartes went on to search for the unarguable truths. "I shall persevere," he wrote in his *Meditations on First Philosophy,* "until I find something that is certain—or, at the least, until I find for certain that nothing is certain."

Like Elliott, Descartes devoted his life's work to the isolation of non-randomness. Also, like Elliott, he appears to have achieved his objective, maybe not completely, but to a considerable degree. In *Rules for the Direction of the Mind,* Descartes writes, "In order to separate what is quite simple from what is complex, and to arrange these matters methodically, we ought, in the case of every series in which we have deduced certain facts, the one from the other, to notice which fact is simple, and to mark the interval greater, less, or equal, which separates all others from this." Conceptually, Elliott and Descartes were certainly in tune. I would not be surprised if Elliott had read Descartes and was influenced by him, given the passion that both men shared for the mysteries of unstable numbers.

It should come as no surprise that Descartes' rejection of all knowledge in favor of cleansing the mind and starting afresh in search of a solution to problems that were yet to be solved satisfactorily, did not endear him to the Establishment of that period, who, like in most periods, claimed to have all of the answers and solutions for just about everything. The most severe and venomous attacks that were levied at Descartes came from the religious authorities. Cartesianism was assaulted as subversive of religion. On one occasion, Descartes was summoned before the magistrates of Utrecht on heresy charges. The matter never escalated into anything more serious than a warning because of the intervention of Descartes' influential friends. If you apply Descartes' philosophy to markets, it is most unlikely that you will have any influential friends to come to your rescue. As the anti-hero of the film *Wall Street* said, commenting on the camaraderie of the securities industry, "If you want a friend, buy a dog!"

Yet, if you want to make sense of these markets and apply the Wave Principle to price formations that look like a picture of a dead man's heartbeat on an oscilloscope, you could do far worse than to adopt the approach of this tough, unyielding, brilliant scholar, this grand and original free-thinker and doubter. Begin now by cleansing your mind, by doubting all that you've been told about markets from those who wish to perpetuate the current dogma for their own interests. Be highly sceptical of the blurbs from the tip sheet writers, along with the sales literature from the broker-age houses that pretends to be investment advice. Question absolutely everything that comes from sources who stand to gain from your activity, whether you gain or lose.

Question the idea that markets are all true auction markets; that prices are arrived at by the orderly interplay of supply and demand; that the future can be predicted by studying the historic fundamental background of the economy or a company, or through the use of standard, trend-following chart techniques. Do not allow yourself to be seduced by silly ideas, such as by buying shares you're supporting industry, or any other nonsense along a similar vein.

From this day forward, promise yourself whenever a stockbroker, investment adviser, money manager, financial journalist, tip sheet peddler, or seer at your local cocktail bar tells you he has some inside information, or that he knows, or can guess, the future of a market, individual commod-ity, stock, bond, or collectible, emulate Descartes. Doubt it! Become one of the financially washed! Stop using that filthy kid stuff! Abandon financial pornography once and for all. You know it's right! You'll be glad that you did! You could save yourself a fortune that will help you go on to make a fortune.

Before you consider using the Wave Principle, banish the concept of absolutes, along with the objective of making predictions with the Wave Principle from your psyche. Replace those damaging perceptions with assessments that consider possibilities and probabilities only. Accept that, while the odds may be in your favor by 100-to-1, there is always that *1* that you're not going to be able to get rid of. Think tactically and strategically with the funds you have to invest. Be aware that acting on the basis of predictions and forecasts will be detrimental to your success.

Submit to only one certainty, the certainty of uncertainty. By so doing, you may then begin to recognize those elements of non-randomness in life and in markets and the sources from which the information you need can be obtained. In so doing, you may then be able to succeed in your application of the Wave Principle to your investment and trading objectives where others have failed.

Getting Started

You will want to use the Wave Principle for developing a cohesive strategy that will help you with your long-term, intermediate-term, and short-term objectives, whichever your inclination. The object will be to determine optimal buying and selling points in accordance with your objectives. If you're a long-term investor, your only interest may be in detecting major trend changes. On the other hand, all investors should make use of optimal, intermediate-term trend changes for fine-tuning their portfolios.

Be acutely aware that markets are technically the strongest after a severe decline and technically the weakest after a sharp rise. After a sharp rise, you will begin looking for the completion of wave formations that will offer you the best opportunity to liquidate. Conversely, after a severe fall, you will then be perusing the formations in order to detect the most favorable buying points.

You must arm yourself with a long-term chart—as long as possible on the market you are interested in. By long-term, I mean going back at least fifty to sixty years. For the Dow Jones Industrial Average, you can get a chart going back nearly two hundred years. Such a chart is unlikely to give you anything more detailed than monthly highs and lows. You will also want a chart showing you weekly highs and lows for at least the past five years, or the last important terminal juncture. A cyclical chart of daily closing prices will also be needed for no less than two years. Finally, you'll want an hourly chart, or every-price chart for no less than three months.

Initially, you will use these charts to determine the various turning points that have occurred in the past, while delineating the relative importance of these turning points. You will use these turning points to fortify your tactics and strategies. As a long-term investor, you will only be interested in participating in the market at the most important cyclical turning points. You will want to be invested in highly leveraged stock positions at the beginning of a move, reducing your leverage as the move proceeds. When the movement is complete, you will then switch your strategy, investing in highly leveraged, fixed-interest securities, employing the same tactics you used for your stock positions during the course of the move.

The long-term investor will remain with his fixed-interest securities—reducing the risk exposure as the cyclical forces gradually become exhausted, anticipating a period when he will re-invest for the next long, equity-market upswing. In this respect, the long-term investor might spend three to five years invested in common stocks and two to three years out of them, depending on the nature of the wave formation.

I am very reluctant to recommend trading to any investor, since, in my experience, very few investors can handle short-term risk. What I do recommend to each and every investor is that at all times the investment portfolio be evaluated for risk. What a company does, or the industry it may happen to be in, I consider to be totally irrelevant. The only characteristic of a company that concerns me is its risk profile, which is usually a matter of financial leverage. In fixed-interest markets, the risk element can be ascertained by the nature of the vehicles; e.g., financial futures, bond options, zero coupon bonds, and long-dated low-coupon bonds will have a higher risk profile than current-coupon, short-dated to medium-dated, fixed-interest issues.

There are two elements of risk, which are market risk and financial risk. Financial risk can be readily quantified through the various risk measurement services applicable to individual stocks. It is a fairly simple matter to quantify financial risk in fixed-interest markets by the ratings and nature of the vehicles. Essentially, an efficient portfolio is one where the reward exceeds the risk. If this is not the case, the portfolio cannot operate efficiently.

Assuming the investor has built an efficient portfolio, the Wave Principle can be used to adjust the portfolio for market risk. Quite simply, the further a market moves upward from an important terminal juncture, the greater market risk is going to be. The investor who wishes to maintain a portfolio with a consistent risk profile should reduce the financial risk as market risk increases. In a market environment of high risk, financial risk should be reduced, and vice versa. The Wave Principle can be an immensely valuable aid for implementing this concept.

Take Five!

If you get ahold of Dave Brubeck's jazz masterpiece "Take Five" and learn to hum it while you're dealing, perhaps that might help. You want the count of five to be indelibly engraved on your investment thinking. That second sequence of five waves down in a zig-zag, or the end of the fifth wave of Wave C of a massive irregular correction, will give fortune-making, buying opportunities.

The five-wave upmove, possibly extended by four more waves, and maybe some more on top of that, will tell you when to start heading for the exits, so you can either let the bears romp by, or join them.

No matter what other factors are involved in your investment decision-making process—economic, fundamental, technical, or whatever—you must always be on the look-out for the completion of that all-important, five-wave drive.

In a bull market, just think of three drives upward, the second bigger than the first, the third smaller than the second, each interrupted by a decline which is smaller than all three in amplitude. When that third rally starts to approach the dimensions of the first in time and space, that's when you want to get ready to abandon your holdings.

In a bear market, envisage a plunge bigger than anything that took place during the bull market, followed by a strong rally. Then look out for three successive plunges, each interrupted by a brief rally. That last plunge will tell you that an end of the bear market is approaching, and you better get ready to start buying with both hands.

There is nothing more to think about, nothing more to be concerned with. The empirical evidence in favor of terminal endings occurring in bull markets and in bear markets, in precisely the manner described, is over-whelming.

When I wrote *Supertiming* in 1978, applying the Wave Principle to the US stock market, I delineated the move that began in the Dow Jones Industrial Averages in 1932 as the beginning of super cycle Wave V of a grand super cycle. It was also my judgement that the pivotal action in the DJIA that began in 1974 was to be classified as cycle Wave V of super cycle Wave V of that grand super cycle that began shortly after the Industrial Revolution.

Back in 1978, I was looking for a bull market that began in late 1974 to continue until 1984. It was my conclusion that the termination of that bull market would also mark the terminal juncture of a grand super cycle that would have been 184 years in duration. My study of the Wave Principle at that time also told me that the corrective action that was likely to follow that bull market would have to be sufficient to correct all of the excesses that had been accumulated during the previous 184 years. In other words, I was expecting the longest and strongest bull market in US stock market history, to be followed by the most savage bear market the United States had ever experienced.

The following comments appeared in the original text of *Supertiming*.

> I certainly have no intention of being fatalistic about the entire affair. At this stage I will merely play the role of an ostrich and stick my head in the sand by saying I am just the student conveying the words of the master.

> If Elliott's treatment of the Wave Principle in its grand super cycle context proves correct, we have two things to look forward to. First, a bull market of the dimensions and time span similar to that experienced by the US market preceding the Great Crash, i.e., about six more years of rapidly rising prices, as the level of equities catches up to the previous rate of inflation in the US. Second, a massive collapse that will make the 1929–1932 C Wave look like a Teddy Bear's picnic.

> But, first things first. Let us set down some precedents of how one should handle the remaining years of the bull phase. We should all know what to do when it terminates. The object at this time is to make sure sales are not made premature and the investor gets the maximum return on capital employed from the move that remains. If you are a long-term investor all you have to do is stick with it, making sure you are not tempted to liquidate your holdings too soon. So, your job will be to spot the terminal point when it occurs.

Those who followed the Wave Principle as it was outlined in *Supertiming* are duly delighted with the results. The bull market continued for the additional six years as the Wave Principle had indicated, extending beyond upon where you want to fix the orthodox top. At this stage, the orthodox top is academic. I abandoned the equity market quite some time ago in order to participate in the big bull market in US bonds, where a good portion of the funds I look after have been committed for quite some time.

The longest and strongest bull market in the history of the United States has come and gone along with corresponding bull markets in other countries. Many have made fortunes during that long and glorious bull market. Many will soon lose all of the fortunes that were made, along with a good chunk of their savings on top. According to my reading of the Wave Principle, that long and agonizing phase that acts to correct the excesses of a grand super cycle spanning nearly two hundred years is now upon us.

As a long-term strategist I am convinced that the big bull market in US stocks is completed. I will now be on the look-out for the next bull market, while waiting for the end of the bull market in bonds and exploiting the bear market swings through short sales, along with the options and warrants which are exercisable into the various indices like the NYSE, Standard & Poors, and XMI.

In *Supertiming* I devoted considerable effort to outlining the strategy to be employed during the final phases of the bull market in anticipation of the next bear market. It is likely to be many years before we see a major terminal juncture of a bull market. I do not believe investors should be holding equities of any kind at this time. But, I do believe that investors should be preparing themselves for the period when it would be advisable to maintain a fully leveraged, one-hundred-percent-invested stance in the US equity market again.

The Next Bull Market

In the years ahead, I expect the following sequence to develop.

1. Wave V of cycle Wave V, of super cycle Wave V, of grand super cycle Wave V has become extended. An irregular correction has been in progress. Wave A has been completed. During the summer of 1991, I was waiting for confirmation that Wave B had been completed. A high-volume break below the level of 2,800 in the Dow Jones Industrial Averages will verify the completion of Wave B. At the time, the DJIA will still be in the early stages of Wave 1 of Wave C, considering the projected magnitude of the current Wave C.

2. Wave C should unfold in a classic fashion, although the duration of the coming bear market is likely to exceed the customary eighteen-month-to-three-year parameters. The bear market itself, beginning at the orthodox top, is likely to be a six- to eight-year affair. Wave C of the remainder of the bear market could easily run three to four years, possibly more.

3. The DJIA will spend more time in a corrective phase than in an impulse phase. The impulse phases are likely to be very fast moving, encompassing massive selling waves in rapid succession. Rallying action will be shallow, slow, and labored, especially following the completion of Wave 1 of Wave C.

4. Given the structure of the preceding bull market, I expect Wave 2 of Wave C to be either a flat or a triangle. There is also the strong likelihood that Wave 2 of Wave C is going to involve a complex inverted pattern. After the completion of Wave 1, during the development of

Wave 2 of Wave C, many investors will begin to believe a new bull market is about to start. They will be wrong. Watch the pattern of Wave 2 very closely. You will know there is little chance of a new bull market starting, since none of the waves in an upward direction will be developing impulse characteristics.

5. Wave 3 of Wave C is likely to be devastating. It will be the longest and most severe of the three downward waves of Wave C. Those who purchased stocks during Wave 2 of Wave C will watch their investment evaporate with a speed that they never thought remotely possible. Corrective action during Wave 3 of Wave C is likely to be very brief and much more limited than the corrective action during Wave 1.

6. Wave 4 of Wave C is likely to take the form of an inverted zig-zag. Wave 4 is unlikely to be complex if Wave 2 was complex. Wave 4 is likely to be strong and protracted, providing the best rallying action the bear market will have had up until then. Wave 4, like Wave 2, will also convince a number of individuals that a new bull market is starting. Be careful during Wave 4 of this Wave C to categorize cycle degrees accurately. You will know it is Wave C, since it will be an inverted zig-zag, involving three waves: one up, one down, and one up. However, the waves of the next-lower degree will have a count of five-three-five. Your vital clue will be that the time and amplitude of minor waves of Wave 4 will be similar to those of Wave 2.

7. All hope will be abandoned when Wave 4 turns out to be a false start in a bull market, along with Wave 2. Most investors will be inveterate bears, projecting prices down to a level that would greatly exceed the amplitude of Wave 3 of Wave C, counting from the top of Wave 4. Pessimism is likely to be so thick during Wave 5 of Wave C that you could cut it with a knife. A bull will be an extinct species during Wave 5 of Wave C. This will be the time for you to start ear-marking those shares you want to purchase when the selling pressure is finally exhausted.

8. As the bear market draws to a close, the level of volume is going to fall quite considerably. Day by day you'll find volume levels quoted at their lowest levels in years. Buying stock during Wave 5 of Wave C will be considered in most circles as the most foolish and dangerous financial escapade anyone could possibly think of. It is most unlikely that Wave 5 of Wave C will end in a panic. The panic will have occurred earlier.

Wave 5 of Wave C is likely to end in a whisper. That will be the time for you to quietly begin building your equity portfolio for the next period of long-term expansion.

9. Wave C of the bear market will be a cycle wave, made up of five primary waves. The primary impulse waves, as will be the intermediate, minor, and minute, each of the corrective waves separating the impulse waves will be inverted, involving three distinct components. The purchase of stock should not be considered until the fifth minor wave, of the fifth intermediate wave, of the fifth primary wave is in the course of development, as the level of volume steadily contracts.

10. With these general rules in mind, the investor should now watch the market unfold, plotting its hourly, daily, weekly, and monthly movement in order to keep abreast of each minor and intermediate movement as it unfolds. During the course of Wave C, there are likely to be several excellent intermediate-term trading opportunities. Long-term investors should simply use intermediate-term trading opportunities for adjusting the risk profile of their portfolios.

Trading Intermediate-Term Action

Trading the intermediate-term swings of Wave C are going to be a bit more tricky than trading the intermediate-term swings of an ongoing bull market. First, you're going to be limited to playing the downside of the market. It would be most unwise to attempt playing the upswings of the corrective phases. The odds will be against you. As an intermediate-term trader during Wave C, your activity must be confined to selling short, buying put options and put warrants. If this is not your cup of tea, leave it alone and be content to let the bears finish their work.

Second, although the time horizon of this cycle Wave C is sufficient for you to generate considerable profits during the bear market, you're going to be faced with some very fast-moving markets. Unless you have access to frequent price data and can handle fast-moving markets, you will be exposing yourself to considerable risk. The loss to the short seller during a bear market, if things go awry, is theoretically unlimited.

Having given you my note of caution, the correct application of the Wave Principle during a bear market will certainly help the experienced and aggressive trader maximize his investment returns, above and beyond that which would accrue sitting in fixed-interest securities or money-market instruments, while interest rates are steadily falling.

1. Always consider the risk/reward potential of any subsequent movements by attempting to project the possible minimum and maximum amplitude of that movement. The Wave Principle should accustom you to selling into strength at the end of a rise and buying into weakness at the end of a decline, while also giving you an idea of how long an ensuing move is going to last and how far it will go. The Wave Principle is the only forecasting tool which is able to quantify this extremely vital trading aspect.

2. When trading, do not use tools which are inconsistent with the objective of the Wave Principle for supportive or confirmatory purposes. Most technical methods add up to little more than trend chasing. After a move has been established, the trader is then advised to participate with no idea of how much of the movement remains in time or space. This could involve a breakout that proves to be false, the penetration of a trend line or moving average, the completion of a reversal pattern or continuation pattern, etc. All of that ancient chart work is pretty much of a hit-and-miss affair. Purchases and sales are habitually laggard, while the trader is often left with a small portion of a total swing, providing the swing has been accurately anticipated to start with. There have been severe criticisms levied at technical methods of the type referred to, which are thought to encourage over-trading and added costs. Often the trader will find several profitable trades are wiped out by merely one loss, when using conventional chart techniques. My first book, written in 1967 and called *Share Price Analysis,* dealt with traditional chart techniques. Over the past quarter of a century dealing in markets, I have abandoned most of the techniques in favor of the tenets of the Wave Principle.

4. You must avoid the temptation of using the Wave Principle as a trend-chasing tool, following the trend, rather than anticipating a trend reversal. You must be patient if you're a trader, acting only in advance of meaningful pivotal points. The object at all times is to attempt to make your purchases as close to an important bottom as possible and to execute your sales as close to an important top as possible. With the proper application of the Wave Principle, you can often anticipate— within one-tenth of a point—where an important top will be and where

an important bottom will be, and adopt your trading tactics accordingly. I know of no other stock market device that can even aim at achieving such an objective.

5. When dealing with Wave C, with which I believe the Dow Jones Industrial Averages is now confronted, after the confirmation of Wave B, the entire time frame of Wave 1 of Wave C should encompass approximately 8 months, measuring from Wave B peak. Traders will want to investigate short positions when completion of Wave B has been confirmed, retaining short positions throughout the remainder of Wave 1 of Wave C. All short positions, put options, and put warrant positions should be closed on the minuette wave of Wave C, into weakness. No positions should be held during Wave 2 of Wave C of any kind.

6. As mentioned previously, Wave 2 of Wave C is likely to be an inverted complex triangle of an inverted complex flat. You will want to use channelling techniques when dealing with Wave 2 of Wave C in order to establish the upper parameter of the formation. When it appears the evolution of threes and fives is nearing completion, you will then want to reposition yourself, taking a bit of extra risk on that occasion, since you know that Wave 3 of Wave C is going to provide you with the biggest rewards.

7. Assuming the pattern unfolds as I described and there appears an inverted flat or an inverted triangle, simple or complex, in Wave 2 of Wave C and you've built up a handsome profit cushion with your holdings during Wave 3, you can actually reverse your position during Wave 4 of Wave C. The rally, which will constitute Wave 4 of Wave C, should be sufficient in duration and amplitude to give you additional trading profits, unlike Wave 2 of Wave C where both bears and bulls are likely to come out on the losing side.

8. Waves 4 and 5 of Wave C should be fairly easy to deal with. The terminal juncture of Wave 3 of Wave C should be easy enough to spot, since it's an impulse wave. You'll have reversed your position from short to long, anticipating a simple zig-zag involving five sub-waves up, three sub-waves down—that you'll sit through—and then five sub-waves up again. On the fifth minor sub-wave, of the second upward drive of Wave 4, you'll be liquidating your long positions with the intentions of going short, buying put options and put warrants again.

9. I've already described the type of atmosphere you can expect during Wave 5 of Wave C, which is due sometime during late 1993, according to my timetable. But, don't hold me to that one. It's a possibility, neither a prediction nor a forecast. When you begin to position yourself for Wave 5 of Wave C during minor Wave 5 or Wave 4, you will modify your strategy, confining your activities to lower-risk vehicles, such as heavily capitalized stocks for your short-selling vehicles along with options and warrants that are at-the-money or close to it, rather than options and warrants that are deeply out-of-the-money. During Wave 5 of Wave C you will be approaching the end of the bear market. At the end of the bear market, you will want to reverse your strategy completely, moving to a highly leveraged, one-hundred-percent-invested stance on the long side of the market.

10. Here are a few more points that should help you trade Wave C successfully to its ultimate conclusion: (a) after the completion of Wave B of the irregular correction has been confirmed, use only moderate leveraging and a medium-risk profile for trading the remainder of Wave 1 of Wave C; (b) from the top of Wave B of the irregular correction, watch for the development of a normal five-wave sequence downward; (c) liquidate all positions at sub-minor wave 5 of Wave 1 of Wave C, anticipating a complete flat or complex triangle. Do not take long positions. Stay out of the market during this period, which could last for several months. Expect the maximum breadth of the pattern to be 50 to 61.8 percent of Wave 1 of Wave C, with a final sell-off confined to the tip of minor Wave 1, of Wave 1, of Wave C. Use the channelling technique to establish the upper parameters of the flat or triangle; (d) expect the duration of Wave 2 of Wave C to be longer than that of Wave 1, although narrower in amplitude. A reasonable time frame would involve 1.6 times the duration of Wave 1. Since you are likely to be dealing with a complex formation, using the time frame as a guide will be helpful, along with the tenets relative to complex formations. As the duration of the move reaches maturity, you will want to position yourself at the upper parameter of the triangle or flat. The approaching Wave 3 of Wave C will give you the best profit-making opportunity of the bear market. You will want to purchase options and warrants that are deeply out-of-the-money, when premiums are low. You can use a broad-brush technique with your short sales. Highly leveraged companies will be extremely vulnerable during Wave 3 of Wave C of the bear

market; (e) following a conventional five-wave count for Wave 3 of Wave C, you will want to close your short positions and put option positions, taking a position on the along side of the market. The Wave 4 zig-zag will not be a new bull market, but it should carry long far enough and last long enough to justify exposure with moderate risk. There will be a decline involving a three-wave count in the zig-zag, which should be ignored; (f) at the fifth sub-minor wave of the zig-zag, which will be Wave 4 of Wave C, you will want to start positioning yourself for the fifth and final wave of the bear market. Risk exposure to the downside of the bear market should only be moderate during this phase; and (g) when pessimism reaches a nadir and volume reaches its lowest level for years, you will be approaching minor wave 5, of intermediate Wave 5, of primary wave 5, of Wave C. It will then be time to start closing your short positions and preparing for a low-risk period, which will be followed by twenty to thirty years of near-uninterrupted expansion.

Confirming Important Turning Points

It was Elliott's intention to make his method as scientific as possible. He was still trying to arrive at this scientific perfection until the day he died, as can be seen from the various modifications introduced in his writing over the years. In the final analysis, considering the difficulties that will be encountered as a consequence of the irregular manner in which waves can develop, along with the possible margins for error that can occur in counting, the effective use of the Wave Principle is still very much an art rather than a science. For this reason, it is always necessary to check and cross-check the projections you will make when using the Wave Principle in your investment approach.

You may certainly dismiss a number of chart techniques that you currently use that might tend to mislead you. But, I would strongly recommend you continue to pay extremely close attention to the fundamental principles of investment analysis along with the economic factors that influence markets. Of course, these factors are not timing devices, but will help you in a confirmatory capacity. As I have stressed and demonstrated, Elliott had a thorough command of the fundamental principles of investment along with the economic factors that influence markets. You will not be able to use the Wave Principle as a substitute for knowledge. Don't even think about it!

In all cases, the time to take immediate action will be the completion of a five-wave count, whether you're dealing with a bull market or a bear market. In a bull market, the five-wave count will involve the completion of three impulse movements interrupted by secondary downward action. In the case of a bear market, the five-wave count will be that of Wave C of a correction, which will involve three impulse movements in a downward direction interrupted by two rallies. Even in the case of complex corrections, the pattern is all in a five-wave count.

Whereas the ending of a five-wave count should be the established criteria for instigating new positions counter to the previous trend, Elliott's rule that says "a corrective wave should not dip below the first wave of the cycle it is correcting" offers an extremely important guide to prevent one of the most common of all counting errors: the mixing of cycle degrees.

For example, the fifth wave of a cycle move is completed when the fifth sub-minuette wave, of the fifth minute wave, of the fifth minor wave, of the fifth intermediate wave, of the fifth primary wave is completed. In order to gain confirmation that the fifth wave of a cycle move has actually been completed, the series of waves to follow should initially involve the correction of a sub-minuette wave that does actually carry below the first wave of that tiny formation.

In turn, the waves of the next-higher degree would follow a similar pattern, a correction in a minute wave series falling below the first wave in the series. This process will continue when a trend is being reversed, until the level of cycle degree is reached. A cycle-wave bear market must follow a cycle-wave bull market. A primary bull market is followed by a primary bear market.

Quite simply, as long as the corrective action of waves in progressively lower degrees does not violate the overall upward direction, ending above the first wave of the cycle degree that is being corrected, the trend can be considered upward. As soon as a breach of that rule occurs, it can then be comfortably assumed that a trend reversal is in the making.

The importance of that trend reversal can be determined by the number of wave degrees in which the corrective wave falls below the peak of the first wave of the same cycle degree. If, after completion of a five-wave sub-minuette series, the sub-minuette corrective wave falls below the peak of the first wave of the series, corrective action of a wave of at least the next-higher degree is taking place. If the corrective wave that follows the completion of a five-wave minuette pattern falls below the first wave of that pattern, you then know that a corrective wave of at least a minor formation is taking place. The principle applies from the sub-minuette pattern all the way through to primary waves, cycle waves, super-cycle waves, and grand, super-cycle waves.

Watching for a shift in the wave count is another important element that can aid in the confirmation of important trend changes. Sub-minuette wave 5, of minute wave 5, of minor wave 5, of intermediate wave 5, of primary Wave 5, of cycle Wave 5, of super cycle Wave 5, of grand super cycle Wave 5, should have five components, as is normal. If suddenly the next series of sub-minuette waves has only three components and the minute waves and minor waves only have three components, a trend reversal could be in the making that acts to retrace the entire grand super cycle.

The small waves can be used as excellent indicators when an important trend reversal is expected or as confirmatory indicators for one that is suspected to have occurred. These tactical devices will not work all of the time, but they will work often enough to give you the all-important edge you need to improve your performance as a trader or investor.

Another device that can help to confirm a trend reversal, in addition to the various other techniques that have been described, incorporates a type of trend line. This is not the trend line used in the traditional sense. Following what appears to be the completion of a five-wave count, tangents are established at the beginning of the count (0) and at the bottom of the fourth wave for the count, extended beyond the time horizon of the fifth wave.

When the price action of the market under study drops below the 0–4 line, there is a high probability that a trend reversal of significant magnitude is taking place. Be on the alert for other small 0–4 lines that are crossed and may be contained within a larger 0–4 line. It is possible for the market to drop below a small 0–4 line and a large 0–4 line at the same time.

You will be able to draw 0–4 lines from long-term five-wave counts; intermediate-term, five-wave counts; and minor five-wave counts. The greater the size of the 0–4 line, the greater the probability of an important turning point when the 0–4 line is crossed. You must only use swings of equal dimensions in time and space when selecting the tangents for your 0-4 lines.

Some traders draw lines as soon as two waves and the pivotal point of a third is completed. This has 0–2 lines. According to those who have tested the method, if after a 0–2 line is drawn, a 0–4 line is drawn that remains at the same angle as the 0–2 line, or is outside the angle of the 0–2 line, when

Figure 60
ZERO 4 LINES

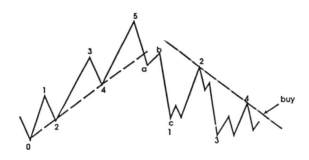

the 0–4 line is penetrated, this adds to the likelihood of important pivotal action. If the bottom of a Wave 4 falls considerably short of the angle drawn from the tangents of the beginning of the formation and the bottom of Wave 2, then the pivotal action following the penetration of the 0–4 line is not considered to be as reliable.

0–2 lines and 0–4 lines can be used in downward formations as well as in upward formations to confirm a turning point. In a downtrend, the investor would be looking for an upward penetration of the 0–4 line.

It has been suggested that traders and investors can do quite well, when applying the Wave Principle, by using nothing more than 0–4 lines. I do not subscribe to that theory. I feel the technique is useful, but should be used in conjunction with the various other confirmatory tenets of the Wave Principle. The following illustration shows how these 0–4 lines and 0–2 lines are constructed.

Applications to Individual Share-price Movements

The examples used throughout the text up until now have all dealt with very broad-based stock market indices. The question arises: Can the Wave Principle be used on the price action of individual shares?

In the majority of cases, the Elliott Wave Principle will not be of much use with regard to individual issues. It is of no value whatsoever in selection, and of marginal value with regard to timing. Elliott always kept in mind the basic principles of his philosophy and applied them in a reasonably consistent manner. His hypothesis was that the principle he discovered worked best when applied to the popular market averages rather than individual issues. This would appear to be logical in view of the emotional rationale behind the Wave Principle. The Wave Principle, as seen in the broad movements of the stock market, is the reflection of mass response to the stimuli of the average. Accordingly, the greater the number that follow particular market averages, the more consistent will be the response. In New York, we have what many consider to be a mathematical monstrosity in the form of the antiquated DJ30, yet this indicator is a far better barometer of the stock market than either the NYSE Composite Index or the S & P 500 Index, despite the far greater number of shares in both of these latter indices.

When it came to the treatment of individual shares, Elliott merely intimated that the best approach was to select issues which moved in harmony with the averages. Elliott also stressed marketability and soundness. His main recommendations were as follows:

1. First select the industrial groups that are performing in harmony with the averages.

2. Then select the shares that are moving in sympathy with the individual groups.

3. Age of Shares: According to Elliott, the life of a share has three stages:

   (a) The first is the youthful, or experimental stage, during which such shares should be avoided, as they have not been properly seasoned.

   (b) The second is the creative stage. Shares that fall within this category have reached healthy development, thus making them a desirable medium for trading providing they are thoroughly seasoned.

   (c) The third, or grown-up stage, represents the period of fullest development. Dividends may be uniformly reliable and fluctuations narrow. For these reasons, the certificates become lodged in portfolios and therefore the shares are less attractive for trading purposes.

4. Always choose shares that are constantly active, medium priced, and seasoned leaders. A share that is frequently or occasionally inactive should be avoided for trading purposes, because waves are not being registered. Inactivity clearly indicates that the share does not enjoy thorough distribution or that it has not yet reached the full stage of development. Furthermore, there are practical dangers in trying to apply the principle to the high flyers, because, typically, even one

primary wave may go through a price rise of several hundred percent. Intermediate moves would thus fluctuate wildly, causing innumerable whipsaws if one tried to act on the price movement.

5. Diversify funds, i.e., employ more or less an equal amount of money in from five to ten companies and not more than one company in each group.

In a broad sense, when using the Wave Principle as an aid to the timing of individual share purchases, the first thing one must watch out for is the five-wave pattern. Purchases should only be made in issues which have not yet completed their five-wave patterns. It would also be imprudent to consider purchases in shares that are well along in their development of a fifth wave.

In this respect, the exact position of the market cycle may not be of much help. Elliott observed that individual issues will complete their own cycles, sometimes ahead of the market cycle, sometimes behind it. In bull markets, each of the individual industrial groups will make their peaks at different times. While many groups will perform in harmony with the averages throughout the bull cycle, as many again will not. The tendency is that just the opposite occurs at the bottom of a bear market, when most industrial groups will reach their troughs in unison.

The Secret of the Markets

While Elliott's work has been available to the US financial community for quite some time, it is yet to receive the recognition it rightly deserves, nor the type of academic examination that might truly advance an understanding of Elliott's methods. By and large, the analytical community has little interest in adopting new techniques until they become fashionable and are assimilable by other analysts and clients . . . particularly institutional clients. The business of markets is transacted by and with people who speak the same language and know the same code words.

In order to have developed as complicated, yet logical a mechanism as the Wave Principle, Elliott must have done practically nothing other than study wave patterns in their various forms in the stock market, commodity markets, and other markets, classifying them, sub-dividing them, superimposing wave patterns on other wave patterns, codifying each structure, checking, cross-checking, then testing, testing, testing in the dozen or so years he worked on his theory, from 1935 until his death in 1947.

Since the business of anticipating the future behavior of prices on markets began, every market strategist who may have been considered a genius by some has also been considered an imbecile and a lunatic by others, particularly those who may have attempted to advance the art of studying price movements. Every investment innovator I know of—fundamentalists, technicians, and academics alike—have all been plagued by a collection of variegated detractors, like dogs who have been bitten in different places by several fleas of multifarious breeds.

The secret of markets is . . . there is no secret and there never will be. That's the secret that not one investment analyst in ten thousand is prepared to admit. There is no touchstone. Stop wasting your time looking for one! There is no guru available to rescue you from the depths of your investment failures and such a messiah is unlikely to ever appear. There is yet to be discovered a universally accepted market theory. And, as Descartes might have pointed out, there is not even the comforting hope that those methods which have attracted the widest following might be the most nearly correct or even workable to any consistent and useful degree. In fact, it would not be unreasonable to assume, as Descartes suspected, that the most intelligent approach is likely to be the most complex, utilized by only a small minority. What is true is that the Wave Principle is a model of precision and logic, with all of its obscurities, compared to the vagueness surrounding most other technical and chart principles which offer little, if any, value to the serious intelligent investor.

It is a sad truth of the Wave Principle that its astute and experienced practitioners—as opposed to several who have used the Wave Principle as a marketing cosmetic—will almost always run counter to popular sentiment, which is not a way to win friends, influence investors, and gain popularity during a lifetime. Those skillful practitioners of the Wave Principle must by instinct and conviction be bearish when the majority are bullish and be bullish when all of the investment community, luminaries, commentators, et al., are in deepest gloom. It creates a sort of closed loop of unpopularity, from which only the very strong minded can detach themselves from.

But now that you have come to the end of your quest, now that you have detected and solved—or at least addressed—all the problems associated with the application of the Wave Principle, I trust that you are strong enough to stand up to such trials. And perhaps, you are even courageous enough to build on Elliott's work, to record your ideas and theories, so that future generations of investors may benefit.

15
The Summer of 1991

Never try to teach a pig to think. It doesn't work. It also annoys the pig.

—ANONYMOUS

It is the summer of 1991. I've just finished having my lunch at Chez Frederick on the Isle St. Honorat, off the coast of Cannes, and I'm heading back to Monaco Port in my 41 foot Bruno Abbotte Primatist power launch. Usually, I have to reserve a table a week in advance if I want to lunch at Chez Frederick in mid-summer. That holds true for most of the gourmet spots on the Cote D'Azur during the high season. On this occasion, I telephoned Henri, the head waiter, only an hour before leaving Cap D'Ail port, where I berth my boat. Henri managed to put together a table for my party of six without a hitch.

Life is good! During the summer of 1991 it was especially good . . . at least for me! I even managed to escape the irksome task of zig-zagging through the variety of craft, from ocean-going yachts to Boston whalers, that are usually scattered in a random fashion, tie-lines criss-crossed, in the inlet waters off the Isle of St. Honorat.

Once outside the three-mile limit, I advanced the throttles on my two 650-horsepower BPM engines and immediately began to feel the delicious sensation of the Mediterranean breeze gushing over my sun-drenched skin as the nose of my craft pointed skyward, playing leapfrog with the tidal waves.

"Hang on!" I shouted to my passengers, trying to make myself heard above the roar of the engines. "We're about to fly!"

The waters of the Mediterranean were as smooth as glass, while the sun added the kind of sparkling effervescence to the sea that is rarely found anywhere in the world outside the Cote D'Azur. Be it an ocean liner, trawler, sea cruiser, sailboat, wind-surfer, or even a dinghy, the boating conditions were sheer perfection. Yet, the number of boats on the water during this glorious day in the summer of 1991 were far fewer than would have been expected. In fact, as I skimmed over the waters on my way to Monaco Port, there wasn't a boat in sight. There was an eerie calm. Of course, there was no shortage of boats in the various coastal ports with "For Sale" signs attached to their bows and hanging from their masts, some of which were in the hands of receivers.

Once past Nice, I turned my boat starboard, approaching the beaches of Cap Ferrat, Villefrance, and Eze sur Mer. The depleted array of sun-tanned, bare-breasted beauties was made more conspicuous by the even smaller number of their bronzed, bare-chested, Neanderthal-like counter-parts that normally forms the complete picture of the French Riviera most summers. The summer of 1991 was a bit different. Some of the hotels along the coast were offering discounts of as much as fifty percent in an effort to fill their empty rooms. Many of the same hotels were operating at occupancy levels of less than fifty percent during the summer of 1991 on the French Riviera.

Maxima, one of the few restaurants on the Cote D'Azur with a two-star rating in the Michelin guide, had closed at the beginning of the summer. The owner of one of my favorite restaurants in Monte Carlo, which closed "temporarily" in July, discreetly advised his patrons that no re-opening was being planned. Empty shops that had been formerly occupied by haute-couture boutiques were rapidly becoming a permanent feature on the Boulevard Des Moulins, the Main Street of Monte Carlo. The well-known Gucci chain had closed its Monte Carlo branch the year before, along with other branches located in various major cities.

You see, the world was in recession during the summer of 1991. That recession was engulfing every corner of the globe, even the French Riviera, the favorite playground of billionaires and millionaires for decades, the international Disneyland for adults. There was no escape from that reces-sion, unless you knew how to use it to your advantage. Very few did. Most were victims.

The entrance to Monaco Port is bordered by an oceanic museum on one side and a building housing the offices of stockbrokers Merrill Lynch on the other. By law, the maximum speed limit of any boat entering a port is three knots per hour in the principality. As my boat edged into the port, I turned my binoculars toward the offices of Merrill Lynch to see if my friend of twenty-five years' standing and stockbroker-to-the-wealthy, Marc Sibony, was still toiling behind the"tape." He was there, alright! The Dow Jones Industrial Averages were making new all-time, intra-day highs. The herd was out in full force.

The Ritual of Self-destruction

On they rush, headlong toward the sea. They scramble over one another. They bite and tear, shriek and squeal. Gripped by a seemingly mad compulsion, thousands of lemmings sweep down the countryside, destroying everything in their path, in a wild and frenzied stampede toward the Arctic Ocean from the hills of Norway, supposedly in search of food. They cross tundra, rivers, even lakes at an ever-quickening tempo. Finally, they reach the water's edge. Then suddenly, something strange and bizarre happens. The quest for sustenance ceases to become a consideration. The instinct of hunger disappears and is replaced with an instinct for self-destruction. Thousands upon thousands of lemmings plunge headlong into the sea, drowning themselves in what takes on the appearance of a bubbling cauldron, seemingly rising to the surface of the waters from the burning fires of hell.

Like the Wave Principle, no one is really certain why this happens. It just happens. Many theories have been advanced, but none are wholly conclusive. Through some mysterious force—a process of natural selection—a few lemmings remain on shore, refusing to take part in the ritual of self-destruction. These remaining lemmings form the nucleus of the lemming population, so that 3.86 years later there will be another herd of lemmings to repeat the ritual of mass suicide all over again. Not unlike the Wave Principle, the life cycle of the lemming, which appears to conform to the Golden Ratio, remains one of the mysteries of that nature's law that governs the behavior of all life forms known on this planet.

During the summer of 1991, gripped by a lemming-like fever, the players on Wall Street were once again heading for their metaphorical sea, as they had done so many times before, at the peak of a bull market or the top of a secondary correction in a bear market. Like a herd of hungry lemmings, greedy stock purchasers were determined to rumble and stumble onward to their financial self-destruction, trampling over anything, or anyone, that might stand in their way.

Their hunger was based on the rhetoric of President Bush and his supportive economic cohorts, who promised an economic recovery during the second half of 1991. Similar promises were made by the Chancellor of The Exchequer, Norman Lamont, in Britain, where investors were also joining the lemming-like mission. The fact that these political exhortations were almost a carbon copy of those continuously made by President Hoover during the three long years of depression during the 1930s, made little impression on investors during the summer of 1991. Investors, and the public, believed what they wanted to believe.

Politicians know it is easy to convince people of the things they want to believe to start with. So do the stockbrokers, dealers, and promoters who exploit the avarice which is undeflected by thought. During the summer of 1991, the public wanted to believe an economic recovery was at hand, or just around the corner, as promised by the politicians. The investment community-at-large duly fuelled the fantasies, as hope triumphed over reason once again.

A great man once said, "You can fool some of the people all of the time and all of the people some of the time." The summer rally of 1991, along with the entire stock market bull run that followed the Gulf War, would appear to have been based on this assertion. The very few in number who cannot be fooled all of the time were not a meaningful consideration in either political or investment circles as the lemmings marched on.

There were two distinct schools of thought relating to the minor up-swing in economic activity that occurred in the United States following the end of the Gulf War. One group of economists held that the Gulf War itself was the cause of the worldwide recession. Therefore, the selective economic strength that appeared in the US economy following the end of the Gulf War represented the incipient stages of a long economic recovery that would continue well into the future, taking a firm hold in the second half of 1991.

President Bush promised an economic recovery during the second half of 1991, and most economists were prepared to subscribe to the premise of the president, like those with their cloudy crystal balls during the Hoover Administration. The track record of those economists who had been endorsing the views of the US president during the recession of the 1990s was certainly less than encouraging.

On 5 July 1990, the *Wall Street Journal* ran an article showing the results of forty leading economists. Eighty-five percent of the economists polled insisted there would be no recession in the United States for twelve months. Those forecasts were made two weeks after the recession of 1990 had officially started. On 19 June 1991, "Blue Chip Economic Indicators," an organization that specializes in reviewing US economic forecasts, surveyed fifty leading Wall Street economists. Only three percent of those surveyed accepted that the US recession began in June 1990 or earlier. Ninety-five percent said the recession would be over no later than the summer of 1991. Several claimed the recession had ended in May 1991.

There is little question that Wall Street economists have been habitually wrong as a group, notoriously failing to predict recessions and being equally wrong for a long, long time, before they suddenly become right in their predictions of economic recovery. But, the word from the herd during the summer of 1991 was the overwhelming prediction that the economic recession had ended, or was about to end, which fuelled the lemming-like behavior of investors on Wall Street during the summer of 1991, when the Dow Jones Industrial Averages made a new, all-time, intra-day high.

The other school of economic thought during the summer of 1991 held that the improvement in economic activity in the United States during the period following the Gulf War was an unsustainable affair, reflecting nothing more than a temporary improvement in sentiment. The slight bulge in a selective number of economic aggregates was seen as lopsided and not in any way indicating the type of performance associated with a strong economic turnaround.

Those who refuse to accept the notion that an economic recovery was either at hand, or in the offing, insisted that none of the phenomena cited by those who believe in the thesis of President Bush, other than a fleeting, modest building of US inventories, promised a great deal of help for the US economy during the second half of 1991. Moreover, these economists, whose views are in the minority, state that the areas which revealed an improvement in economic activity following the Gulf War were not in any way related to the causes of the 1990 economic downturn to start with.

The consequences of past speculative excesses in fixed investment and debt creation were expected to produce continuing economic woe. During the summer of 1991, retail sales were once again beginning to reflect consumer restraint. While corporate profits may have firmed in the second quarter, there was the expectation that US corporate profits would resume their decline in the second half.

In the minds of the very few whose forecasts were unfettered by the instincts of the herd, the effects of the Gulf War had fully spent their force by the summer of 1991, while the initial causes of the 1990 downturn— long-term structural weakness in fixed investment and long-term secular problems in the financial sector—remained a stark reality. This situation was expected to last for quite some time. The economists who shared this view feel that paying for past excesses will be a painful and slow process in the United States.

By the time share prices began to falter on Wall Street during the summer of 1991, most investors had already submerged themselves in their sea of financial self-destruction. All who had intended to buy during the early summer months had already bought, as indicated by the fall in the volume of trade, as the summer months progressed.

On 6 August 1991, the Federal Reserve allowed interest rates to move lower. The Dow Jones Industrial Averages rallied by 38 points in response, buoyed by the enthusiasm of those ne'er-do-wells who cling to the notion that interest rate relationships are a static force and are capable of making an automatic contribution to economic activity.

On 7 August 1991, it was revealed that the decision of the Federal Reserve to lower interest rates was based on a report from the twelve regional Federal Reserve banks, who had concluded that the improvement in US economic activity during preceding months had been slow and uneven.

The periodic *Beige Book* summary of economic conditions, produced by the twelve Federal Reserve banks, was published a day after the Federal Reserve acted to lower short-term interest rates in order to stimulate the flagging economy. The survey said that retail sales in the United States were generally flat. It also said there was some pick-up in manufacturing business, but the recovery was not uniform. Demand was seen as stronger for consumer goods than for capital equipment. The demand for consumer goods was seen as unsustainable.

The *Beige Book* also said that employment prospects in the United States were less than encouraging. Several districts reported state and local governments as well as service industries cutting back on employment. The pick-up in home sales that followed the end of the Gulf War was seen to be losing steam. Commercial real estate and non-residential building showed no improvement whatsoever, while business loan demand was weak in most districts. Credit standards had tightened considerably over the two quarters that had just passed. Credit quality was considered to be steadily declining.

The message was concise and clear. The *Beige Book* flatly denied the glowing economic forecasts that had been made during the preceding weeks and months. An economic recovery was nowhere near as certain as many had been led to believe. Those who maintained that the United States was about to experience a double-digit recession had considerable fortification from the Federal Reserve's *Beige Book*.

The Message of the Wave Principle

With the US economy and the financial system more vulnerable than ever during the summer of 1991, it seemed to be just a matter of time before further developments would trigger a sharp decline in the US stock market. Perhaps it would be the let-down which must inevitably follow after unrealistically high hopes about bank mergers inter alia. Or maybe it would be a sudden rash of selling from abroad due to the worldwide credit crunch at the time.

Other possible triggers for a collapse in share prices in the United States could also include a rise in interest rates, more insurance company failures, a flight to Treasury bills and bonds, another collapse in the junk bond market . . . or perhaps some event investors were not thinking about at the time . . . like the deposition of Soviet President Mikhail Gorbachev . . .

There was also the element of stock-price valuations. During the summer of 1991, the shares of companies listed on the New York Stock Exchange were selling at an average of nearly eighteen times current earnings. Considering the prospect that earnings themselves were starting to fall sharply, you didn't need a Ph.D. in quantum mathematics to come to the conclusion that a massive adjustment was long overdue on Wall Street during the summer of 1991.

The factors which pointed to the likelihood of a sharp decline in share prices were firmly in place during the summer of 1991. But, these factors had been in place for quite some time, yet the Dow Jones Industrial Averages had recently risen to a new all-time high, along with the Financial Times Stock Exchange Index. Elliott Wave theorists had also been up in arms for quite some time, shrieking that a devastating collapse was at hand, like the fellows who walk along the streets in sandwich boards.

Bob Prechter, undoubtedly the most widely publicized of all Elliott Wave theorists, stated on 24 April 1991:

In the stock market, the long-term Elliott Wave pattern and the sentiment indicators are bearish. Although, a major decline could begin at anytime.

The ideal development from here would be a sell-off into late May, at least to below 2,850, then a rise in July to register its high for the year. The extent of any decline may affect whether or not the rise will carry to a new high, but as discussed in prior issues, the maximum upside potential this year should be limited to 3,250, which also happens to meet the rising resistance line which touches the 1987 and 1990 peaks. Keep in mind that the wave structure and time cycles do not require any further advance, while long-term patterns do require a drop to below Dow 1,700, ideally to 1,100.

For investors, the crucial facts are that the market (1) is within ten percent of its high, (2) is vulnerable to a sixty-percent decline beginning at any time, and (3) is not a safe place to invest.

In dissecting the forecast of Bob Prechter that was made in April 1991, one can certainly find fault and claim errors of judgement. By hindsight, it can be said that by following Prechter's advice, investors would have missed out on the summer rally that took the Dow Jones Industrial Averages up to a new all-time high. Prechter could also be accused of being less than definitive and hedging his bets with certain phraseology. Observations of this nature ignore the primary functions of the Wave Principle, along with the most important element of Prechter's forecast.

There was a sell-off in May 1991 that took the DJIA down to the area of 2,850. The May 1991 low was the lowest level reached following Prechter's forecast. From the May 1991 low, the DJIA did rise to a new all-time high in July, precisely as Prechter had forecast four months before. At the same time, at no time during those four months had the DJIA exceeded the ten-percent parameter which Prechter saw as the upper limits of any rally.

While Prechter's detractors may whine and complain about missing the summer rally, a market that has a sixty-percent risk factor while offering nothing more than a ten-percent reward factor, is a market that should be avoided. With the aid of the Wave Principle, Prechter said, "Investors should stay out." This advice was the most appropriate that could have been given at the time.

A Fallen Idol

Unfortunately, Bob Prechter has become somewhat of a fallen idol, undeservedly so. Bob is a fine analyst and has a command of the Wave Principle which rivals that of A. Hamilton Bolton and A.J. Frost. Bob should have seen it coming. As Shakespeare would have said, "Those whom the gods would seek to destroy they must first drive mad."

Bob Prechter was blessed with the opportunity of becoming associated with A.J. Frost. Frost worked with A. Hamilton Bolton for many years and was among the few astute practitioners of the Elliott Wave Principle at the time. After working with Frost for several years, just shortly after my book was published in England, *The Elliott Wave Principle As Applied to the UK Stock Market,* Prechter co-authored the book *The Elliott Wave Principle: Key to Stock Market Profits* with A.J. Frost.

When the book was published back in the late 1970s, both Prechter and Frost agreed that the Dow Jones Industrial Averages was in a bull market and capable of reaching the level of 2,700. Frost parted company with Prechter when Prechter decided he knew more than the teacher, and revised the forecast upward to DJIA 3,880. Frost was not pleased and could not find justification for the higher figure in accordance with any tenets of the Wave Principle that he had worked with over the years.

A.J. Frost, who was seventy-nine years old at the time and a man of unyielding intellectual integrity, and also a veteran of many, many Elliott Wave cycles, vehemently disagreed with the higher projection that Prechter had made and subsequently disassociated himself from any further work produced by Prechter. I am not prepared to venture any opinion on whether this disassociation was beneficial or justifiable.

Prechter's forecast of DJIA 3,880 was interrupted by the Crash of '87, which saw the DJIA plunging downward to the never, never land, instead of careering upward as Prechter predicted it would. Yet, it was Prechter's forecast of DJIA 3,880—which proved demonstrably wrong—that was given such overwhelming publicity by Wall Street and that rocketed Prechter to fame and fortune. Prechter now admits that the forecast took on a life of its own, which was probably well beyond what he had ever intended, when he made his forecast of DJIA 3,880.

Since the Crash of '87, very little has been heard of Bob Prechter, who now seems to be resting in seclusion; his forecasts no longer monitored by the media, followed only by those subscribers who have decided to stick with him. When Prechter first made his forecast of DJIA 3,880, the US bull market was climbing steadily. Whoever was willing to stick his neck out and make the highest forecast was bound to attract the most publicity. Bob Prechter, waving the Elliott Wave Principle, stuck his neck out and made that forecast. Everybody loves a bull. The more bullish, the more rapturous that love!

That love may be endearing, but it is certainly not enduring. People frown on those who make forecasting errors, in their unyielding self-righteousness. But, the herd is prepared to forgive and forget, provided the forecaster remains bullish. But, nobody loves a bear. Bob Prechter has committed the deadliest combination possible for any stock-market forecaster: he has made a bad forecast, and he has also turned bearish. I know precisely how deadly that combination can be from my own personal experience.

During the early 1970s, I, too, was the darling of the media in Britain. I was quite bullish at the time. My forecasts were monitored and applauded by the press. In May 1972, when the Financial Times Stock Exchange Index broke upwards to 545, I predicted the bull market would continue until the level of 700 was achieved, anticipating a further upward drive of 155 index points. My forecast was published with considerable enthusiasm and delight by the media. Shortly after I made that forecast, share prices turned sharply downward, engulfing the UK stock market in its worst bear market in history. Before the bear market was over, the Financial Times 30 Share Index lost nearly seventy-five percent of its value.

When the Financial Times 30 Share Index broke backward through the level of 500, during the latter part of 1972, I reversed my forecast, turning from bull to bear. The media never acknowledged my shift in stance or that my "bad forecast" only involved a margin of error of less than ten percent. In their indignant self-righteousness, the media had chosen to continue to harp on my original forecast, as if it were set in stone and no other had been made since.

In late 1974, I accurately forecast the level at which the bear market in Britain would end. In my book *The Elliott Wave Principle As Applied to the UK Stock Market,* I predicted that Britain would experience " . . . the longest and most glorious bull market in its stock market history," which duly occurred as I said it would.

In early 1981, I predicted a new bull market in US bonds that would be longer and stronger than any US bond bull market in fifty years, lasting some ten to fifteen years. That bull market in US bonds was still under way during the summer of 1991.

There were many other forecasts of similar accuracy to which I attribute the use of the Wave Principle. Yet, for nearly twenty years, I have had to suffer a continuous barrage of ridicule, insult, and degradation from one particular journalist in the United Kingdom who has chosen to ignore all of the forecasts I have made in the past twenty years, choosing only to remember my sin of turning bearish after being bullish back in 1972.

My heart goes out to Bob Prechter. Bob certainly has my respect and sympathy, along with many other fine analysts like Joe Granville, Jim

Dines, George Lindsey, Roger Babson, and others, who were hoisted to the rooftops of glory by the poisonous pens of the media, so they could later be pricked into oblivion with the same quills.

In late 1988, Prechter's forecast for the Dow Jones Industrial Averages was 400 . . . no big figure. While Prechter was the most bullish of the bulls, he ultimately became the most bearish of the bears, having interpreted Elliott Wave Theory as having completed that important and significant fifth wave, of a fifth wave, of a fifth wave, the wave to end all waves.

Frost and Prechter were again in disagreement on the correct interpretation of the Elliott Wave Theory in late 1988. Frost was convinced that Prechter would have to alter his short-term bearish view to get on the right track again. According to A.J. Frost back in late 1988, "There is no better investment than the stock market." The Dow Jones Industrial Averages were standing at 2,016 at the time and have since moved to 3,056, a gain of over fifty percent in less than three years.

Unlike Prechter, Frost never considered the Crash of '87 to have altered his longer-term bullish projection. According to A.J. Frost, during the upward movement of 1986, there was a peak in Wave IV at 1,738.75 of the DJIA. In order for the cyclical bear market to be confirmed by the Wave Principle, that Wave IV peak would have to be violated. The lowest close for the DJIA during the Crash of '87 was 1,738.41. On a closing basis, the DJIA remained within one percent of the Wave IV peak. At no time did Frost believe the Crash of '87 to have confirmed cyclical bear market conditions. He placed the plunge in the category of a corrective wave in a continuing bull market, rather than an impulse wave in a bear market, the latter being Prechter's interpretation.

Back in late 1988, Frost was expecting to see the fifth and final wave of the structure— which Prechter believed had already occurred—taking the DJIA above the level of 3,000 during the final stages of its development. His amazing time frame called for that achievement sometime during 1991. Bear in mind that Frost's forecast, based on the Wave Principle, was made two-and-one-half years ago.

Frost maintained that the US stock market was heading for a secular top. Essentially, Frost was looking for a period of euphoria followed by a period of panic sometime this year. According to Frost, the period from 1992 to 1994 may be reminiscent of 1931–1932. Referring to the post-1991 period, Frost says, "I feel we're coming into a period of decline right through 1992–1994, experiencing a whole series of Black Mondays, Tuesdays, Wednesdays, and Fridays. I think it's going to be just pitiful."

Supplementing his Elliott Wave considerations, Frost looks for three preconditions to confirm the major terminal juncture that he expects. The first is the position of the debt/loan ratio. A.Hamilton Bolton was the innovator of this tool, which measures the ratio of spending to short-term debt in the United States. Transactions which take place in New York are actually excluded from the figures due to the inordinate size of fiscal turnover in the city, which is not considered to be representative of monetary conditions of the nation in aggregate.

A.J. Frost's additional preconditions are an inverted yield curve, where short-term rates are higher than long-term rates, along with a wide divergence between the broad market of shares and the Dow Jones Industrial Averages. This breadth divergence would involve a steadily rising DJIA against a laggard advance/decline line, which begins to move in the opposite direction of the DJIA, indicating professional distribution under the umbrella of strong leading index movements, as was taking place during the summer of 1991. The three preconditions cited by Frost have already taken place.

A.J. Frost has never gone on record in terms of indicating how sharp the fall in share prices that he envisages is expected to be. Reading between the lines of his commentary, it would seem that his projections were falling into line with those of Bob Prechter. Prechter has since modified his parameters, forecasting a level of 1,100 for the DJIA rather than 400. Unfortunately, the decline in share prices during the summer of 1991 was not sufficiently protracted for a bear market or ostentatiously obvious enough to give either Frost's or Prechter's forecasts the credibility they deserve. Investors will probably have to see the DJIA down to about 1,000 before the forecasts of these pioneers receive widespread acknowledgement.

Alternative Counts

I have shown you the manner in which two professional analysts, Bob Prechter and A.J. Frost, both with an extensive knowledge of the Wave Principle along with many years of experience in applying this to the real world, are in total disagreement in terms of the precise position of the DJIA with the long wave cycle. During the summer of 1991, Prechter was convinced that Wave V had been completed during the summer of 1988 and that the upward drive from the lows of the 1987 crash was corrective

Wave B of a corrective pattern. Frost was equally convinced that super cycle Wave V—which might also be grand super cycle Wave V—had not yet been completed.

Yet, where both parties were in total agreement is that when Bob Prechter's Wave B reaches a terminal juncture, or when A.J. Frost's super cycle Wave V is complete, there's going to be one almighty, thundering bear market that's going to make the Crash of '87 look like a minor tertiary correction and possibly make the Crash of '29 like a teddy bear's picnic.

This you will probably find comforting: there are two interpretations that lead to the same conclusions. Although the interpretations are different, at least you know where you are going when the drive that began after the Crash of '87 is complete. The Dow Jones Industrial Averages, according to Frost and Prechter, are going down . . . a long way down for a long, long time.

Oh, if life could be so simple! We would all be disgracefully rich, picking up a billion or two when needed in the time it takes to count from one to five and pause for a count of a,b,c. I hate to tell you this, but during the summer of 1991, the two different interpretations offered by Frost and Prechter, along with the likely outcome, were not the only interpretations being offered by followers of the Wave Principle. There were others who neither agreed with the interpretations of Frost and Prechter nor the conclusions that both men had come to.

Glen Neely, seemingly a newcomer to the field of Wave Principle analysis, compared to the experience of A.J. Frost and Bob Prechter, established the Elliott Wave Institute in 1983 for the purpose of teaching Elliott Wave theory to serious students of the stock market. Glen Neely published *Elliott Wave in Motion* in 1988, which was intended to be an upgraded, expanded version of the work of R.N. Elliott, for the purpose of providing a more-scientific basis upon which wave principle analysis could be conducted.

In the United States, Glen Neely's Elliott Wave philosophy, techniques, and methods of sequential analysis have come to be known as "The Neely Method." There are certain divergences between "The Neely Method" and R.N. Elliott's basic tenets which I, personally, am somewhat suspicious of. In my research, I have never been able to fault the Wave Principle as Elliott had intended it to be and have found efforts to improve on the Wave Principle producing most unsatisfactory results.

Neely's approach to the Wave Principle is based on a perspective which incorporates a graphic representation by way of a price chart, or record-of-price action, representing an illustration of mass psychology. The current price of any security in the marketplace is held to be the product of millions of transactions, carried out by hundreds of thousands of people all over the world. The analysis of the price action in accordance with the principle of R.N. Elliott is therefore an analysis of the emotions and reactions of the masses as they unfold in time. Graphically, the application of the Wave Principle allows the market operator to organize and interpret the meaning of this mass psychology and its future implications, since it is asserted that mass psychology will follow certain structural relationships which are peculiar to the Wave Principle.

Neely, as other Elliott practitioners, subscribes to the view that various patterns, formations, channels, etc. follow certain rules and guidelines and, since these movements will occur in a relatively specific sequence, the investor who is aware of previous relationships is alerted to the possibilities of future relationships.

Philosophically, there can be no argument with Neely's perspective. There then comes a point of departure in Neely's work which I find conceptually alien to R.N. Elliott's basic philosophies and the principles of dealing in markets.

"My approach is far more pattern specific," says Glen Neely. "Elliott, as it was presented forty or fifty years ago, did not go into enough detail to explain very complex market conditions that permits considerable personal bias and a variety of interpretations. What I have tried to do over the past ten years is constantly add new rules to each individual type of formation, so that the criteria necessary to create that pattern is extremely rigid. In this way, the analysis will not lend itself flexibility or opinion.

"Everything the market does should be logically explainable," Neely adds. "My approach has a strong emphasis on the logical integration of information and market reaction and structure. Most Elliott Wave analysts have opinions all the time. I only have opinions once every six months, once a year, or whatever. It all depends on when the market allows me to have an opinion."

Markets are based on shifting opinions and nothing more. You never beat the market. At best, you join it! Neely appears to be trying to adopt a rational approach to a totally irrational environment in a mechanical way, unaware that the Wave Principle has no meaning if used in a manner where the world is considered as a static environment, prone to inflexiblity, rather than a dynamic one, ever changing, ever evolving. R.N. Elliott and most of the successful practitioners of the Wave Principle would never dare make that mistake.

Nevertheless, Glen Neely must be acknowledged as having a thorough understanding of the Wave Principle and a practical working knowledge of the subject. During the summer of 1991, his interpretation was indeed an interesting one.

Neely asserts that the peak in the Dow Jones Industrial Averages that was reached in the summer of 1987, before the Crash of '87, was part of an Elliott Wave diagonal triangle that had been developing for close to one year and was part of a terminal formation. Neely's interpretation of the wave pattern that was developing from the lows of 1986 to the highs of 1987, necessitated a complete retracement within three months of the 1987 peak. Neely's term of reference called for a drop from the 2,700 level of the DJIA to 1,900, or less, in order to validate the analysis. The Crash of '87 was the acid test for Glen Neely in terms of confirming the precise wave count, along with what may come next.

The Crash of '87, having reaffirmed the position of the DJIA in the context of the Elliott Wave Principle for Neely, has led him to the conclusion that the DJIA had gone about as far as it was likely to go during the early summer of 1991. Neely felt that upside potential for the DJIA from the June 1991 peak was virtually non-existent for the twelve to twenty-four months to follow. It was also his contention at the time that the US stock market was on the verge of the sharpest decline since the Crash of 1987, which would take the Dow Jones Industrial Averages back to the lows of 1990.

Here, there is a strict departure from the forecasts of Prechter and Frost, who believe a decline of a far greater magnitude is in store on the scale of a 1930s-type long-term-cycles bear market, where the DJIA could lose ninety percent or more of its value. Frost believes such an event is pre-ordained, since we are about to complete the calamitous primary Wave V, of cycle Wave V, of super cycle Wave V. According to Frost, Primary Wave V has already been completed. Although Neely is not specific on the point, it would appear that this count told him that primary Wave V had not yet begun.

During the summer of 1991, Neely was looking for a quick and dirty decline to take the DJIA back to an area near the 2,100 level. In his mind's eye, based on his wave analysis, a decline of about 1,000 points for the DJIA was likely to occur in a time frame of two to ten weeks, once it gets under way. The decline, which was expected to be of similar magnitude, but slightly longer duration than the Crash of '87, was then expected to be followed by a long and labored recovery, taking the DJIA back to the level of the summer-of-1991 high.

After the DJIA plunges to the 1990 low and then recovers to the summer-of-1991 high, Neely's analysis then calls for an extended sideways movement for a year or more. "The pattern we have been in according to the wave theory," says Neely, "is one of psychological extremes or polarization of opinion. This means, every time a low is approached, members of the public become incredibly bearish. On a long-term scale, that bearishness should be relatively pervasive for the next five or ten years. As we approach the major highs, all those who prefer to be bullish and are looking at the international scene with all of the nice things that are happening there, will begin to get very excited about the upside potential. The battle between those two forces will mean they continually neutralize each other. In my opinion, that is going to create a sideways market for at least five years, where the market may move up to as high as 400 for the cash S&P and the low of May 1988. The market should predominantly go nowhere."

As most astute investors are fully aware, markets will always do whatever they have to do to make absolutely certain that most investors are mostly wrong, most of the time. During the summer of 1991, markets were divided into two extremes. There were those who were anticipating an economic recovery at any time, accompanied by a New World Order and an expansion in world trade as a side effect that would push share prices into the stratosphere. There were others anticipating Armageddon, a 1930s-type depression and stock market crash of overwhelming magnitude. During the summer of 1991, few, if any, investors were giving any thought whatever to a "Mister In-between" kind of environment, incorporating transition and low economic growth accompanied by a stock market that simply traded sideways, bordered by strict parameters. On that score, Glen Neely has an interesting point to make.

Beat The Dealer!

A few years ago, a mathematician wrote a book called *Beat The Dealer*. It was a book that described a system which would enable the user to consistently win at the casino game of blackjack. Unlike most "systems," this was not a book dealing with theoretical probabilities that might, or might not, have practical application in real life. This was a method which could be utilized in the real world of professional gambling, by professionals and amateurs alike.

In fact, so effective was the mathematical method that was devised by the author, that after accumulating several hundred thousand dollars with his system, he was banned from playing at most of the casinos in the United States and Europe. Others began using the method with equal success, who were also banned from casinos, but only after the casinos had suffered considerable loss. Eventually, the manner in which blackjack was dealt at casinos had to be changed, since it was seen that there was a method where the player could have a distinct advantage over the "house," and that advantage was a considerable one. Before the method was devised, the game of blackjack was played with one deck of cards in casinos. The use of the method devised by this mathematician necessitated the introduction of four decks of cards in the "shoe" instead of one, restoring the advantage usually enjoyed by the casino operator.

Games of chance fall into two categories, ones involving natural selection—which is random—and those involving finite correlation. A roulette wheel does not have a memory. Equally, a pair of dice has no recollection of the numbers preceding the last throw. The players may have such a recollection, but the dice do not. The result of each spin of the wheel, each throw of the dice, is totally independent of all that has gone on before. These are games of natural selection.

In some casinos, there are thirty-six numbers on the roulette wheel along with a *0* and a *00*. Yet, if you bet on a number you will only be paid 35-to-1. On the theoretical completion of two sequences where all of the numbers will have appeared, the casino operators will win thirty-eight times, while the players will only win thirty-six times. In other words, the number of possibilities exceed the payout ratio, giving the casino operator a distinct advantage. In dice games, the same applies.

When the number of possibilities exceeds the payout ratio, in a game of natural selection, the player must lose with the progression of play. The greater the number of plays, the greater the chance of loss. This is a mathematical certainty. When the game is one of natural selection, there is no chance whatever of any player shifting the odds in his favor, unless he cheats. I do not recommend cheating.

The game of blackjack, as it was originally played in casinos with one deck of cards, is not a game of natural selection. It is a game where the odds favoring the player change as each card leaves the deck. When we get down to the very last card in the deck, the odds favoring the player can be overwhelming, since it is possible for the player to have a reasonable knowledge—without cheating—of what the remaining card is. Yet, predicting what cards would come up next was not an aspect of the method devised by this mathematician for beating the casino.

In a deck of fifty-two cards, there is a fixed relationship between the suits, number of "picture cards," and the cards which have numbers. There is also a payout that corresponds to the fixed relationship based on the mathematical chances of holding a hand of "21." When the very first hand is dealt, the mathematical chances in terms of the payout favor the casino, even if the player takes a card, or refuses to take a card, based on what would produce the most favorable outcome on the basis of mathematical certainty. But, as the cards are dealt, the mathematical probabilities change significantly. At times, the nature of the cards remaining in the deck can offer possibilities that are decidedly in favor of the player or decidedly in favor of the casino, where the player stands very little chance of winning. This can be predetermined without a great deal of effort. I know! I've done it!

First, it is a very simple matter to arrive at a state of play in the game of blackjack where the way that you play gives you the best possible chance against the house, leaving you with the minimal possible disadvantage. There are simple basic rules that anyone can commit to their psyche until it becomes a matter of habit. Then comes the point of departure.

In a full deck of cards, the ratio of picture cards to numbered cards is marginally in favor of the casino during the state of play, provided the player uses the gaming strategy that will reduce his disadvantage to the minimum. After the first hand is dealt, the ratio between the numbered picture cards will have changed. During the second hand that is dealt, that change will have either benefited the player or the casino, based on the nature of the change. According to the mathematical probabilities, if the ratio of pictured cards to numbered cards has increased as the second hand is dealt, the change in relationship favors the player. If the ratio of numbered cards to picture cards has increased after the first or subsequent hands have been dealt, the change benefits the casino.

Basically, the method designed to effectively beat the game of blackjack involved a risk-evaluated strategy incorporating a money management technique. The risk-evaluated element called for a method of playing the game in basically the same way the dealer would play the game. The dealer has finite rules that he cannot deviate from. The player must also adopt finite rules which give him the smallest disadvantage. Where the player has flexibility and the dealer does not, are in his money management techniques. The dealer has to deal every hand; the player does not. The dealer has no choice over the amount of stake, other than the house limit, whereas the players can choose what he wants to bet, providing it doesn't exceed the house limit.

In the system which has been used to effectively beat the dealer in the game of blackjack, the player draws cards and adopts a finite method of play, placing him on par with the dealer to the nearest possible extent. Then, by determining whether or not the remaining number of cards favor him or not, he decides how much to bet. If the ratio of high cards to low cards favors the dealer, he will reduce his bet or not bet at all. If the ratio of high cards to low cards is in his favor, he will increase his bet.

Not only is it possible to apply these principles to the application of the Wave Principle, it is quintessential. The most important observation to be made through a comparison of this winning method for the game of blackjack—which has been proven beyond question—with that of dealing in markets, is the element of prediction. As can be readily seen, the element of prediction is only of relatively minor significance. Risk evaluation and that which can be quantified are the critical elements in all forms of speculation.

Profits or Predictions?

Most of those who have exploited the Wave Principle and have gained popular recognition are in the prediction business, rather than the money-making business. These are two distinct, different businesses calling for a variety of different skills. In the prediction business, the idea is to make lots and lots of predictions, focusing on those that are right and ignoring those that are wrong. The object is to provide the impression that most of your predictions were right even though they may not have been. There is also the subtle technique of offering vast rewards in the future, which often necessitates over-dramatizing the forecasts.

The prediction business, like any business, is a very competitive one. In order to succeed in the prediction business, you have to use techniques which are similar to your competitors and hopefully improve on those techniques. However, the road to success in the prediction business really has very little to do with making accurate predictions. R.N. Elliott's predictions were absolutely brilliant. Elliott certainly never achieved the notoriety and financial success of Joe Granville. No less astounding were the predictions of A. Hamilton Bolton, who had completely mastered the Wave Principle, yet had never been rewarded with the fame and fortune acquired by Bob Prechter, whose experience with the Wave Principle could not possibly be as comprehensive.

Success in the prediction business is about making forecasts that people like to read and which are popular. The emphasis is also on giving the appearance of being accurate, rather than making accurate predictions. Rising to the heights of popularity in the prediction business also means making predictions that attract attention, wording your prediction in a god-like manner for maximum impact. None of that has anything at all to do with the business of making money in the stock market, while acting on the basis of predictions—even on the limited occasions when those predictions may be correct—is not the appropriate conceptual approach to dealing with either the Wave Principle or markets in general. You must stop thinking in terms of predictions and begin to think only of quantifiable possibilities and probabilities. Then, and only then, will you be able to acquire a winning approach to markets. Winning may not be everything, but losing isn't anything.

Unlike the prediction business, the profit-making business in markets is readily quantifiable by the bloodless verdict of your personal balance sheet. If you've been making consistent profits in markets over the years, the tools and methods you have been using are the right ones. If your profits have been somewhat erratic, or, on balance, you have more losses than profits to show for your efforts, then the tools and methods you have been using are the wrong ones. This is unarguable. The only way you can appear to be right when you've been ruefully wrong is by engaging in self-deception, which is the kiss of death for anyone involved in investment markets. The profit-making business is a far more demanding taskmaster than the prediction business.

I have deliberately demonstrated the manner in which those with a great deal of experience have come up with the different interpretations of the Wave Principle during the summer of 1991 and also three different predictions. If you are in the prediction business, you will be none too happy about the idea that during the summer of 1991, the Wave Principle was subject to the possibility of three totally different outcomes, possibly more. But, if you're in the money-making business, the actual outcomes and predictions shouldn't make a bit of difference. Although the Wave Principle may have been subject to three different interpretations during the summer of 1991, all three interpretations had one thing in common.

Whatever the nature of the prediction, the Wave Principle was shouting, in no uncertain terms, that the summer of 1991 was not the time to be buying stocks.

In my illustration of the system that provided a winning system for blackjack, it should have been evident that predicting precisely what card was going to come out of the deck next was not an essential element for winning. The ability to anticipate the precise nature of the next card may be useful, but over-concentration on attempting to predict precisely what card would come up next would tend to overshadow the more vital aspects of the winning strategy. This also holds true for the Wave Principle.

When using the Wave Principle, you will be able to calculate precisely what level the Dow Jones Industrial Averages—or whatever other market you choose—is going to move to and when it is going to get there. The results you obtain when making these predictions will seem impressive. But, those results will be absolutely useless to you unless they are part of a profit-making strategy.

The Wave Principle should not be used as a tool for making predictions. It should be used as a tool for assisting in the accumulation of wealth by helping you evaluate risk and reducing or increasing your exposure to a market accordingly. When the wave count is completely obscure and offers an exceptionally wide array of possibilities, simply adopt a posture of what I describe as "masterly inactivity." In other words, when in doubt, stay out!

After you see the completion of five primary waves, predicting how far the next bear market will go and how long it will last is as much fun as any other game you can play with your clothes on. But, far more important than making that kind of prediction will be the automatic compulsion to reduce your exposure if you're long on the market and consider going short, regardless of how long or how deep the next correction is going to be. The Wave Principle tells you that upon completion of five primary waves, the next correction is going to be deeper than any correction that was seen since the beginning of the primary cycle run. That's really all you have to know if your objective is to operate with a strategic advantage.

During the course of your dealings in markets, you will always strive to make your sales as close to intermediate- and long-term tops as possible and make your purchases close to bottoms. The Wave Principle will help you to anticipate where those tops and bottoms are going to be with greater accuracy than any technical market tool ever devised. But, when the moment of truth comes and it is time to buy or sell, the incorporation of the Fibonacci Summation Series is going to be far more useful than a strategy linked to executing purchases or sales based on an index level you may have—or somebody else may have—calculated as a possible, or probable, terminal juncture several months before the time has come to act decisively.

A detailed analysis of the Wave Principle will be able to tell you what a market is likely to do at any hour, of any day, in any future year, with a degree of clarity well beyond the reach of any other analytical device. Yet, this feature belies the more meaningful and useful role the Wave Principle has to play as a strategic weapon in your battle for investment survival.

As long as your focal point is the money-making business, as opposed to the prediction business, you should be able to achieve the maximum benefit from the Wave Principle, with an immediate improvement in your investment returns.

I might say, "Good Luck!" But, once you have mastered the Wave Principle, luck will only play a minor role in your prospective investment performance.

Appendix

The Wave Principle
R.N. Elliott

ORIGINAL PUBLISHER'S NOTE:

During the past seven or eight years, publishers of financial magazines and organizations in the investment advisory field have been virtually flooded with "systems" for which their proponents have claimed great accuracy in forecasting stock market movements. Some of them appeared to work for a while. It was immediately obvious that others had no value whatever. All have been looked upon by THE FINANCIAL WORLD with great skepticism. But after investigation of Mr. R.N. Elliott's Wave Principle, THE FINANCIAL WORLD became convinced that a series of articles on this subject would be interesting and instructive to its readers. To the individual reader is left the determination of the value of the Wave Principle as a working tool in market forecasting, but it is believed that it should prove at least a useful check upon conclusions based on economic considerations.

THE EDITORS OF *The Financial World*

INTRODUCING "THE WAVE PRINCIPLE"

Since the beginning of time, rhythmic regularity has been the law of creation. Gradually man has acquired knowledge and power from studying the various manifestations of this law. The effects of the law are discernible in the behavior of the tides, the heavenly bodies, cyclones, day and night, even life and death! This rhythmic regularity is called a cycle.

Historical Significance

The first great advance in the scientific application of the law was made in the time of Columbus by Leonardo da Vinci in his illuminating study of the behavior of waves. Other great men followed with special applications: Halley with his comet, Bell with sound waves, Edison with electrical waves, Marconi with radio waves, and still others with waves of psychology, cosmic waves, television, etc. One thing in common that all these waves or forms of energy have is their cyclical behavior or ability to repeat themselves indefinitely. This cyclical behavior is characterized by two forces—one building up and the other tearing down. Today Hitler is said to be timing his conquests in accordance with this natural law as interpreted in the movements of the stars—but the destructive forces are accumulating and at the proper time will become dominant—completing the cycle.

Because of this phenomenon of repetition or rhythmic recurrence, it is possible to apply the lesson learned from other manifestations of the law in a very practical and profitable way. The trade cycle and the bull and bear movements of the stock market are also governed by the same natural law. Some fifty years ago Charles Dow through his observations of the important changes in the stock market gradually built up the Dow Theory, which now is accepted in many quarters as having special forecasting significance. Since Dow's studies, the store of information regarding market transactions has been greatly multiplied, and important and valuable new forecasting inferences can be drawn from certain behavior.

Through a long illness the writer had the opportunity to study the available information concerning stock market behavior. Gradually the wild, senseless and apparently uncontrollable changes in prices from year to year, from month to month, or from day to day, linked themselves into a law-abiding rhythmic pattern of waves. This pattern seems to repeat itself over and over again. With knowledge of this law or phenomenon (that I have called the Wave Principle) it is possible to measure and forecast the various trends and corrections (minor, intermediate, major and even movements of a still greater degree) that go to complete a great cycle.

FIGURE 1

This phenomenon is disclosed in Figure 1. The full wave or progressive phase of the cycle consists of five impulses: three moving forward and two moving downward. Waves 1, 3 and 5 are in the direction of the main trend. Wave 2 corrects Wave 1—and Wave 4 corrects Wave 3. Usually the three forward movements are in approximately parallel planes; this may also be true of Waves 2 and 4.

FIGURE 2

Each of the three primary waves that together make a completed movement is divided in to five waves of the next smaller or intermediate degree. This subdivision is shown in Figure 2. Note carefully that there are five smaller or intermediate waves making up the Primary Wave 1, five in Primary Wave 3, and five in Primary Wave 5. The Primary Wave 2 corrects the completed Primary Wave 1 consisting of five intermediate waves; Wave 4 in turn corrects the five intermediate waves that make up Primary Wave 3.

FIGURE 3

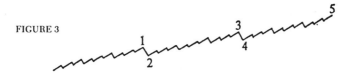

Each intermediate forward wave is in turn divided into five minor waves as shown in Figure 3. When the fifth minor wave of the fifth intermediate phase of the fifth primary movement has spent its force, a formidable top has been constructed. Upon completion of a movement of this magnitude, the destructive forces become dominant; the primary trend turns downward and a bear market is in progress long before the economic, political or financial reasons for the change in outlook are clearly apparent.

THE WAVE PRINCIPLE   PART II

In the preceding discussion of the Wave Principle as applied to the forecasting of stock price movements, it was pointed out that a completed movement consists of five waves, and that a set of five waves of one degree completes the first wave of the next higher degree. When Wave 5 of any degree has been completed, there should occur a correction that will be more severe than any previous correction in the cyclical movement.

Completed Movement

The rhythm of the corrective phases is different from that of the waves moving in the direction of the main trend. These corrective vibrations, or Waves 2 and 4, are each made up of *three* lesser waves, whereas the progressive waves (1, 3 and 5) are each composed of *five* smaller impulses. In Figure 4, the completed movement is shown, being identical to Figure 3 except that Waves 2 and 4 of the "zigzag" pattern are shown in greater detail. These Waves 2 and 4 are thus shown to consist each of three component phases but as these two waves are also "completed movements," they are also characterized by

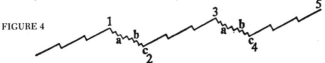

FIGURE 4

five-wave impulses; that is, the "a" and "c" phases (the first and third movements of the correction) are also each composed of five smaller waves, while "b" (the correction of the correction) is composed of three lesser waves. This question of corrections will require more extended discussion later on, as some forms and types are so complicated in structure that their presentation at this stage might be confusing.

The student using the Wave Principle to forecast price changes does not require confirmation by a companion average, inasmuch as the Principle applies to individual stocks, to various groups (steel, rails, utilities, coppers, oils, etc.), and also to commodities and the various "averages," such as those of Dow Jones, Standard Statistics, *New York Times, New York Herald Tribune,* the *Financial Times* of London, etc. At any given time it will be found that some stocks are advancing and others are declining; but the great majority of individual stocks will be following the same pattern at the same time. It is for this reason that the wave pattern of the "averages" will correctly reflect the cyclical position of the market as a whole. The larger the number of stocks included in an average, the more sharply outlined the wave impressions will be. This means that if stocks are widely distributed among a large number of individuals, the response to cyclical influences will be registered more definitely and rhythmically than if the distribution is limited.

Price Ranges Used

No reliance can be placed on "closings," daily or weekly. It is the highest and lowest ranges that guide the subsequent course of the cycle. In fact it was only due to the establishment and publication by Dow Jones of the "daily range" in 1928 and of the "hourly range" in 1932, that sufficient reliable data became available to establish the rhythmic recurrence of the phenomenon that I have called the Wave Principle. It is the series of actual "travels" by the market, hourly, daily, and weekly, that reveal the rhythmic forces in their entirety. The "closings" do not disclose the full story, and it is for this reason (lack of detailed data) that the phase-by-phase course of the London stock market is more difficult to predict than the New York market.

The complete measurement of the length of a wave is therefore its continuous travel between two corrections of the same or greater degree. The length of a wave of the lowest degree is its travel in one direction without any sort of correction, even in the hourly record. After two corrections have appeared in the hourly record, the movement then enters its fifth and last stage, or third impulse. So-called "resistance" levels and other technical considerations have but little value in forecasting or measuring the length or duration of these waves.

Outside Influences

As the Wave Principle forecasts the different phases or segments of a cycle, the experienced student will find that current news or happenings, or even decrees or acts of government, seem to have but little effect, if any, upon the course of the cycle. It is true that sometimes unexpected news or sudden events, particularly those of a highly emotional nature, may extend or curtail the length of travel between corrections, but the number of waves or underlying rhythmic regularity of the market remains constant. It even seems to be more logical to conclude that the cyclical derangement of trade, bringing widespread social unrest, is the cause of wars, rather than that cycles are produced by wars.

THE WAVE PRINCIPLE Part III

Because, after the Fifth Wave of an advancing movement has been completed, the correction will be more severe than any yet experienced in the cycle, it is desirable to determine beforehand where the top of this wave will be. With such knowledge, the investor can take the necessary steps to assume a defensive policy and convert profits into cash under the most favorable market conditions. He will also be in a strong position to repur-chase with confidence when the correction has run its course.

The previous article stated that "The complete measurement of the length of a wave is therefore its continuous travel between two corrections of the same or greater degree." By repeatedly measuring the length of these waves as they develop, under a method known as channelling, it is possible to determine at the time of completion of Wave 4 approximately where Wave 5 should "top."

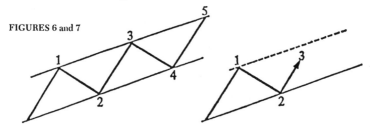

FIGURES 6 and 7

Figure 6 shows a normal completed movement or "cycle," in which Waves 1, 3 and 5 each have approximately the same length. Forecasting the ultimate movement by the channelling method must wait until Waves 1 and 2 have been completed. At such time it is possible to ascertain the "base line" for the lower limits of the channel by extending a straight line from the starting point of Wave 1 through the stopping point of Wave 2. This is shown in Figure 7. Wave 3, normally parallel to Wave 1, should end in the approximate vicinity of the tentative or dashed upper line of the channel.

This tentative upper line is drawn parallel to the base line from the top of Wave 1 and extended forward. But conditions may be so favorable that Wave 3 takes on temporary strength and exceeds the normal theoretical expectation, as shown in Figure 8.

FIGURES 8 and 9

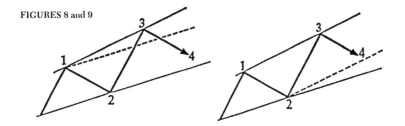

When Wave 3 has ended, the actual upper channel line is drawn from the top of Wave 1 through the top of Wave 3. And for forecasting the bottom of Wave 4 reaction, a tentative or dashed base line is drawn from the bottom of Wave 2 parallel to the actual Wave 1-Wave 3 upper channel line. In Figure 9 the theoretical expectancy for termination of Wave 4 is shown, as well as the actual termination.

With the second reaction, or Wave 4, terminated, the final and all-important channeling step can be taken. The base line of the channel is extended across the stopping points of the two reactionary phases (Wave 2 and 4), and a parallel upper line is drawn across the top of Wave 3. Wave 1 is disregarded entirely, unless Wave 3 was exceptionally strong. When the base and upper parallel lines are drawn as suggested, the approximate termination of Wave 5 will be forecast, as shown in Figure 10.

FIGURE 10

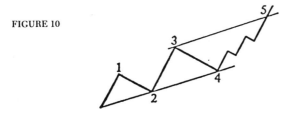

This channeling method is, of course, subordinate in importance to the rhythm of the various phases that make up the completed movement. Waves 1, 3 and 5 should each be composed of five waves of the next lower degree. Theoretically Wave 5 should wind up at about the intersection with the upper parallel line drawn as above described. Sometimes, however, Wave 5 develops excessive strength. Patterns in which this "throw-over" should occur will be discussed in subsequent articles.

THE WAVE PRINCIPLE   Part IV

A completed price movement has been shown to consist of five waves, with the entire movement representing the first wave of the next larger degree. By classifying the degree of the various phases, it is possible to determine the relative position of the market at all times as well as the economic changes that should follow.

The longest reliable record of American stock prices is the Axe-Houghton Index (published in *The New York Times Annalist*) dating from 1854. Long range forecasting under the Wave Principle must therefore start with the completion of the bear market that terminated in 1857. The great tidal movement that commenced in 1857 and ended on November 28, 1928 (the orthodox top) represents one wave of a cycle of the largest degree. Whether this extended movement was the First, Third or Fifth wave of the *Grand Super Cycle* necessarily depends upon what happened previous to 1857. By breaking this historic wave down into its component series of five-wave movements, and by breaking in turn the fifth wave of the next smaller degree into its five waves, the student will have actual examples of the various degrees that markets traverse. To avoid confusion in classifying the various degrees of market movements, it is suggested that the names and symbols devised below be used in their respective order:

Degree of Movement	Symbol and Wave Number	Duration
Grand Super Cycle	gsc I (?)	1857–1928
	sc I	1857–1864
	sc II	1864–1877
Super Cycle	sc III	1877–1881
	sc IV	1881–1896
	sc V	1896–1928
	c I	1896–1899
	c II	1899–1907
Cycle	c III	1907–1909
	c IV	1909–1921
	c V	1921–1928
	((I))	June 1921–Mar. 1923
	((II))	March 1923–May 1924
Primary	((III))	May 1924–Nov 1925

Degree of Movement	Symbol and Wave Number	Duration
	((IV))	Nov. 1925 –March 1926
	((v))	Mar. 1926–November1928
Intermediate	(I) – (V)	
Minor	I – V	
Minute	1 – 5	
Minuette	A – E	
Sub-Minuette	a – e	

Price movements illustrating the Intermediate and smaller degrees will be discussed in subsequent articles.

The longest of these waves lasted for over 70 years and included a long series of "bull" and "bear" markets. But it is the combination of the smaller hourly, daily and weekly rhythms that complete and measure the important *Intermediate* and *Primary* cycles that are of great practical importance to every investor.

When the Dow Jones Industrial Averages reached 295.62 on November 28, 1928, the price movement completed the fifth *Minuette* impulse of the fifth *Minute* wave of the fifth *minor* phase of the fifth *Intermediate* movement of the fifth *Primary* trend in the fifth *cycle* of the fifth *Super Cycle* in Wave 1, 3 or 5, of the *Grand Super Cycle*. For that reason, although the actual top of 386.10 was not reached until September 3, 1929, the point reached on November 28, 1928, is designated as the "orthodox" top. This may sound confusing to most readers, but the patterns in which "irregular tops" higher than "orthodox tops" occur will be discussed in due course.

THE WAVE PRINCIPLE Part V

The scope and duration of any price movement are influenced by what happened in the previous cycle of similar or larger degree. The movement that started in 1896 and took 33 years to complete, culminating on September 3, 1929, at 386.10 was so dynamic that the corrective bear cycle was correspondingly severe.

Orderly Decline

Within less than three years, prices were reduced to 10.5 percent of the peak level. Despite its high speed, the downward course of the bear cycle followed a well-defined and rhythmic pattern of waves. Furthermore, it kept within the limits of the pre-measured channel. It was, therefore, possible to determine beforehand approximately where the bear market would end and the new bull market begin. Because of the amplitude of the previous cycles, the new bull market would necessarily be of a large degree, lasting for years. When taking a position for such a movement, the long term investor would be warranted in maintaining his investments until the end of the fifth major wave was in measurable sight. From that point he should be extremely careful.

FIGURE 11

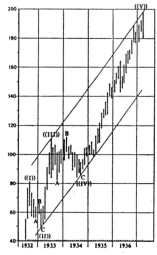

Phases of the Primary Movement, 1932-1937

Wave ((I)) from 40.56 July 8, 1932 to completion of Wave ((V)) at 195.59 on March 10, 1937. (Dow-Jones Industrial Monthly Averages)

Wave	From	To
((I))	40.56 July 8, 1932—	81.39 Sept. 8, 1932
((II))	81.39 Sept. 8, 1932—	49.68 Feb. 27, 1933
A	81.39 Sept. 8, 1932—	55.04 Dec. 3, 1932
B	55.04 Dec. 3, 1932—	65.28 Jan. 11, 1933
C	65.28 Jan. 11, 1933—	49.68 Feb. 27, 1933
((III))	49.68 Feb. 27, 1933—110.53 July 18, 1933	
((IV))	110.53 July 18, 1933—	84.58 July 26, 1934
A	110.53 July 18, 1933—	82.20 Oct. 21, 1933
B	82.20 Oct. 21, 1933—111.93 Feb. 5, 1934	
C	111.93 Feb. 5, 1934—	84.58 July 26, 1934
(V)	84.58 July 26, 1934—195.59 Mar. 10, 1937	

Previous discussions have dealt with the fundamental theory of the Wave Principle. It is now appropriate to show the application of the theory to an actual market. In Figure 11, the completed five-wave movement of the extreme monthly price ranges of the Dow Jones Industrial Averages from July 8, 1932 to March 10, 1937, is charted arithmetically. The series of minuette, minute, minor and intermediate waves all resolved themselves— in the monthly, weekly, daily and hourly records—to form and complete each of the five Primary Waves. Wave ((I)), ((III)), and ((V)) were each composed of five lesser or intermediate degrees. The corrective Waves ((II)) and ((IV)) were each composed of three distinct phases, as shown by the A-B-C patterns. The extent and duration of each important phase are shown in the accompanying table.

When Wave ((IV)) is finished and Wave ((V)) is underway, much closer attention to the market is required. Accordingly, the channel (see Part III, FW, Apr. 19) was carefully noted. A base line was drawn from the bottom of Wave ((II)) through the bottom of Wave ((IV)), and an upper line parallel thereto was extended forward from the top of Wave ((III)). See the accompanying table and chart.

Bearish Indication?

In November, 1936, immediately after the President was reelected by an overwhelming majority vote, external conditions appeared to be so favorable for the bull market that it was extremely difficult even to think of being bearish. Yet according to the Wave Principle, the bull market even then was in its final stage. The long term movement that started in 1932 had by November 12, 1936, reached 185.52, and the various five-wave advances of the preceding 53 months were in the culminating stage of the Primary degree. Note how close the price level was to the upper part of the channel at that time. Yet it required another four months to complete the pattern.

The final and relatively insignificant wave, necessary to confirm that the end was at hand, developed during the week ended Wednesday, March 10, 1937. In that week both the Industrial and Rail averages moved forward on huge volume to a moderately higher recovery level, and according to one of the most widely followed market theories thereby "reaffirmed that the major trend was *upward.*"

The Industrials reached 195.59—compared with the November, 1929, panic bottom of 195.35 and the February, 1931, rally top of 196.96. In that week the advancing prices met the top of the channel. The President's remarks about prices for copper and steel being too high did not take place until April, and by that time the bear movement was well under way.

THE WAVE PRINCIPLE   Part VI

In the 1932–1937 Primary bull movement (see Fig. 11, Part V, FW, May 3), Waves ((I)) and ((III)) ran at high speed. Naturally they terminated in a short time. But Wave ((V)) was so gradual and orderly that it lasted longer than the time interval required for the previous four waves combined. In the discussion of this movement, it was stated that by November, 1936, it was evident that the bull market was in an extremely advanced stage, but that it required another four months to complete the pattern. Although the largest phases of the Fifth Primary were in the culminating stage, the smallest component phases (Minuette, etc.) were still developing.

Figure 12 illustrates how the fifth wave of an important degree becomes extended by the development of five waves of the next smaller degree, and five more of a still smaller degree. Thus, an Intermediate trend will end on the fifth Sub-minuette impulse of the fifth Minuette wave of the fifth Minute phase of the fifth Minor movement of the fifth Intermediate swing. Note that as Wave (V) advances, the corrections tend to become smaller and of shorter duration. Compare with 1935–1937. The termination of a fifth wave marks the point at which an entire movement of the same degree is to be corrected by a reverse movement of similar degree.

FIGURE 12

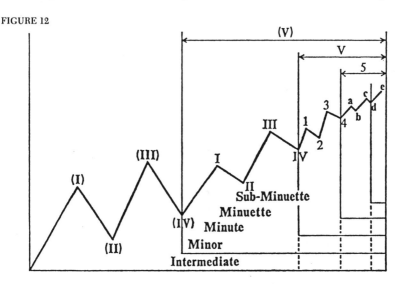

Confusion in the identification of the waves of the smaller degrees, developing toward the end of the fifth wave of the important degree, is sometimes caused by "throw-overs." A throw-over is a penetration, in an advancing movement of the upper parallel line of the channel (see Part III, FW, April 19), and in a declining movement of the lower parallel line of the channel. Volume tends to rise on a throw-over, and should be very heavy as applied to the fifth Intermediate wave of a Primary movement. Failure of the fifth wave of any degree to penetrate the channel line, accompanied by indications of a sustained decline, is a warning of weakness. The extent of the weakness depends upon the degree of the wave. Sometimes, such weakness furnishes a new base for the recommencement of the fifth wave. Throw-overs are also caused by the scale of the chart study of the movement. They are more likely to occur in an advancing movement on arithmetic scales, and in declining movements on logarithmic scales.

Sometimes the fifth wave will "stretch"—that is, deploy or spread out. The fifth wave, instead of preceding in the normal one-wave pattern of the same degree as the movement as a whole, simply stretches or sub-divides into five waves of lower degree. In rhythmic forecasting, this stretching applies to the fifth wave itself, rather than to the terminating cycle of which it is a part. Such spreading out is a characteristic of markets that are unusually strong (or weak, if a down movement). An example of stretching occurred in the 1921–1928 upswing, representing the culmination of a 72-year advance.

THE WAVE PRINCIPLE   Part VII

The rhythm of corrective movements is the most difficult feature of the Wave Principle. Intensive study of the detail of the correction will sometimes be necessary in order to determine the position of the market and the outlook. Mastery of the subject, however, should prove extremely profitable. All corrections are characterized by *three* broad waves, but the detail and extent can vary considerably, and thus different patterns are formed. Various factors (time, rate of speed, extent of previous movement, volume, news items, etc.) tend to influence and shape the corrective pattern. Based on the writer's market research and experience, there appear to be four main types or patterns of corrections. These types have been designated as (1) Zig-zag, (2) Flat, (3) Irregular, and (4) Triangle. Discussion of the Triangle, in its various forms, must be presented in a separate article. The other three forms are diagrammed in Figures 13, 14 and 15.

Small corrections that run their course in a comparatively short time are exemplified in Figure 13. Corrections of a larger degree are described in Figure 14. Figure 15 affords a diagram of the market action when the Primary or Intermediate trends turn downward. Some of these corrections, particularly those of the Irregular type, may extend over a period of years and embrace movements that are commonly mistaken for "bull markets."

FIGURES 13, 14, 15

The three-wave or A-B-C formations that characterize the Zig-zag, Flat and Irregular corrections are clearly shown in the accompanying diagrams. The Zig-zag type was discussed briefly in Part II (Fig. 4, FW, Apr. 12). It differs from other corrections in that both the first and third waves (A and C) are composed of five smaller vibrations. The second ("B") wave of the Zig-zag corrections is composed of three impulses. Sometimes, in a high-speed movement, the first leg ("A") may appear continuous, and resort to the smaller or hourly studies may be necessary to detect the flow.

The first and second waves of both Flats and Irregulars each consist of three vibrations of a degree smaller than that of the previous movement. Of the three movements making up the second or "B" phase of both Flats and Irregulars, the first and third ("a" and "c") are each composed of five still smaller impulses. In a Flat all of the three waves have approximately the same length.

An Irregular correction is distinguished by the fact that the second or "B" wave advances to a secondary top higher than the orthodox top established in the primary movement. Liquidation in the third or "C" wave is therefore usually more intensive than in the first phase. Normally "C" terminates below the bottom of "A," although there are instances of "C," the third phase, being abbreviated. In the larger and important corrections, such as Primary and Intermediate, the "C" or third phase of the Irregular correction may consist of three smaller five-wave sets, as shown in Figure 15.

By analyzing and placing the type of correction that is being experienced, the student has a basis for determining both the extent of the correction, and the extent of the following movement. Channeling (see Part III, FW, Apr. 19) can help in determining the extent. The application of these corrective patterns to specific markets will be shown and discussed in subsequent articles.

THE WAVE PRINCIPLE   Part VIII

Triangular corrections are protracted trend hesitations. The main move-ment may have gone too far and too fast in relation to the slower economic processes, and prices proceed to mark time until the underlying forces catch up. Triangles have lasted as long as nine months and have been as short as seven hours. There are two classes of triangles, horizontal and diagonal. These are shown in Figures 16 and 17.

The four types of horizontal triangles are (1) Ascending, (2) Descend-ing, (3) Symmetrical, and (4) the rare Reverse Symmetrical. In the last named the apex is the beginning of the triangular correction. In the other forms the apex is the end of the correction, which, however, may terminate before the apex is actually reached.

All triangles contain five waves or legs, each of which is composed of not more than three lesser waves. Outlines that do not conform to this definition fall outside the law of the Wave Principle. All waves in a triangle must be part of a movement in one direction; otherwise, the "triangle" is only a coincidence.

FIGURES 16, 17, 18

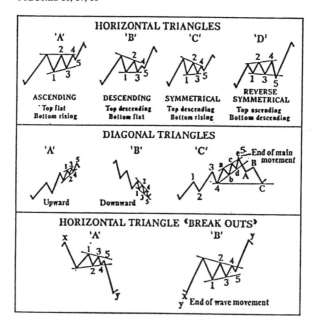

The entire travel within the triangle represents a wave of the main movement. The horizontal triangle occurs as Wave 2 or Wave 4. If it occurs as Wave 2, the main movement will have only three waves. At the conclusion of a horizontal triangle, the market will resume the trend that was interrupted by the triangle, and the direction of that trend will be the same as that of triangular Wave 2. The "break-out" from the horizontal triangle (in the direction of triangular Wave 2) will usually be fast and represent the final wave of the main movement, and be followed by reversal of the trend. The extent of the "break-out" will usually approximate the distance between the widest parts of the triangle. Diagrams A and B, Fig. 18 illustrate the "breakout" from horizontal triangles.

Diagonal triangles are either (1) upward or (2) downward. They can occur as either Wave 3 or Wave 4 of the main movement. Usually they occur as Wave 5, and are preceded by four main waves. But the completion of the diagonal triangle represents the end of the main movement. The second wave within the diagonal triangle will be in the direction opposite to that of the main movement, and will indicate the direction of the reversal to follow conclusion of the triangle. At the conclusion of the fifth wave in this form of triangle, the rapid reversal of trend will usually return the market to about the level from which the triangle started. See diagram C, Fig. 17.

Triangles are not apparent in all studies. Sometimes they will appear in the weekly scale, but will not be visible in the daily. Sometimes they are present in, say, The New York Times average and not in another average. Thus, the broad and important movement from October, 1937, to February, 1938, formed a triangle in the Standard Statistics weekly range, but was not visible in other averages; the second wave of this triangle pointed downward; the fifth wave culminated on February 23; the drastic March break followed.

THE WAVE PRINCIPLE   Part IX

The "extension," though not frequent, is one of the most important market phenomena measurable by the Wave Principle. In an extension the length (and degree) of the wave becomes much larger than normal. It may occur as a part of Wave 1 or 3, but is usually a part of Wave 5 of the main movement. The extended movement is composed of the normal five-wave phase, followed by a three-wave retracing correction, and then by a second advancing movement in three phases. Of the normal five waves, the fifth vibration is usually the largest and most dynamic of the series—thus becoming, in effect, an extension of the extension.

A warning of the approach of this dynamic phase of Wave 5 is conveyed when Waves 1 and 3 are short and regular and confined within the channel, and when the first corrective vibration of the extension is completed near the top of the channel. The length of important extensions may be several times the breadth of the original channel.

Channelling is also useful in measuring the travel of the extension. Thus, in Figures 19 and 20, the line "b-d" represents the base line, and the dashed upper parallel line "c-e" measures the normal expectancy for the "first top" of the extension.

FIGURES 19 and 20

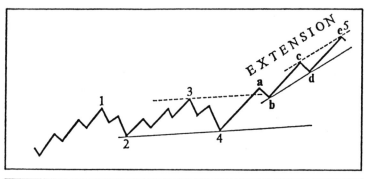

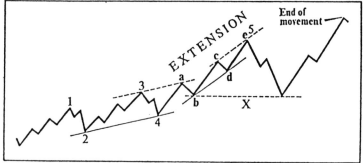

The completion of the normal or first five waves of an extension is never the end of the cyclical movement, but does constitute a distinct warning that the bull cycle is approaching an end, as only two more broad waves (one down and one up) would fully reflect the maximum force of the bull market.

After the first five waves of the extension have been completed, a severe correction (that is usually in three waves, but may be triangular) sets in. This correction becomes Wave A of an irregular cyclical correction. Wave A generally carries the market down (breaking the extension channel) to about the beginning of the extension, although a protracted period of backing and filling may serve to mitigate the severity of this corrective phase. The dashed line marked "X" in Figure 20 indicates the average expectancy for the completion of Wave A.

When Wave A has been completed, the main or cyclical movement is resumed in three broad phases that carry the market into new high ground— even though "e" in Figures 19 and 20 may have been the "orthodox top" of a major or primary bull movement. But this new top, or "irregular top," is the final high point for the bull market. This three-wave advancing phase becomes Wave B of the irregular cyclical correction.

The completion of Wave B marks the beginning of Wave C of the irregular cyclical correction, that in this phase is a bear market of major importance. Wave C should carry the market down in five fast waves to about the bottom of Primary Wave IV of the preceding bull movement. Example: following the dynamic extension in 1928; Wave A, down from November to December, 1928; Wave B, upward to September, 1929; Wave C, downward to July, 1932.

Extensions also occur in bear markets. Thus, the five waves of an extension were completed October 19, 1937, with the market reaching 115.83; followed, in this case, by a broad triangular correction (instead of the irregular A-B-C pattern) covering a period of four months, eventually reaching 97.46 on March 31, 1938. Wave 2 of this triangular correction was in the same direction as the downward cyclical trend.

A tremendous extension occurred in commodity price movements, particularly that of electrolytic copper, in the spring of 1937. In individual stocks, the "orthodox top" of International Harvester was reached at 111-112 in January, 1937; Wave A, in a backing and filling movement that reduced the severity of the correction, carried the stock to 109 in April; Wave B reached a new cyclical top of 120 in August (the general market topped in March), and Wave C brought the stock down to about 53 in November.

THE WAVE PRINCIPLE   Part X

Following the completion of the bull market from 1932–1937 (see Figure 11, FW, May 3, 1939), a three-phase cyclical correction was in order. The first phase should and did consist of five large waves. The first phase of this correction was the decline that ran from 195.59 (Dow Jones Industrial Averages) on March 10, 1937, to 97.46 on March 31, 1938. The accompanying Figure 21 shows the weekly range of the market during this period, on an arithmetic scale. Despite the highly emotional nature that prevailed at certain stages, the rhythmic forecasting principle continued to function. The minute details registered in the daily and hourly patterns are, of course, not entirely visible in the weekly range. For this reason, the essential details of price and time of the five big waves making up this first cyclical phase are given:

Cyclical (A)—from 195.59 on March 10, 1937, to 163.31 on June 17, 1937.

Cyclical Wave (B)—from 163.31 on June 17, 1937, to 190.38 on August 14, 1937.

Cyclical Wave (C)—from 190.38 on August 14, 1937, to 115.83 on October 19, 1937.

Cyclical Wave (D)—from 115.83 on October 19, 1937, to 132.86 on February 23, 1938.

FIGURE 21

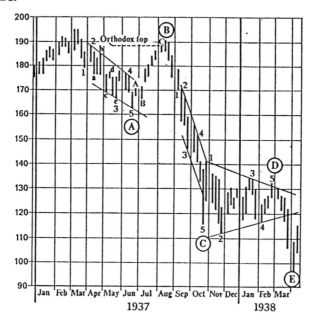

Cyclical Wave (E) — from 132.86 on February 23, 1938, to 97.46 on March 31, 1938.

Cyclical Wave (A) was composed of five minor waves, as follows:

1—195.59 on March 10 to 179.28 on March 22.

2—179.28 on March 22 to 187.99 on March 31.

3—187.99 on March 31 to 166.20 on May 18.

4—166.20 on May 18 to 175.66 on June 5.

5—175.66 on June 5 to 163.31 on June 17.

Wave 3 in Cyclical Wave (A) was composed of five vibrations.

Cyclical Wave (B) was composed of three waves, and an "irregular top":

A—163.31 on June 17 to 170.46 on June 24.

B—170.46 on June 24 to 166.11 on June 29.

C—166.11 on June 29 to 187.31 on August 4.

The "irregular top" was completed on August 14, 1937, forecasting a severe cyclical decline.

Cyclical Wave (C) was composed of five large waves, with an "extension" developing in the fifth wave. Had it not been for this extension, the normal completion of the first phase of the cyclical correction would probably have been in the neighborhood of 135-140.

The analysis of Wave (C) is as follows:

1—190.38 on August 14, 1937, to 175.09 on August 27, 1937.

2—175.09 on August 27, 1937, to 179.10 on August 31, 1937.

3—179.10 on August 31, 1937, to 154.94 on Sept. 13, 1937.

4—154.94 on Sept. 13, 1937, to 157.12 on Sept. 30, 1937.

5—157.12 on Sept. 30, 1937, to 115.83 on Oct. 19, 1937.

In Cyclical Wave (C), there were three "sets" of five vibrations in the downward trend, with the first, third and fifth minor waves each being composed of five impulses. Wave 4 was a fairly important upward correction, in the familiar A-B-C formation. The "extension" that developed in the fifth vibration of Wave 5 indicated that (1) the ground thus lost would be immediately recovered, (2) that the secondary decline would carry the market into new low ground for the cyclical correction, (3) that following this secondary decline, the normal protracted period of backing and filling might form a triangle, with the final down thrust completing the first phase of the cyclical correction, and (4) that a very substantial recovery would follow, in at least five large waves—thus forecasting the 1938 March–November "bull market."

Cyclical Wave (D), as indicated by the "extension" that occurred in Wave (C), was composed of a huge triangle:

Triangle Wave 1—in three vibrations, from 115.83 on October 19, 1937, to 141.22 on October 29 as follows:

A—115.83 on October 19 to 137.82 on October 21.

B—137.82 on October 21 to 124.56 on October 25.

C—124.56 on October 25 to 141.22 on October 29.

2—141.22 on October 29, 1937, to 112.54 on November 23.

3—112.54 on November 23 to 134.95 on January 12, 1938.

4—134.95 on January 12 to 117.13 on February 4.

5—117.13 on February 4 to 132.86 on February 23.

None of the "legs" in this triangle was composed of more than three waves. Following the completion of the fifth wave in the triangle, the downward movement of the cyclical correction was resumed.

Cyclical Wave (E) was composed of five lesser waves, as follows:

1—132.86 on February 23 to 121.77 on March 12.

2—121.77 on March 12 to 127.44 on March 15.

3—127.44 on March 15 to 112.78 on March 23.

4—112.78 on March 23 to 114.37 on March 25.

5—114.37 on March 25 to 97.46 on March 31.

The first large phase of the cyclical correction of the 1932–1937 bull market was thus finally completed, and the market was ready for the second important upward phase of the cyclical correction. This correction extinguished 63.3 per cent of the 155.03 points recovered in the 1932–1937 movement.

THE WAVE PRINCIPLE   Part XI

In using the Wave Principle as a medium for forecasting price movements, the student should recognize that there are cycles within cycles, and that each such cycle or sub-cycle must be studied and correctly placed in respect to the broad underlying movement. These sub-cyclical or corrective phases in a bull market are often important enough to be mistaken for "bear markets." The strong but sub-cyclical correction from March 31, 1938 to November 12, 1938, had a "bull pattern" of five important waves making up its first phase, and was (and still is) regarded by many as a real bull market. Broadly speaking, extended rallies or corrections of bear cycles are composed of three phases, and this is also true of extensive bearish corrections of bull movements.

Wave Characteristics

The character of the waves making up an extended movement is affected by a number of factors that may seem irrelevant to the inexperienced. Examination of any completed movement seems to support the fatalistic theory that the extend or objective of the price movement is fixed or predetermined. The time of the entire cycle is also possibly fixed, but the time of the component phases appears to be variable. The variations in the time cycle appear to be governed by the speed or rate of the price movement, and vice versa. Thus, if the market movement has been violent and rapid in one phase, the next corresponding phase is likely to show a marked slowing down in speed. Example: The first primary wave of the 1932–1937 bull cycle advanced 40 points or 100 per cent in nine weeks, averaging 4.4 points per week. The second bull phase advanced 60 points or 120 per cent in twenty weeks, averaging 3 points per week. The third or final phase crept forward 110 points or 130 per cent in 138 weeks, averaging 0.8 points per week. High speed at the end of long movements usually generates similar speed in the first wave of the reversal: compare the March, 1938, downward movement with the following April reversal.

At certain stages volume seems to play an important part in the price movement, and volume itself will expand or contract to help control and complete the price cycle. Study of the time cycle and volume cycles is sometimes distinctly helpful in clarifying the position of the price spiral. Volume tends to increase in the third wave of the cycle, and to maintain about the same activity in the fifth wave. As the bottom of the volume cycle is approached, erratic price changes in high priced stocks or inactive stocks with thin markets, can distort the small waves in the trend of the averages to such an extent as to create temporary uncertainties. But these waves of volume are also useful in determining the extent and time for completion of price phases, and also in determining the time and direction and even the speed of the following movement. This is especially true in fast swinging markets like those that characterized 1938. The best results therefore will follow from correlation of the volume and time cycles with the component phases of the broad price movement, as the price patterns and all degrees of volume are governed precisely by the same Wave Principle phenomenon.

To maintain a proper perspective, the student should chart at least two and preferably more broad averages, using the weekly range, the daily range, and the hourly record, and showing the accompanying volume. The weekly range should be sufficient properly to evaluate the broad changes in trend, but the monthly range studies will also undoubtedly appeal to many investors. The daily range, by affording close observation of the smaller changes, is essential in correct interpretation of the cyclical progression, and is quite necessary for determining the precise time of important reversals in trend.

Critical Points

The minute changes recorded in the hourly study not only afford valuable and extensive material for practice in wave interpretation, but are especially useful in times when the market is moving at such high speed that the pattern is not clearly registered in the longer-time charts. Thus, the small triangle that appeared in the hourly record of October, 1937, signalled an immediate acceleration or extension of the downward movement; the dynamic October 18–19 "panic" followed. At other critical points the hourly study has also proved valuable, as in locating the "orthodox top" before the final irregular top, thus selecting the time for strategic liquidation near the crest. As the first hourly phase following the break in March, 1938, developed in five minuette waves, it thus afforded a strong confirmation that the important trend had actually changed.

THE WAVE PRINCIPLE   Part XII

The application of the Wave Principle to the movements of the general stock market has been discussed in a number of previous articles. This—the concluding article in this series—applies the Wave Principle to the movements of an individual stock.

Previous articles have discussed the theory of the Wave Principle and its application to broad market movements. The broader the category, the more clearly the wave impressions are outlined. The wave pattern of the comprehensible stock price averages—such as the Dow Jones, *The New York Times,* or Standard Statistics—will correctly reflect the cyclical position of the market as a whole. Therefore, purchases and sales of a diversified list of representative stocks in accordance with the movements of the averages will result in profits, as their aggregate market value will swing in sympathy with the general market. But for the seeker of maximum profits consistent with safety, it is not enough to buy or sell a group of stocks without separate analysis of each individual stock. These individual studies may reveal that some companies are experiencing a cycle differing greatly from that of the market as a whole. A prominent example was the case of American Can in the spring of 1935.

The accompanying charts depict the analysis of American Can by the Wave Principle. In Figure 22 the complete monthly price range history is shown from June, 1932—the beginning of the bull movement—to June, 1935, the time when the "orthodox top" occurred. The action of the stock from that point on to completion of the cyclical correction in December, 1937, is shown in "trend lines." This monthly record condenses the weekly and daily details into the five broad Primary Waves that complete a cyclical movement. These relatively broad charts also help materially in maintaining the proper perspective.

When the important Fifth Primary Wave of the cycle commenced in May, 1934—or in other words, when the Primary Wave IV reaction was completed—it became necessary to study the market action more closely. Hence Figure 23, which shows the weekly price record of the Fifth Primary Wave. And after this Primary Wave had progressed through Intermediate Wave 4, it became important to follow the daily price ranges, as shown in Figure 24. The Fifth Intermediate Wave started in March, 1935; and five Minor waves were completed by June, 1935. This signalled the "orthodox top" of the main bull movement in American Can at 144.

FIGURES 22, 23, 24, 25

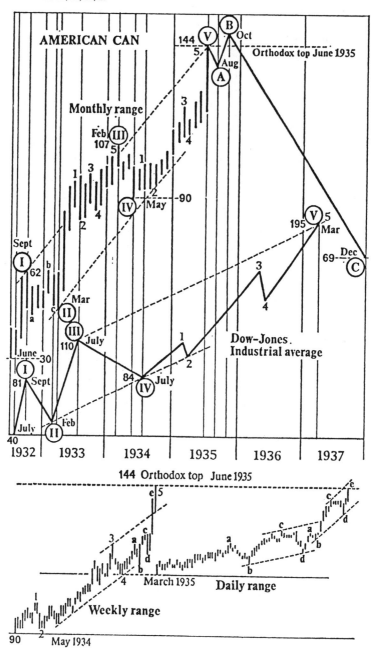

Following the "orthodox top" of the bull cycle in American Can, there developed a reaction to 136-137 in August, 1935—forming Wave A. Then a rally to 149-150 in October, 1935—forming Wave B, the irregular but final top. From this point developed the long Wave C, in five intermediate movements, terminating at 69 in December, 1937.

At the time of the "orthodox top" in American Can, the investor would have observed the striking difference between the cyclical positions of that stock and of the general market. See Figure 25, which outlines the trend lines of the important Primary Waves of the Dow Jones Industrial Averages. In March, 1935, American Can was in the final stages of a bull cycle (Fifth Intermediate Wave of the Fifth Primary). On the other hand the general market was just commencing the Fifth Primary Wave, and still had to experience five upward Intermediate Waves. By June, 1935, the long term investor in American Can would have realized (1) that any further appreciation in that stock would be highly uncertain; and (2) that much greater profits were available in the general market with minimum risks. From that point the general market advanced nearly 80 points or 65 per cent.

Bibliography

APPEL, Gerald. *Winning Market Systems.* Capitalist Reporter,New York, New York 1973.

BALAN, Robert. *The Elliott Wave Principle Applied to Foreign Exchange Markets.* B.B.S. Financial Publishing, 1989.

BECKMAN, Robert. *Share Price Analysis.* Investors Bulletin, London, England, 1969.

BECKMAN, Robert. *The Elliott Wave Principle As Applied to the UK Stock Market.* Tara Books, Hampshire, England, 1976.

BECKMAN, Robert. *Supertiming: The Unique Elliott Wave System.* Library of Investment Study, California, 1979.

BECKMAN, Robert. *The Downwave.* Milestone Publications, Hampshire, England, 1988.

BECKMAN, Robert. *Into The Upwave.* Milestone Publications, Hampshire, England, 1988.

BECKMAN, Robert. *Crashes.* Sidgwick & Jackson, London, England, 1988.

BOLTON, A. Hamilton. *The Elliott Wave Principle: A Critical Appraisal.* The Bank Credit Analyst, Toronto, Canada, 1960.

BRETZ, William. *Juncture Recognition in the Stock Market.* Vantage Press, New York, New York, 1972.

CLEMENCE, Richard V., and DOODY, Francis C. *The Schumpeterian System*. Kelly, New York, New York, 1956.

COGAN, Peter L. *The Rhythmic Cycles of Optimism and Pessimism*. William Frederick, New York, New York, 1968.

COOTNER, Paul. *The Random Character of Stock Price Movements*. The M.I.T. Press, Cambridge, Massachusetts, 1964

DEWEY, Edward R. and DAKIN, E.F. *Cycles: The Science of Prediction*. Henry Holt and Co. New York, New York, 1947.

DINES, James. *The Dines Letter* Belvedere, California.

DREW, Garfield, *New Methods for Profit in the Stock Market*. Pitman, New York, New York, 1948.

ELLIOTT, R.N. *The Wave Principle*. Elliott, 1938.

ELLIOTT, R.N. *Nature's Law: The Secret of the Universe*. (Elliott, 1946)

ELLIOTT, R.N. *The Elliott Wave Course*. Investment Educators, Chicago, Illinois 1962.

FLUMIANI, C.M. *The Reconstruction of the Elliott Wave Principle*. Stock Market Chartist Club of America, Wibraham, Massachusetts, 1970.

FRASER, Ian. The Elliott *Wave Principle*. Article included in *The Encyclopedia of Stock Market Techniques*. Investors Intelligence, Larchmont, New York, 1962.

FROST, A.J. and PRECHTER, Robert. *The Elliott Wave Principle: Key to Stock Market Profits*. New Classics Library, New York, New York, 1978.

GANN, W.D. *Truth of the Stock Tape*. Financial Guardian, New York, New York, 1923.

GARRETT, William C. *Investing for Profit with Torque Analysis of Stock Market Cycles*. Prentice Hall, New Jersey, 1972.

GLEICK, James. *Chaos: Making a New Science*. Sphere Books, London, England, 1988.

GREINER, P.P. and WHITCOMB, H.C. *The Dow Theory and the 70-Year Forecast Record*. Investors Intelligence, Larchmont, New York, 1968.

HAMBRIDGE, Jay. *Practical Application of Dynamic Symmetry: The Law of Phyllotaxis*. Yale, 1920.

HAMILTON, William P. *The Stock Market Barometer*. Barron's, New York, New York, 1922.

JILER, William L. *How Charts Can Help You in the Stock Market*. Commodity Research, New York, New York, 1962.

KING, J.L. *Human Behavior and Wall Street*. Swallow Press, Chicago, Illinois, 1974.

KLEIN, F.C. and PRESTBO, J.A. *News and the Markets*. Regner, Chicago, Illinois, 1973.

KONDRATIEFF, N.P. *Die langen Wellen de Konjunktur*. The Long Waves of the Economy, 1928.

KROW, Harvey A. *Stock Market Behavior*. Random House, New York, New York, 1969.

MALKIEL, Burton G. *A Random Walk Down Wall Street* . W.W. Norton & Co. New York, New York, 1973

MERRILL, Arthur. *Behavior of Prices on Wall Street*, Analysis Press, Chappacqua, 1966.

NEELY, Glen. *Elliott Wave in Motion*. Windsor Books, New York, New York, 1990.

NOTLEY, Ian S. *Market Trend Analysis, Market Trend Analysis Practical* Draper Dobie, Toronto, Canada, 1976.

O'CONNOR, William. *Stocks, Wheat and Pharoahs*. Wener Books, New York, New York, 1961.

PRECHTER, Robert. *The Major Works of R.N. Elliott*. New Classics Library, Georgia, 1980.

RHEA, Robert. *The Dow Theory*. Barron's, 1932

ROSENAU, David. *The Kondratieff Wave* (with J.B. Schuman). World Publishing, New York, New York, 1974.

SCHEINEMAN, W.K. *Why Most Investors are Mostly Wrong Most of the Time*. Weybright and Talley, New York, New York, 1973.

SCHILLINGER, J. *The Mathematical Basis of the Arts* 1956.

SCHULZ, John. *The Intelligent Chartist*. Trend and Value, New York, New York, 1962.

SCHUMPETER, Joseph. *Theory of Economic Development*. Harvard University Press, Cambridge, Massachusetts, 1934.

SCHUMPETER, Joseph. *Business Cycles*. McGraw-Hill Book Co, New York, New York, 1939.

THORP, Edward. *Beat The Dealer*. Random House, New York, New York, 1966.

TOMPKINS, Peter. *Secrets of the Great Pyramid*.

VAN GELDEREN, J. *Springvloed; Beschouwing Over Industriele Ontwikkeling en Prijsbeweging*. (Springtide: Reflections on Industrial Development and Price Movement.) (c. 1920).

Index